HOOD'S DEFEAT NEAR FOX'S GAP

Prelude to Emancipation

CURTIS L. OLDER

CASEMATE

Philadelphia & Oxford

Published in the United States of America and Great Britain in 2023 by
CASEMATE PUBLISHERS
1950 Lawrence Road, Havertown, PA 19083, USA
and
The Old Music Hall, 106–108 Cowley Road, Oxford OX4 1JE, UK

Hardcover Edition: ISBN 978-1-63624-273-6
Digital Edition: ISBN 978-1-63624-274-3

A CIP record for this book is available from the British Library

Printed and bound in the United Kingdom by CPI Group (UK) Ltd, Croydon, CR0 4YY
Typeset in India by DiTech Publishing Services

For a complete list of Casemate titles, please contact:

CASEMATE PUBLISHERS (US)
Telephone (610) 853-9131
Fax (610) 853-9146
Email: casemate@casematepublishers.com
www.casematepublishers.com

CASEMATE PUBLISHERS (UK)
Telephone (0)1226 734350
Email: casemate-uk@casematepublishers.co.uk
www.casematepublishers.co.uk

Confederate Drummer Boy. (Artist Paul Martin)

One little incident had touched my heart more than all the
corpses that strewed the ground where Withington had charged.
Sitting on the stone fence, a little higher up,
was found the body of a little boy in gray,
a musician, perfectly dead and rigid,
his arm extended and his finger pointing towards our lines.

Union Brigadier General Orlando B. Willcox
Forgotten Valor

DEDICATION

For Addy

with all my love!

Contents

Foreword

The battlefields of Antietam, Harpers Ferry, and South Mountain are viewed as travel destinations by countless American Civil War scholars worldwide, both professional and amateur. People intrigued by this world-changing war, particularly during a few days in September 1862, viewed the Maryland Campaign as the most important. One cannot understate the significance of these events from various standpoints.

I met Curt Older in September 2016 when he gave a presentation to the Boonsboro Historical Society on his book, *The Land Tracts of the Battlefield of South Mountain*. I was interested in his research on land records rather than the battlefield, but Curt and I have stayed in touch ever since. Over the years, he would sporadically ask questions regarding local roads, landmarks, and terrain. I knew Curt was up to something but did not ask what. As it turned out, his continuing study of the Battle of South Mountain presented some questions to which he needed answers. He felt various issues he uncovered disagreed with the accepted story and began researching to satisfy his curiosity. By 2020, Curt had come up with a theory but now had to test its credibility.

Our mutual friend and the first choice for local information, Doug Bast, had recently passed away, and Curt contacted me. I tried to dissuade him, professing my lack of American Civil War knowledge. But Civil War knowledge was not what he wanted. We began to correspond regularly. I advised on the region's terrain—geographical and environmental—the historic roads, and even the people's history in some instances as he tried to fit the puzzle together.

I can attest to Curt's unbiased research diligence and accurate placement of primary source data on the ground. Several times, I took it upon myself to visit sites he suspected, which appeared in almost 160-year-old sources. Time and again, I was amazed how the sites still matched those descriptions—surprised at the subtle landmarks casually mentioned in personal letters from 1862 that still fit the locations despite nature's attempts to disguise the evidence and, in some cases, the neglect of humanity in preserving them.

Some of the ideas presented in this book disagree with accepted narratives. While my knowledge of American Civil War military history remains superficial, the process of confirming historical documents through geographical features, physical evidence, and unassociated corroborating documents was a sure one. Like his original "land tracts" research, Curt has physically proven the locations suggested in this book.

One other aspect, which, while not "proof" but supporting, was the tactical sense made by the movements Curt proposes in this book. Operational objectives and the strategies to accomplish them on any battlefield transcend time. From a command, goal, and procedures standpoint, Curt's explanation of the actions by Brigadier General John Bell Hood's two brigades on September 14, 1862, made perfect sense in what was a desperate operation with an evolving objective.

Whether you visit the battlefield in person or through the magic of online satellite images, topographical maps, and other sources, I am confident you will ultimately agree with Curt's analysis.

Ted Ellis
Sharpsburg, Maryland
August 2021

Preface

The road through Fox's Gap dates to at least 1727 when it was part of the Great Philadelphia Wagon Road. From 1755 until 1763, it was the main road from Frederick Town to Swearingen's Ferry. After the creation of Sharpsburg in 1763, the route became the Sharpsburg Road.

The route still exists today, as it has for over 295 years, but has various names along its path. As one travels east from Sharpsburg to just north of Middletown are Geeting Road, Dog Street Road, Reno Monument Road, and Marker Road. The road played a significant role in the historical events of the Braddock Expedition and the American Civil War.

It was never my objective to write a book about the Battle of South Mountain. Other talented authors covered the battle in prior years, and I thought writing about any military engagement would be the most challenging writing any author could undertake. There were just too many moving parts to a fight to adequately comprehend them. I did intend to include a chapter on the struggle in another book.

However, when my analysis of the battle at Fox's Gap came down to the last few hours of the encounter related to Brigadier General John Bell Hood, previously written accounts did not add up. There was no primary source evidence to support the written versions concerning Hood. From a military standpoint, to believe that Hood's force of 2,000 men defeated a Union force of 13,000 men at Fox's Gap did not add up.

The Battle of South Mountain was a turning point in the American Civil War and the critical event in President Abraham Lincoln's decision to issue his Preliminary Emancipation Proclamation. The focus of this book is the role of Confederate Brigadier General John Bell Hood in the battle.

Many a hiker on the Appalachian Trail comes to Fox's Gap unaware of its long history. It is the history of the American journey, from early settlers and founding fathers to the agony of civil strife and reconstruction. I have sought to preserve this history, this Fox's Gap, and this Old Sharpsburg Road.

I owe an outstanding debt of gratitude to Ted Ellis of Sharpsburg, Maryland. He provided critical topographical and geographical information about the battlefield areas, questioned my ideas about the battle, and suggested valuable insights. This book would have been impossible without Ted's "feet on the ground."

My mother's membership in the Daughters of the American Revolution motivated me to join the Sons of the American Revolution after the completion of my service in the United States Navy. The patriotic flavor of these organizations and their concern for our national heritage, when coupled with interests of a military nature, motivated my research into the secrets that Fox's Gap might hold.

Perhaps an adage, "I would rather be lucky than good any day," might be most appropriate at this juncture. Divine intervention must have occurred when I stumbled upon some of the material used in this book.

Reviewers of this book included Ted Ellis, Tim Ware, David Lientz, and Tom Kirkham.

Of course, any errors, oversights, or omissions, of which there will be some, are entirely mine.

Curtis L. Older
September 14, 2022

List of Maps

CHAPTER ONE

The Approaching Battle

Prelude to Emancipation

A turning point in the American Civil War was the Maryland Campaign, and the turning point of that campaign was the Battle of South Mountain, known in the South as the Battle of Boonsboro. The Battle of South Mountain, September 14, 1862, was a historic, consequential, and critical battle in the War Between the States. South Mountain precipitated America's bloodiest day three days later at the Battle of Antietam, about eight miles farther west.

The Union Army's two victories in the Maryland Campaign gave President Abraham Lincoln the necessary resolve to issue his Preliminary Emancipation Proclamation on September 22, 1862.[1] South Mountain marked the first battle where Confederate General Robert E. Lee ordered a retreat and acknowledged a defeat. The Battles of South Mountain and Antietam efficaciously removed any thought by Great Britain of supporting the so-called Confederate States of America during the war. British involvement effectively ended with the issuance of the Preliminary Emancipation Proclamation.[2]

Many Civil War authors included the Battle for Crampton's Gap and the battles fought at Fox's and Turner's Gaps as part of the Battle of South Mountain. Timothy Reese, the author of *Sealed with Their Lives, The Battle of Crampton's Gap*, makes a case for considering the Battle of Crampton's Gap as a distinct and separate battle.[3] An analysis of the battle at Crampton's Gap will not be part of this book.

After General Lee assumed command of the Army of Northern Virginia during the Peninsula Campaign, he and his army remained on the offensive. The Confederate Army of Northern Virginia followed their victory at Second Bull Run, fought on August 29 and 30, by invading Maryland. The Maryland Campaign took place from September 4 through September 20.

Historic roads passed over the South Mountain at two mountain gaps, Fox's and Turner's, that became the scene for the Battle of South Mountain. Old National Pike traversed Turner's Gap, and Old Sharpsburg Road passed through Fox's Gap.

Turner's Gap, about two and one-half miles southeast of Boonsboro, MD, lay a mile north of Fox's Gap.

The Confederate Army held Turner's and Fox's Gaps, about 55 miles northwest of Washington, D.C., on September 14. My analysis will focus on the fight at Fox's Gap, the fighting scene throughout most of the 14th. Discussion of the Battle of Turner's Gap will be only as it directly pertained to the conflict at Fox's Gap.

The North had little to cheer about before September 1, 1862. The Union Army lost in the Eastern Theater at First Bull Run, the Peninsula Campaign, and Second Bull Run. The Union military's main achievements were, heading into September 1862, Major General Ulysses S. Grant's successes at Forts Henry and Donelson, the Battle of Shiloh, and Union naval victories on the North Carolina coast and along the Mississippi River. Rumors that England might give political recognition to the Confederacy were widespread.

In a remarkable chain of events between September 8 and 22, the Union's fortunes changed dramatically. On September 8, General Lee sought to persuade Jefferson Davis, president of the so-called Confederate States of America, that the military and political situation was such that Davis should offer the North terms to end the war.[4] The "Confederate States of America" would become an independent nation. Confederate confidence at this juncture of the war was near its peak, while that of the North was frail.

The Maryland Campaign would be General Robert E. Lee's biggest miscalculation and a consequential war turning point. Clarification of the war's outcome came during the four days of September 14 through 17 in the gaps of South Mountain and along the Antietam Creek at Sharpsburg. Many of the men who fought in the Battle of South Mountain considered it the decisive turning point of the Maryland Campaign.

The Union and Confederate Armies in September 1862 had no notion of President Lincoln's plan to issue his Preliminary Emancipation Proclamation upon a Union victory in the next battle. Both sides continued to plan their campaigns unaware of the historic significance that would attach to the outcome of their next combat—which began at 9:00 am at Fox's Gap on Sunday, September 14.

Heading into the week of September 14, the 60-day clock on the Second Confiscation Act was about to expire:

> The act's defining characteristic was that it called for court proceedings to seize land and property from disloyal citizens (supporters of the Confederacy) in the South and the emancipation of their slaves that came under Union control.[5]

Lincoln signed the Act on July 17, but the Act was only applicable to Confederate areas already occupied by the Union Army. The First and Second Confiscation Acts aided the growing movement towards emancipation.

The answers to some of the most critical questions concerning the war began to make themselves known at 9:00 am on Sunday, September 14, along Old Sharpsburg Road at Fox's Gap in Maryland. Fifty-five miles to the southeast, at what is today called the Lincoln Cottage near the Soldier's Home, about three miles from the White House in Washington, D.C., President Abraham Lincoln anxiously awaited developments and contemplated his Preliminary Emancipation Proclamation.[6]

Over the years, various authors have researched and written about the battle. Ezra A. Carman, John M. Priest, D. Scott Hartwig, Brian M. Jordan, John Hoptak, and Stephen W. Sears were some of the most significant.[7] I will disagree with these previous authors as to the movement of Brigadier General John Bell Hood's two brigades during the last hours of the battle. However, I owe gratitude and appreciation to earlier authors who researched and wrote about the conflict. Without their efforts, the battlefield might have become lost to history. In fact, the past three decades have witnessed special attention given to the battlefield due to an increased concern for preservation. In 2000, the state of Maryland created the South Mountain State Battlefield, which probably contains secrets yet to be found.

The primary focus of this book will be on Confederate Brigadier General John Bell Hood's advance south from Old National Pike towards Old Sharpsburg Road late in the afternoon on the 14th. Virtually every author who wrote about the Battle of South Mountain misstated Hood's movements and his level of success. Until this book's publication, students of the Civil War misunderstood the conclusion of the battle at Fox's Gap.

I have chosen to take an analytical approach, rather than a narrative approach, to the battle at Fox's Gap, and will focus on the movement of Brigadier General John Bell Hood's two brigades during the late afternoon. The study will use primary source evidence and direct or firsthand eyewitness accounts by the events' participants on both the Union and Confederate sides of the battle. Ted Ellis, a lifelong resident of Sharpsburg and local authority, provided me with his analysis of the geography of the South Mountain battlefield. Ted's knowledge of the geographic features of the Turner's and Fox's Gap area helped make the words of the participants in the battle come alive.

There has been general agreement among historians about much of the combat for Fox's Gap; however, many details were difficult to substantiate. Unfortunately, many participants at South Mountain died in the ensuing Battle of Antietam and left no written record of their involvement at South Mountain. A re-examination of various components of the battle at Fox's Gap was overdue. The following analysis will emphasize the Union Army's objective to flank Turner's Gap via Fox's Gap.

Union Major General George B. McClellan, informed by a lost copy of General Robert E. Lee's Special Order No. 191 near Frederick, Maryland, knew Lee had divided his army.[8] This knowledge allowed McClellan to strike at the separated parts of Lee's army and destroy them in detail.

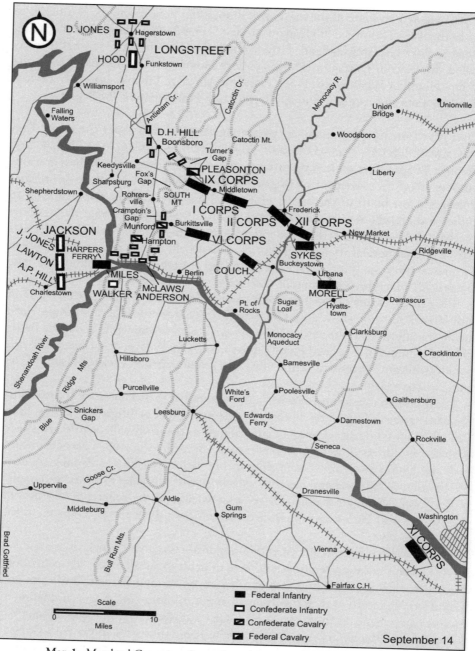

Map 1: Maryland Campaign, September 14, 1862. (Map by Bradley Gottfried)

McClellan hoped to confront the Confederates on the north end of the line while inserting Major General William B. Franklin's Sixth Corps into the center of the Rebel position in Pleasant Valley. Doing so would cut the Rebel army in two and deploy Franklin's roughly 13,000 men to relieve Colonel Dixon S. Miles's besieged command at Harpers Ferry.

Under the command of Major General Ambrose E. Burnside, the Union Ninth Corps was at Middletown, MD, about three miles from Turner's Gap, on the night of September 13. Confederate troops under Major General Daniel H. Hill held both Turner's and Fox's Gaps, although rather loosely, early on September 14. Hill positioned two brigades at the gaps in response to an order given by Lee for Hill to do so once Lee learned of the rapidly advancing Federals. Hill subsequently called up his other three brigades as the Federal assault began at 9:00 am on September 14.

General Lee, who never planned to defend South Mountain, ordered eight infantry brigades under Major General James Longstreet and the independent brigade under Brigadier General Nathan "Shanks" Evans to march from their encampments around Hagerstown, Maryland, and reinforce Hill. These events set the stage for a day-long battle atop South Mountain that saw Hill's and Longstreet's men struggle to hold Turner's and Fox's Gaps. Among the reinforcements, Longstreet brought the men under Brigadier General John Bell Hood, consisting of Colonel Evander M. Law's and Colonel William T. Wofford's Brigades.

The research presented in this book substantiates that previous writers missed the location of Hood's advance south of Old National Pike in the late afternoon of September 14. The placement by all other authors of Hood's two brigades, long thought to be accurate, was not credible. Hood's command suffered a decisive defeat one half-mile west of Fox's Gap. This book documents the extent to which Hood's men lost the fight and, in so doing, corrects errors in the history of the Battle of South Mountain that lingered for too many years. The Union army won a great victory on the Fox's Gap battlefield, and the evidence presented in this book confirms it.

Understanding the Battlefield Geography

The reader may find it helpful to refer to Appendix A for more information on the features of the battlefield area.

By 1730, the Great Philadelphia Wagon Road passed through what became Fox's Gap.[9] Along with his family, John Frederick Fox settled along the road about a half-mile west of the mountain crest sometime in the 1750s.[10] During the Braddock Expedition of 1755, Major General Edward Braddock, Governor Horatio Sharpe,

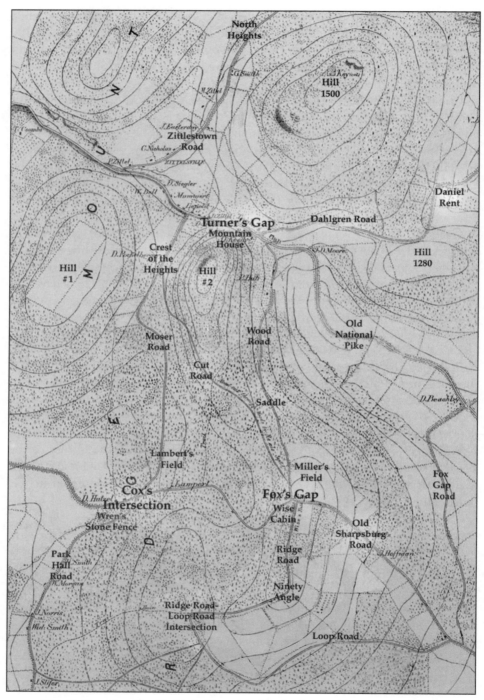

Map 2: (Locations identified in bold on *Atlas Map* by Curtis Older) (Declan Ingram)

George Washington, and Colonel William Dunbar's Regiment passed through Fox's Gap in their failed attempt to capture Fort Duquesne from the French and their Indian allies at the Forks of the Ohio, today Pittsburgh, PA.[11] With the creation of Sharpsburg in 1763, the road became known as Sharpsburg Road and later Old Sharpsburg Road, the name it was known by during the Battle of South Mountain.

Robert Turner patented a land tract called Nelson's Folly at the present site of Boonsboro, Maryland, in 1750.[12] There does not appear to be another Turner, other than Robert, for whom to name Turner's Gap. Construction of the first road through Turner's Gap came in 1756 with the creation

George Washington. "First in War, First in Peace, and First in the Hearts of His Countrymen."

of Fort Frederick.[13] In the early 1800s, the National Road or National Turnpike replaced the wagon road through Turner's Gap. The National Road was the first road financed by the United States Congress and the first macadam road built in the United States.[14]

By September 14, 1862, the road through Turner's Gap was identified as the National Road on the Map of the Battlefield of South Mountain in the *Atlas to Accompany the Official Records of the Union and Confederate Armies* (*Atlas Map*). Union Brigadier General Jacob D. Cox identified the road as the National Road on his map of the Battlefield of South Mountain in his *Military Reminiscences*.[15]

Before we analyze the infantry and artillery movements in the battle for Fox's Gap, we must clearly understand the geography and physical characteristics of the battlefield. This understanding is essential to make sense of the command decisions made by both Union and Confederate officers. A failure to properly recognize the geographical characteristics of the battlefield and how they impacted the decisions made during the battle led to the inability to correctly analyze the movements of Hood and his two brigades during the late afternoon of September 14, 1862.

The contested battles fought at Fox's Gap and Turner's Gap were over a handful of land tracts surveyed and patented in the 1700s and early 1800s. Parcels of land in the 1700s received a name to identify them. The battles for Fox's and Turner's Gaps primarily took place over a plot of land named Addition to Friendship.[16]

Overlaid on Map 4 are the land tracts of Addition to Friendship, Flonham, and the Miller's Field tract of John Miller. According to Steven Stanley, a cartographer who specializes in Civil War maps, when the Confederates, led by Colonel Thomas L. Rosser and Major John Pelham, arrived at Fox's Gap, Pelham's guns took up a position in Miller's Field east of Wood Road.[17] Rosser's 5th Virginia Cavalry straddled Old Sharpsburg Road, perhaps 200 feet east of the mountain crest at Fox's Gap, and Rosser sent a screen of skirmishers further down Old Sharpsburg Road to the east. Rosser and Pelham's men arrived the night before at the direction of Major General J. E. B. Stuart.

The Addition to Friendship tract contained 202 acres of land. Frederick Fox, a son of John Fox, laid out the acreage in a 1797 survey, and he received the patent in 1805.[18] The tract consisted of approximately 105 acres on Turner's Gap's east side and

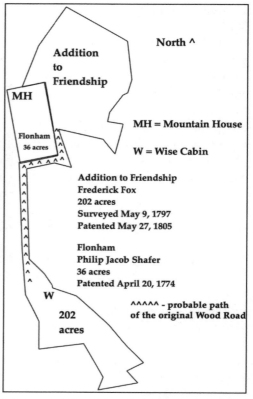

Map 3: Battle for Addition to Friendship, 1797 Land Survey by Frederick Fox. (Map by Curtis Older)

85 acres at Fox's Gap along Old Sharpsburg Road. The remaining 12 acres of Addition to Friendship ran along the east side of South Mountain's East Ridge and formed a connecting corridor between the two more significant segments.

The corridor connecting Turner's and Fox's Gaps became Wood Road and was about a mile long. The useable portion along much of Wood Road was narrow, as the ground fell off quickly to the east and to a lesser degree to the west. Over the years, modifications came to Wood Road near Turner's Gap. Today the Appalachian Trail runs along much of the original Wood Road.

The Addition to Friendship tract was contiguous to a lot named Flonham, patented by Philip J. Shafer in 1774.[19] The northern portion of Flonham became the site of the Mountain House. The Mountain House at Turner's Gap probably dates to after the construction of the turnpike in 1807; I believe the building of the Mountain House was after 1826 when Henry Miller acquired the five acres of land for its construction. An Edward L. Boteler purchased the land from the Miller family in 1855 and held it until 1867. The Mountain House, known today as the Old South Mountain Inn, still stands as a landmark south of Old National Pike at Turner's Gap.[20]

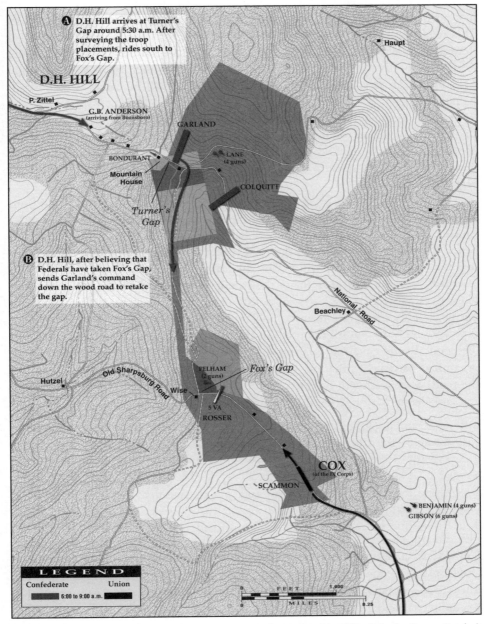

Map 4: Fox's and Turner's Gaps, 6:00 am to 9:00 am, September 14, 1862. (Map by Steven Stanley)

Area Roads

Two roads ran south from Old National Pike to the Rohrersville area in 1862. In his *Military Reminiscences,* Union Brigadier General Jacob D. Cox referred to the first north-south road west of Fox's and Turner's Gaps as the "Rohrersville Road."[21] This road will be the primary focus of the discussion that follows. The road lay between the West Ridge and the East Ridge of South Mountain. While not the official or locally known name for this road on September 14, it was the name used by Union Brigadier General Cox. Hereafter it will be called Moser Road, its name today.

Ted Ellis estimated the distance from the Mountain House to the Old National Pike and Moser Road intersection shown on the *Atlas Map* in 1862 as 1,300 feet.[22] Moser Road intersected Old Sharpsburg Road about a half-mile west of Fox's Gap. Today, from Old Sharpsburg Road south to the Rohrersville area, the road is Park Hall Road.

A second road, labeled on the *Atlas Map* as the "Road to Rohrersville," ran from Boonsboro to the Rohrersville area and intersected Old Sharpsburg Road two miles south of Boonsboro and a mile and a half west of Fox's Gap. Today, Maryland Route 67 roughly approximates the road to the Rohrersville area from Boonsboro in 1862. This second route will not be the primary focus of our discussion.

Roads were the critical factor in the strategy employed by both the Union and Confederate forces in the Battle of South Mountain. Roads were how the armies moved cannon, ammunition, and supply wagons to provide support to their infantry. Infantry sought to control the roads in the battlefield area because these were their lifeblood. Roads gave the infantry a means of determining their location in an unfamiliar battlefield situation. The case was made clear in the struggle to control the roads associated with the Fox's Gap battlefield.

Confederate Major General Hill told us about two roads used by his artillery:

> There were two mountain roads for artillery on the right [south] of the main turnpike [Old National Pike]. The defense of the farther one [Ridge Road] had cost Brigadier General Samuel Garland Jr. his life. It was now entrusted to Rosser of the cavalry, who had reported to me, and who had artillery [Major John Pelham] and dismounted sharpshooters [5th VA Cavalry]. Brigadier General George B. Anderson was entrusted with caring for the nearest and best road [Old Sharpsburg Road]. [Captain James W.] Bondurant's battery was sent to aid him in its defense.[23]

Hill did not clearly describe the two roads south of Old National Pike usable by Confederate artillery. I interpreted Hill to identify one road as the road somewhat along or near the mountain's East Ridge. This road consisted of Wood Road between Turner's and Fox's Gaps and Ridge Road south of Old Sharpsburg Road. The mortal wounding of Garland, according to most accounts, was south of Old Sharpsburg Road along Upper Ridge Road. The second and best road that Hill identified was Old Sharpsburg Road. Hill perhaps omitted including Moser Road in his description since it was an uncontested road until late in the battle.

The West Ridge and the East Ridge

Ted Ellis of Sharpsburg, a local authority on the geography of the area, described the two mountain ridges on the west and east sides of Moser Road and Park Hall Road, the first north-to-south roads west of Turner's and Fox's Gaps:

> West Ridge (Hill #1)—The west mountain ridge, running along the near west side of Moser Road, begins to rise about one mile south of Old Sharpsburg Road and passes through Hill #1. Park Hall Road, south of Old Sharpsburg Road, curves around the southernmost point of the West Ridge. The west crest extends north to Pennsylvania Route 16 and is the primary ridge of the mountain north of the Washington Monument, located about a mile north of the Mountain House.

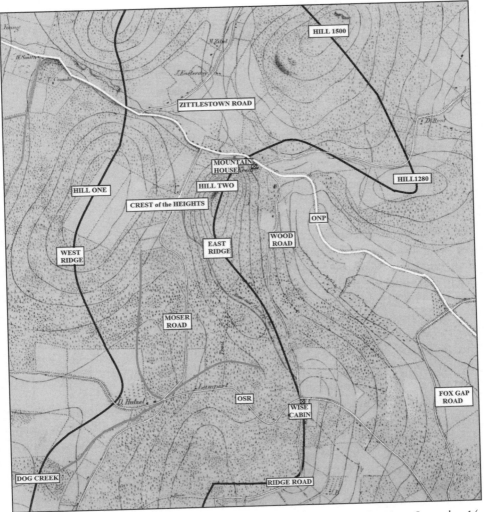

Map 5: West and East Ridges of South Mountain, Turner's Gap and Fox's Gap Area, September 14, 1862. (Map by Ted Ellis)

> East Ridge (Hill #2)—The east mountain ridge is on the east side of Moser Road. The Frederick and Washington county line follows the highest part of this mountain ridge from the Potomac River to near the Washington Monument, located about a mile north of the Mountain House. There the county line shifted from the East Ridge to the West. The Lambs Knoll peak at 1,680 feet was the highest point on the east crest of the mountain, a mile and one-half south of Old Sharpsburg Road.

The Battlefield of South Mountain Map in the *Official Records* showed the words "Blue Ridge Mountains" running along the West Ridge of South Mountain between Old National Pike and Old Sharpsburg Road.

Knowledge of the two ridges significantly alters the interpretation of Hood's statements we will analyze later. For this reason, perhaps, Ezra Carman, Antietam historian and author, placed Hood's two brigades at Fox's Gap rather than a half-mile west. Carman did not acknowledge that the two mountain crests extended south of Old National Pike. According to Carman:

> A narrow valley divides the mountain into two crests or ridges north of the turnpike. Though deep at the gap [Turner's Gap], the valley becomes a slight depression about a mile to the north.[24]

Carman referred to the area near the Washington Monument, approximately a mile north of the Mountain House. Carman's assessment was correct; it just was not complete. He did not acknowledge or was unaware of the two ridges south of Old National Pike.

The Confederate Defensive Posture

The Confederate "defensive posture" on September 14, 1862, at Turner's Gap between the West Ridge and the East Ridge of South Mountain was at a higher elevation than the area east of the East Ridge, the direction from which the Union Army began their attack. The Confederates probably considered the Crest of the Heights, between Hill #1 and Hill #2 along Moser Road, part of the "top of the mountain" during the battle. Perhaps Hood sought to defend the "top of the mountain" during his late afternoon march south from Old National Pike. Hood likely considered the immediate area of Fox's Gap, near Miller's Field and the Wise Cabin, as lost to the Union upon hearing reports from Brigadier General Thomas F. Drayton's men as Hood advanced to the south.

As will become evident from the following material, the only route of escape from the area of the "Confederate defensive posture," as shown on Ted Ellis's map, was northwest along Old National Pike to Boonsboro. The route was through Zittlestown gorge. Union troops under Cox eliminated Old Sharpsburg Road as a route of escape by the evening of September 14, as the following evidence will substantiate.

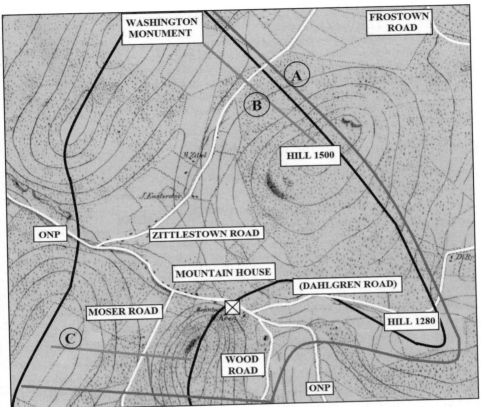

Map 6: Confederate Defensive Posture at Turner's Gap, September 14, 1862. A—Confederate Defensive Perimeter; B—Crest of the Heights between Washington Monument and Hill 1500; C—Crest of the Heights between Hill #1 and Hill #2; Black—West and East Ridges of South Mountain. (Identified on the *Atlas Map* by Ted Ellis)

Miller's Field

Ted Ellis described his findings from his inspection of Miller's Field as follows:

> The most significant factor concerning Miller's Field was its convex or curved shape. One cannot overstate this point. Miller's Field's highpoint was 240 yards north of Old Sharpsburg Road and 75 yards east of Wood Road, as measured on the United States Geological Survey topographic quadrangle. The field sloped away from the highpoint in every direction, North, South, East, and West. Old Sharpsburg Road turned southeast on the east side of the East Crest. From the Saddle, northwest of Miller's Field, one could not see Old Sharpsburg Road.
>
> Even in the open field, an individual could not see Old Sharpsburg Road from more than 50 yards north of the high point. One could not see Old Sharpsburg Road from along Wood Road until they reached a point within 200 yards north of Old Sharpsburg Road. The shape of Miller's Field made it impossible for the Federals on Old Sharpsburg Road to see the Saddle

of the East Ridge. It was impossible for the Confederates at the Saddle to see the Federals in Miller's Field until they were nearby.

The Confederates probably had forward observers hidden along the East Ridge crest on the west side of Wood Road near Old Sharpsburg Road to warn of any Union movements in that direction. The Confederates could have placed guns at the Saddle, but they would have fired blindly at Old Sharpsburg Road. When initially placing his men on Miller's Field the night of September 13, Major General J. E. B. Stuart would have put them on the high ground in the center of the field for maximum utility.

Some Preliminaries to the Battle

In Special Order #191, issued on or about September 9, General Lee divided his army and ordered Major General Thomas "Stonewall" Jackson to move his command to Martinsburg, Virginia.[25] Jackson would later march on Harpers Ferry, held by Union troops, and seek its surrender. Major General Lafayette McLaws's command and Brigadier General John Walker's command also would assist in the capture of Harpers Ferry. Major General James Longstreet was to move his command to Boonsboro, Maryland, while Major General Hill's Division was to act as the rearguard on the march from Frederick, Maryland. Longstreet then marched with two Confederate divisions to Hagerstown while Hill established his base at Boonsboro. The Old National Pike, at the time of the battle, was somewhat equivalent to Interstate I-70 today.

During the afternoon of September 13, Federal cavalry and their infantry support pushed Confederate Major General J. E. B. Stuart's cavalry west of Middletown towards Turner's Gap. Upon receiving notice from Stuart, Hill ordered two of his brigades under Brigadier General Samuel Garland Jr. and Colonel Alfred H. Colquitt and the artillery batteries of Captain James W. Bondurant and Captain John Lane in Boonsboro to reinforce Turner's Gap. Lieutenant Colonel Allen S. Cutts's Battalion of the Reserve Artillery, which included Bondurant's and Lane's artillery, had been assigned to Hill's Division only a short time before.[26]

Colquitt's force had about 1,400 men.[27] Garland's Brigade had a troop strength of slightly over 2,500 men on September 2 but fell to approximately 945 on the 14th.[28] The 23rd North Carolina Regiment's history indicated Garland's Brigade numbered less than 1,000 men on September 14.[29]

Stuart and his Jeff Davis Cavalry Legion arrived at Turner's Gap from the east about 4:00 pm on September 13, just as Colquitt's Brigade arrived from Boonsboro. After informing Colquitt that the enemy's force consisted of cavalry and one or two infantry brigades, Stuart remained at Turner's Gap with his cavalry until darkness and then retired to Boonsboro.[30]

Later that evening, after observing the campfires of an entire Federal Corps to the east, Colquitt notified Hill in Boonsboro. Hill quickly warned Lee of the evolving situation confronting the Confederate defense of Turner's Gap. Lee was at Hagerstown with Longstreet's Corps, having arrived there on September 11. Lee's response was to request Hill and Stuart to fortify the Confederate defenses at Turner's Gap. Both

Hill and Stuart were in Boonsboro when Lee's messages arrived, but, for reasons unknown, they failed to communicate with each other. Communications between Lee and Hill were via dispatch until Lee returned to Boonsboro with Longstreet and his men during the late afternoon on the 14th.

Stuart explained the orders he gave the evening of the 13th:

> On reaching the vicinity of the gap near Boonsborough, I found General Hill's troops occupying the gap [Turner's]. I turned off General Hampton, with all his cavalry except the Jeff Davis [Cavalry] Legion, to re-enforce [Colonel Thomas T.] Munford at Crampton's Gap, which was now the weakest point of the line. I remained at the gap near Boonsborough until night, but the enemy did not attack the position. No place for cavalry operations, a single horseman passing from point to point on the mountain with difficulty, so I left the Jeff Davis [Cavalry] Legion here. I directed Colonel Rosser, with a detachment of cavalry and the Stuart Horse Artillery [Pelham], to occupy Braddock's [Fox's] Gap. I started on my way to join the main portion of my command at Crampton's Gap, stopping for the night near Boonsborough.[31]

Clarification of Stuart's remarks in his report was necessary. Stuart inferred the Jeff Davis Legion spent the night of the 13th at Turner's Gap. "The Jeff Davis [Cavalry] Legion, detached to guard Solomon's Gap in Elk Ridge near Harpers Ferry on the 14th, rejoined the army on the 16th and rejoined its brigade the following afternoon."[32]

What was evident and usually overlooked in Stuart's order of the 13th was his recognition of the importance of Fox's Gap, while all other preparations focused on Old National Pike. Stuart's placement of Colonel Rosser's cavalry unit of approximately 200 men and Pelham's artillery section of two guns at Fox's Gap fully 12 or more hours before the battle at Fox's Gap began on September 14 was genuinely astounding![33] Stuart read the minds of Union Brigadier Generals Alfred Pleasonton and Jacob D. Cox and virtually knew what they would do a dozen or so hours before they chose to attack first at Fox's Gap. Stuart and Pleasonton probably were taught a similar strategy as students at West Point. Stuart saw that Fox's Gap provided the Union forces with a way to flank Turner's Gap from the rear.

Stuart's Cavalry Division consisted of three batteries: Chew's (Virginia) horse battery in Robertson's Brigade, the Washington (South Carolina) Battery or Hart's (South Carolina) horse battery in Hampton's Brigade, and Stuart's (Virginia) Horse Artillery under Pelham.[34] Captain R. Preston Chew's Battery fought at Crampton's Gap, while Captain J. F. Hart's Washington (SC) Battery was not in the battle at South Mountain, or if it was, its location was unknown. Pelham's artillery saw significant action at and near Fox's Gap.

Troops under Hill's command formed the dispersed Confederate Army's rearguard on September 14. With the Confederate Army widely divided, holding the South Mountain passes was critical to prevent McClellan's Union Army of the Potomac from getting between Jackson's Confederate Army at Harpers Ferry and Longstreet's Confederate Army at Hagerstown. If Jackson's force achieved the surrender of the 13,000-man Union garrison stationed at Harpers Ferry, Jackson's men would move to Williamsport and then Hagerstown to join Longstreet.

Hill sent three 10-pound Parrott guns and one Whitworth rifled gun of Lane's Georgia battery a half-mile east of the Mountain House just south of the road to Daniel Rent's Farm (today Dahlgren Road).[35] These guns occupied the top of Hill 1280, as identified by D. Scott Hartwig (see preceding map).[36] After the war, the road from Turner's Gap to Frostown became known as Dahlgren Road.[37] Madeline V. Dahlgren, the widow of Admiral John A. Dahlgren, purchased the Mountain House property in 1876.[38]

Union Major General George B. McClellan's Headquarters were just south of Old National Pike between Bolivar Heights and Middletown, as noted on the *Atlas Map*. Today, the location is near Bolivar Court, which runs between Old National Pike and Bolivar Road.[39]

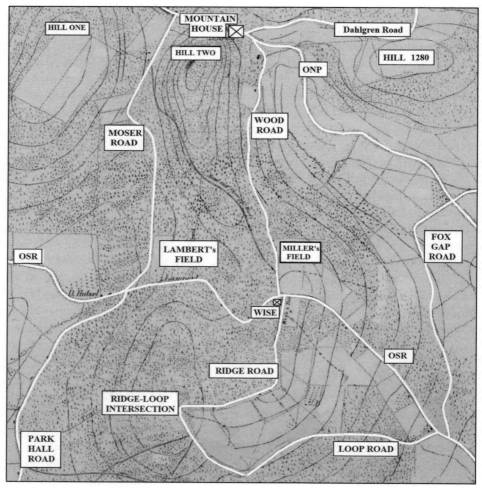

Map 7: Close-up of Turner's and Fox's Gaps, September 14, 1862. (Map by Ted Ellis)

The following discussion will focus on the primary source evidence provided by officers and soldiers in the Union Army present at the battle. McClellan described the overwhelming Union success in the fight for the Fox's and Turner's Gap's battlefields on September 15, at Bolivar, Maryland. "If I can believe one-tenth of what is reported, God has seldom given an army a greater victory than this."[40]

Major General Ambrose Burnside, commander of the Union First and Ninth Corps, wrote the following:

> A topographical survey is being done. It will show the country's nature and the troops' disposition. I feel sure that history will demonstrate this to have been one of the many brilliant engagements of the war.[41]

One critical military factor prevented Lee from reuniting his Confederate Army late on September 14 or 15. The Union Ninth Corps held Cox's Intersection, today the intersection of Moser Road and Reno Monument Road (formerly Old Sharpsburg Road), one half-mile west of Fox's Gap. If the Confederates at Turner's Gap moved south towards Cox's Intersection, they would run headlong into the Union Ninth Corps under Cox. Union Major General Joseph Hooker's First Corps at Turner's Gap would follow Lee's troops from the north in close pursuit. Thus, Lee could not move his forces from Turner's and Fox's Gaps to Sharpsburg along Old Sharpsburg Road.

McClellan's objective in keeping a wedge between Lee's Army near Turner's Gap and Jackson's troops at Harpers Ferry was intact on September 14. Lee never ordered his troops to retreat before South Mountain. The only viable route of Lee's retreat was through Boonsboro by Zittlestown gorge. For these reasons and the overwhelming defeat of the Confederates on the battlefield, the Union's success at Turner's and Fox's Gaps was a great victory by the Union's high command and the common soldier.

Miller's Field, the Wise Cabin on the right. Old Sharpsburg Road left to right, September 14, 1862.

I will not delve into the chain of events that led up to the Battle of South Mountain. Numerous authors have previously covered that aspect of the Maryland Campaign. If Lee had any plans or thoughts of moving his army into Pennsylvania, they ended with the Battle of South Mountain. However, Sharpsburg and the banks of Antietam Creek offered Lee the opportunity of one more battle in Maryland at a location of Lee's choosing. The capitulation of the Union forces at Harpers Ferry to Jackson on September 15 at 8:00 am gave Lee that chance. In the South, the Battle of Antietam on September 17 was called the Battle of Sharpsburg.

It was evident from the correspondence of McClellan to the Union high command that a primary objective of his on September 15 continued to be the ability of the Army of the Potomac to remain between, and to keep separated, Jackson's and Lee's forces. The following chapter will present primary source evidence from the Union perspective regarding Confederate Brigadier General John Bell Hood's advance with two brigades south of Old National Pike during the late afternoon on September 14.

CHAPTER TWO

Fox's Gap—Union Perspective

The morning of Sunday the 14th of September was a bright one.

UNION BRIGADIER GENERAL JACOB D. COX[1]

Cox's Intersection

A primary objective of this book will be to confirm the correctness of the following statement by Union Brigadier General Jacob D. Cox about the combat for Fox's Gap during the Battle of South Mountain:

> The order came to me as the senior officer upon the line, and the signal [was] given. On the left [west], Longstreet's men were pushed down the mountainside beyond the Rohrersville and Sharpsburg roads, and the contest there was ended.[2]

Previous authors who wrote about the Battle of South Mountain rejected this statement by Cox. Authors, including Ezra Carman, contended that two brigades under Hood advanced south from Turner's Gap along or near Wood Road just before sundown. They claimed that Hood recaptured part of the ground lost at Fox's Gap in the late afternoon by Drayton. Most authors placed the totality of Union forces near Miller's Field and Wise's Field at Fox's Gap at the battle's end. None of the authors placed Union troops at Cox's Intersection.

Rohrersville Road was the name Cox gave to the first road that ran north to south on the west side of Turner's and Fox's Gaps. Today, Rohrersville Road, identified by Cox, bears the name of Moser Road between Old National Pike and Old Sharpsburg Road and Park Hall Road between Old Sharpsburg Road and the Rohrersville area. In Cox's quote, Sharpsburg Road was Old Sharpsburg Road at the time of the battle. Old Sharpsburg Road is Reno Monument Road running through Fox's Gap today.

I will use the term "Cox's Intersection" to identify the "Rohrersville and Sharpsburg roads" intersection described by Cox. Today, this is the Moser Road and Reno Monument Road intersection about one half-mile west of Fox's Gap. I will provide primary source evidence to establish that Cox's Intersection was where

Union Brigadier General Jacob D. Cox, 1861–5. (Courtesy Oberlin College Library Special Collections)

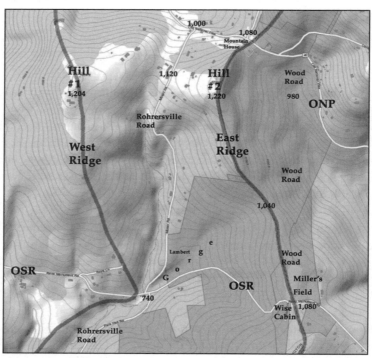

Map 8: Cox's Intersection, Moser and Park Hall Roads at Old Sharpsburg Road. (Locations identified in bold on current topographical map by Curtis Older)

Brigadier General John Bell Hood attacked with his two brigades about dark on September 14, 1862, where Hood lost many men killed and wounded, and as Cox said, where the battle ended.

The Initial Union Strategy

Union Brigadier General Jacob D. Cox described the initiation of events in the Battle of South Mountain on the morning of September 14 as follows:

> At my camp in front of Middletown, I received no orders looking to a general advance on the 14th; but only to support, by a detachment, Pleasonton's cavalry in a reconnaissance toward Turner's Gap.
>
> I rode forward again and found Pleasonton. [Colonel Eliakim P.] Scammon had given him a clue of our suspicions, and they had reached a good mutual understanding in the personal interview. I found that he was convinced that it would be unwise to make an attack in front and had determined that his cavalry should merely demonstrate upon the main road and support the batteries while Scammon should march by the Old Sharpsburg Road and try to reach the flank of the force on the summit. I told him that given my fear that the enemy's strength might be too great for Scammon, I had determined to bring forward Colonel George Crook's Brigade in support. If it became necessary to fight with the whole Division, I should do so, and in that case, I should assume the responsibility myself as his senior officer. To this, he cordially assented. [3]

Cox made the case undeniably clear that the Union's objective in marching by Old Sharpsburg Road was a flank attack against the Confederates at Turner's Gap. Pleasonton thought a frontal attack would be unwise, and Cox agreed. Cox's and Pleasonton's idea was a flank attack against the enemy's rear at Turner's Gap.

Brigadier General Alfred Pleasonton commanded a Union Cavalry Division at South Mountain. He provided the following statement in his after-action report on September 19:

> Scammon's [infantry] brigade I directed to move up the mountain on the left-hand road [Old Sharpsburg Road], gain the crest, and then move to the right [north] to the turnpike [Old National Pike] in the enemy's rear. [4]

There is every reason to believe the initial Union strategy of Pleasonton and Cox remained in place throughout the day. Union Major Generals McClellan, Burnside, Reno, and Brigadier General Pleasonton were together in the afternoon at Pleasonton's position at a knoll near Old National Pike. From that point, they issued their orders. As the battle began, Pleasonton specifically told Colonel Scammon the objective of his 1st Brigade was to flank the enemy's rear.

Pleasonton was straightforward with his statement. After gaining the crest, Scammon should attack "in the enemy's rear." We cannot read into Pleasonton's directive that after Scammon gained the ridge, he should attack along Wood Road and reach Turner's Gap by that route. A correct reading of Pleasonton should focus on "in the enemy's rear."

Pleasonton also informed us about the area roads:

> I also learned that there were two roads, one on the right and the other to the left of the gap, both of which entered the turnpike beyond [west of] the gap and would assist us materially in turning the enemy's position on both flanks.[5]

Pleasonton confirmed that today's Zittlestown Road and Moser Road met Old National Pike on the *west side* of Turner's Gap. It was evident that Pleasonton did not refer to Wood Road or Dahlgren Road, which met Old National Pike on the *east side* of Turner's Gap. (See Map 9)

Wood Road met Old National Pike 300 feet east of the Mountain House during the battle on September 14. That intersection was not in the enemy's rear. We can conclude that Pleasonton intended Scammon to attack Turner's Gap from the west and rear using Moser Road. Using the *Atlas Map*, Ted Ellis estimated the distance west from the Mountain House to the Moser Road and Old National Pike intersection as 1,300 feet.

Pleasonton also credited Major General Jesse L. Reno for the great Union success in the battle:

> He [Reno] was eminently successful in driving the enemy until he fell when he gallantly led his command to a crowning victory. Reno's clear judgment and determined courage rendered the triumphant results obtained by the operations of his corps second to none of the brilliant deeds accomplished on that field.[6]

It was evident that Pleasonton considered the Ninth Corps effort at Fox's Gap an overwhelming victory.

While Pleasonton's role during the Battle of South Mountain was somewhat unclear, there was no reason to believe he was unaware of the events during the day and evening of the battle. Cox informed us that by 4:00 pm, "McClellan had arrived on the field, and he with Burnside and Reno was at Pleasonton's position at the knoll in the valley, and from that point, a central one in the middle of the curving hills, they issued their orders."[7]

Cox's statement placed McClellan at his headquarters, as shown on the *Atlas Map*. This location was east of Bolivar Road and south of Old National Pike. It was almost directly north of the Fox Inn. Ted Ellis indicated that location was the only "knoll" nearby separate from the mountain. It was decidedly higher than the surrounding valley and gave the best view of the battlefield, left and right.

There was no reason to believe that Pleasonton did not inform Reno, Burnside, and McClellan of Pleasonton's original strategy to flank the Confederates by the two roads west of Turner's Gap. Had the fight been renewed on September 15, the Union Army threatened to capture the Zittlestown Road and Moser Road intersections with Old National Pike from the north and the Moser Road and Old National Pike intersection from the south. Pleasonton's initial strategy to flank Turner's Gap, in which Cox concurred, remained intact throughout September 14 and would have been brought to fruition on September 15.

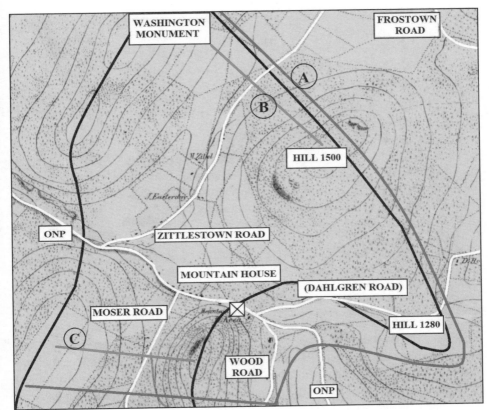

Map 9: Initial Union Strategy, September 14, 1862. A—Confederate Defensive Perimeter; B—North Crest of the Heights; C—South Crest of the Heights; Black—West and East Ridges of South Mountain. (Identified on *Atlas Map* by Ted Ellis)

Union Brigadier General Alfred Pleasonton directed the placement of Lieutenant Samuel N. Benjamin's four cannon and Captain Horatio G. Gibson's six cannon on an isolated 700-foot-wide rise of high ground at about 8:00 am on September 14.[8] This knob, approximately 75 feet higher than the surrounding terrain, was near Fox Gap Road (See Map 10), east of Old Sharpsburg Road. The location of the cannon was closer to the Fox Gap Road and Old Sharpsburg Road intersection than the Bolivar Road and Old Sharpsburg Road intersection.

Brigadier General Cox posted an additional six Union cannon near the same rise before 9:00 am. These six guns consisted of four 10-lb Parrotts under Captain James R. McMullin and Captain Seth J. Simmonds's section of two 20-lb Parrotts.[9] The position was near one half-mile beyond where any fighting occurred on the east side of South Mountain.

Edward O. Lord's *History of the Ninth New Hampshire Regiment* indicated Benjamin's four guns fired at Confederate artillery on the north side of Old

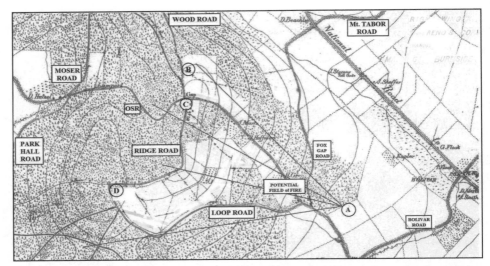

Map 10: Union Cannon Effectiveness at Fox's Gap. Point A—16 cannon near Fox Gap Road—725–30 ft. elevation; Point B—north side of Miller's Field—1,060 ft. elevation; Point C—Wise's Cabin—1,060 ft. elevation; Point D—Ridge-Loop Intersection—1,100 ft. Elevation. September 14, 1862. (Identified on *Atlas Map* by Ted Ellis)

National Pike and at Fox's Gap.[10] The effective range of the Union cannon from their positions near Fox Gap Road included any point on the east side of the East Ridge of South Mountain, from Fox's Gap to Turner's Gap. The locations subject to Union cannon fire included the Ridge-Loop Intersection, Wise's Cabin, and the north side of Miller's Field.

Based solely upon period line-of-sight and elevations, Union cannon near Fox Gap Road could target Confederate artillery at Fox's Gap. However, Union infantry near the mountain crest needed to be out of the line of fire, limiting the Union guns' effectiveness. A likely target of the 16 Union cannon was Bondurant's artillery at or near Miller's Field late in the battle. Due to the convex shape of Miller's Field, it is difficult to see how Confederate cannon at the northwest corner of Miller's Field near Wood Road could have been effective during the battle. That location was below the elevation near the center of Miller's Field and Old Sharpsburg Road was out of sight.

It was reasonable to believe that the 16 Union cannon maintained their fire towards Fox's Gap, primarily around the Wise Cabin, Miller's Field, and Wood Road, during the two-hour lull in the infantry fight between noon and 2:00 pm.[11] Many Union cannon also aimed their fire toward the Confederate artillery north of the Old National Pike and near Turner's Gap.

The Battle Begins

A Confederate brigade led by Brigadier General Samuel Garland Jr., which consisted solely of North Carolina infantry regiments, moved along Wood Road

Battle of South Mountain at Fox's Gap, September 14, 1862. (Library of Congress)

before 9:00 am. They moved from their positions at Turner's Gap to occupy posts along the entire Ridge Road at Fox's Gap.[12] Ridge Road ran from Old Sharpsburg Road to the Ridge-Loop Intersection. Confederate cavalry under Colonel Thomas L. Rosser and two cannon under Major John Pelham occupied the Ridge-Loop Intersection at the beginning of the battle.

The NinetyAngle was about the midpoint of Ridge Road and where Upper Ridge Road met Lower Ridge Road. Upper Ridge Road connected with Old Sharpsburg Road, and Lower Ridge Road ran south to the Ridge-Loop Intersection. The NinetyAngle was where the Ridge Road began to angle to the southwest from a primarily north to south line. Four additional guns under Captain James W. Bondurant near the NinetyAngle helped fortify the initial Confederate position.[13]

The infantry battle for Fox's Gap began at 9:00 am Sunday, September 14, 1862, with Union infantry led by Lieutenant Colonel Rutherford B. Hayes, who initiated an attack against the Confederates about one-half-mile south of Fox's Gap.[14] Another member of the 23rd Ohio infantry that day besides Hayes was Sergeant William McKinley. Hayes and McKinley later became United States presidents.

The Union infantry approached Fox's Gap from the east by way of Old Sharpsburg Road with the objective to flank the Confederates holding Turner's Gap one mile to the north. Hayes and his men moved along a path known as Loop Road and Loop Road Spur to initiate an attack farther south against the Confederate right, or southern, flank positioned along Lower Ridge Road and at the Ridge-Loop Intersection.

Today, Lambs Knoll Road roughly follows the route of Ridge Road that passed near the Ridge-Loop Intersection. Most of the land between Loop Road and Ridge Road was open ground or farm fields on September 14.

Map 11 shows the current battlefield view on the south side of Old Sharpsburg Road at Fox's Gap. Part of Loop Road followed the David's Will land tract's southern border. The military crest ran somewhat parallel to Ridge Road as it appeared on the map. According to Wikipedia:

> The military crest was an area on the forward or opposite slope of a hill or ridge just below the topographical crest. A person can obtain maximum observation of the decline down to the mountain's base.[15]

In his *Maps of Antietam*, Bradley Gottfried identified the Confederate and Union positions between 6:00 am and 8:00 am on September 14 (Map 12).[16] Gottfried placed Rosser's 5th VA cavalry just east of the NinetyAngle along Ridge Road and Pelham's guns a short distance beyond them to the southeast. Gottfried indicated Rosser's 5th VA cavalry consisted of 200 men.[17]

Union Major Rutherford B. Hayes, 1861. (Courtesy Rutherford B. Hayes Presidential Library & Museums)

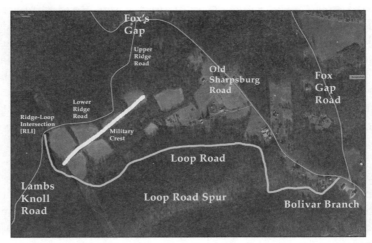

Map 11: Loop Road and Military Crest at Fox's Gap. Aerial view of where the battle began overlaid on 2021 image. (Map by Curtis Older)

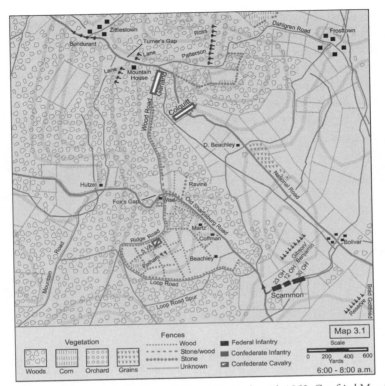

Map 12: Fox's and Turner's Gaps, 6:00 am to 8:00 am, September 14, 1862. Gottfried Map 3.1. (Map by Bradley Gottfried)

Where the Battle for Fox's Gap began. Ground level a half-mile south of Fox's Gap. (Photograph by Curtis Older, September 14, 2012)

Bradley Gottfried's Map 3.3, 9:30 am to 10:00 am, showed the Confederate forces at Fox's Gap in the early morning of September 14.

Union Brigadier General Jacob D. Cox's Kanawha Division captured most of Ridge Road from the Confederates during the morning fight at Fox's Gap, leading Confederate Major General Daniel H. Hill to conceive a counterattack to retake Ridge Road during the afternoon.[18] Hill designated Confederate Brigadier General Thomas F. Drayton's Brigade to occupy the perimeter of Miller's Field and serve as

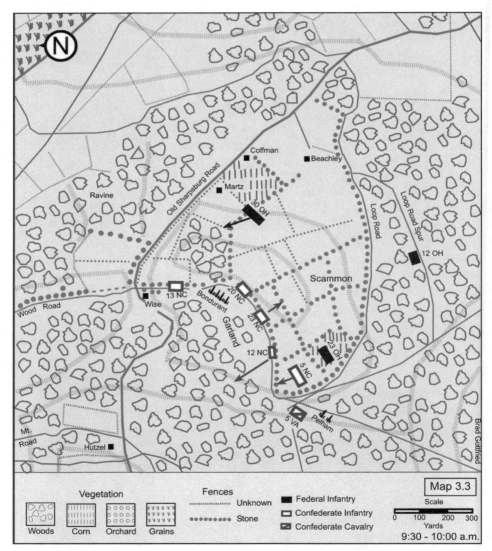

Map 13: Fox's Gap, 9:30 am to 10:00 am, September 14, 1862. (Map by Bradley Gottfried)

Wise Cabin at Fox's Gap, about 1880. (Courtesy U.S. Military Institute, Carlisle, PA)

the hinge of the Confederate movement. Confederate brigades under Colonel George T. Anderson, Brigadier General Roswell S. Ripley, and Brigadier General George B. Anderson would swing towards Ridge Road after starting along Old Sharpsburg Road and Park Hall Road west of Fox's Gap.

We now turn to the primary source evidence from the Union perspective that buttressed the conclusion the Union Ninth Corps occupied Cox's Intersection between 5:30 and 6:00 pm on September 14. Because elements of the Union Ninth Corps occupied that junction and elements of the Union First Corps were near the Mountain House and also just north of the Moser Road and Old National Pike intersection, Lee and his Confederate high command withdrew their forces to Boonsboro before marching to Sharpsburg and Antietam Creek. The option of fighting a second day at Turner's Gap offered no reward to the Confederates and most assuredly a significant defeat.

The Confederates did not want to fight through Cox's Intersection to rejoin Jackson's force at Harpers Ferry. Selection of that option meant the Confederates would meet the Union Ninth Corps head-on in their attempt to cross Old Sharpsburg Road, and the Union First Corps would advance through Turner's Gap in close pursuit.

Union Primary Source Evidence

Our discussion about Confederate Brigadier General John Bell Hood's advance late in the day towards Old Sharpsburg Road begins with evidence supplied by the

Union command. Brigadier General Cox, commanding the Kanawha Division of the Ninth Corps at Fox's Gap, described the following in his *Military Reminiscences*, published in 1900 shortly after his death:

> The order came to me as the senior officer upon the line, and the signal [was] given. On the left [west], Longstreet's men were pushed down the mountainside beyond the Rohrersville and Sharpsburg roads, and the contest there was ended.[19]

Rohrersville Road, to which Cox referred, is Moser Road and Park Hall Road today, extending from Old National Pike at the north to the Rohrersville area at the south. This road was the first north-to-south route west of Turner's and Fox's Gaps and led to Pleasant Valley. The road lay between the West Ridge and the East Ridge of South Mountain. Moser Road was the road to which Pleasonton referred as a route on the south side of the turnpike by which the Union Army could flank Turner's Gap from the rear.

Concerning Cox's published military works, historian Homer C. Hockett said that Cox, in general, was "recognized as an elegant and forceful writer, of fine critical ability and impartial judgment, one of the foremost military historians of the country."[20] His books are still cited today by scholars as objective histories and, in his memoirs, incisive analyses of military practice and events.

Cox's Gorge

A portion of Cox's after-battle report filed on September 20 follows:

> About 4:00 pm, most of the re-enforcements being in position, the order was received to advance the whole line and take or silence the enemy's batteries immediately in front. The order was immediately obeyed, and the advance was made with the utmost enthusiasm. The enemy made a desperate resistance, charging our advancing lines with fierceness, but they were everywhere routed and fled with precipitation. In this advance, the chief loss fell upon the division of General Orlando B. Willcox, which was most exposed, being on the right [east], as I have said above; but it gallantly overcame all obstacles, and the success was complete along the whole line of the corps. The enemy's battery was found to be across a gorge, beyond the reach of our infantry. Its position was made untenable, and it was hastily removed and not again put in position near us.
>
> Brigadier General Samuel D. Sturgis's division was now moved forward in front of General Willcox's position, occupying the new ground gained on the slope's farther side. The enemy made a brisk attack upon the extreme left [south] about dark but was quickly repulsed by Colonel [Harrison S.] Fairchild's Brigade of [Brigadier General Isaac P.] Rodman's division, with slight loss.
>
> About 7:00 pm, the Rebels made another effort to regain the lost ground in front of General Sturgis' division and part of the Kanawha Division. This attack was more persistent, and a very lively fire was kept up for about an hour, but they were again repulsed and retreated in mass from our entire front under cover of the night.[21]

In his *Military Reminiscences*, Cox described the following:

> The batteries on the north of the National Road had been annoying to Willcox's men as they advanced, but Sturgis sent forward Captain George W. Durell's Battery from his division as soon

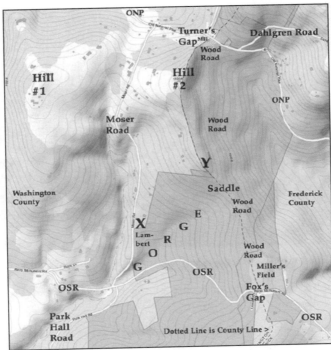

Map 14: Topographical Map showing Cox's Gorge. Afternoon Confederate Artillery Positions at X and Y, September 14, 1862. (Map by Curtis Older)

as he came up, and this gave special attention to these hostile guns, diverting their fire from the infantry. Hooker's men of the First Corps were also pushing up the mountain on that side of the turnpike by this time, and we were not again troubled by artillery on our right [east] flank.[22]

Cox was unmistakable when he told us that after the arrival of Durell's Battery, part of Brigadier General Samuel D. Sturgis's 2nd Division, the Union right or east flank at Fox's Gap was not again troubled by Confederate artillery. Much of the bothersome Confederate artillery was on the north side of Old National Pike, at least one mile away. It was reasonable to assume that any Confederate cannon along Wood Road, probably under Bondurant, had been removed by this hour in the battle. Upon Drayton's defeat, Bondurant's Confederate artillery probably retreated by 5:00 pm from the north side of Miller's Field.

Cox also told us that:

> A staff officer now brought word that McClellan directed the whole line to advance. At the [Union] left [Fox's Gap battlefield], this could only mean to clear our front decisively of the enemy there, for the slopes went steadily down to the Rohrersville Road [Moser and Park Hall Roads].[23]

Cox indicated that he intended to push his troops down the mountain's western slope to Park Hall Road and Cox's Intersection.

Cox's Gorge at the Lambert Property near Cox's Intersection, April 2022. (Photograph by Ted Ellis)

Cox highlighted the Confederate use of the road he labelled as "Rohrersville Road" in the following key description:

> Along our center and left where the forest was thick, the enemy was equally repulsed, but the cover of the timber enabled them to keep a footing nearby, whilst they continually tried to extend so as to outflank us, moving their troops along a road which goes diagonally down that side of the mountain from Turner's Gap to Rohrersville.[24]

Ted Ellis indicated the faint stream shown in the Cox's Gorge image above was from a spring in the gorge. Ted's opinion was that the stream coming from the ravine would be highly weather dependent like most headwater mountain streams. The wettest time of the year occurred in March, and the driest in mid-September. Therefore, this stream probably was dry at the battle in 1862.

Confederate cannon fire against Union forces on the Fox's Gap battlefield significantly diminished or ended after 5:00 pm. Confederate cannon, probably under Rosser and Pelham, a short distance north of the gorge near Cox's Intersection, no longer bothered Union forces. Rosser and Pelham probably moved their units to Hill #1 or near the Mountain House.

The Journal of Captain William Bolton

Captain William Bolton of the 51st Pennsylvania credited Durell's guns with clearing the mountain of the enemy just before the 51st PA advanced to the summit of Old Sharpsburg Road:

> The 51st was soon put into position in front of Durell's battery as its support and ordered to lie down close to the ground. The battery was belching its deadly missiles up the mountain gorge at a fearful and terrible rate over our heads, a regular artillery duel between two contending

armies. The enemy was well posted on the very top of the mountain. They had to depress their guns to reach us, and we had to elevate ours. The duel lasted until sundown, and General Reno, who commanded the old Ninth Corps, was near his old brigade, directing the artillery fire in person.

The artillery having cleared the mountain of the enemy, the 51st was soon ordered to advance towards the summit.[25]

Bolton gave direct evidence that Union artillery commanded the area of Miller's and Wise's Fields after the arrival of Durell's Battery and Sturgis's Division, occurring no later than 6:30 pm. Confederate artillery at the northwest corner of Miller's Field along Wood Road could have threatened the Union far right or far east flank on the Fox's Gap battlefield.

Bolton's statement that the artillery cleared the mountain of the enemy was significant. Bolton's account told us that Brigadier General Orlando B. Willcox's 1st Division, and Colonel William H. Withington's 17th Michigan in particular, cleared Drayton's infantry from the area of Miller's Field and the Wise Cabin. Durell's Battery then commanded the immediate vicinity of Fox's Gap.

Durell's Battery probably controlled the mountain top shortly after 5:00 pm. The precise timing of Withington's charge and the commencement of Durell's artillery fire are unknown, but those two actions must have been slightly overlapping or in close sequence.

Before Reno's shooting, the Union forces had at least a dozen cannon in Miller's Field and near the Wise Cabin. The writings of Willcox and Bolton, among others, supported this conclusion. Bolton informed us that General Reno himself ordered Durell's battery of six guns to advance to the crest near Wise's Cabin and Miller's Field. We are unsure when and where the 5th U.S. Artillery, Battery A, of Rodman's 3rd division took up their positions. Rodman's Battery would have increased the number of Union cannon near Miller's Field and Wise's Field to 18 guns.

Late in the afternoon, Reno came on the field that his old brigade was occupying on the right of the Old Sharpsburg Road. His black piercing eyes flashing fire as it were, ordered Durell's Battery to limber up and go in a gallop up the narrow road leading to the mountain's crest.[26]

It was certain this occurred before 6:30 pm.

Cox indicated the Confederates disappeared into the woods beyond Fox's Gap by 5:00 pm. Miller's Field was a 13¼-acre open field in the immediate northeast quadrant at the Wood Road and Old Sharpsburg Road intersection. John Miller owned the land on September 14. After Drayton's defeat, the Confederates retreated into the woods to the west and northwest of Miller's Field.

On the west side of Fox's Gap, Old Sharpsburg Road descended into a ravine adjacent and south of the gorge identified by Cox in his September 20 report. The low point of the ravine was at Cox's Intersection, i.e., the Moser Road and Old Sharpsburg Road intersection. The gulch identified by Cox ran northeast from the corner for about one half-mile to the midway point along Wood Road. See "G O R G E" on Map 14.

Cannon crew at Fox's Gap. Light 12-pounder Model 1857, September 14, 2012. (Photograph by Curtis Older)

The map shows that the cannon beyond the gorge that Cox identified were near position X along Moser Road. This position was near Lambert's Field, along the east side of Moser Road. The Confederate cannon were those of Pelham and Rosser's 5th VA cavalry, who occupied the space after they retreated from the Ridge-Loop Intersection at about 11:00 am.

As indicated above, no Confederate artillery at Turner's Gap or along Dahlgren Road was a threat to the Union right or east flank on the Fox's Gap battlefield after the arrival of Durell's Battery of 10-pounder Parrott (rifled) guns about 5:00 pm. Therefore, the enemy's battery to which Cox referred was across the gorge near point X along Moser Road, as shown on Map 14.

Cox implied the cannon were near his troops. Thus, Cox's statement indicated that Union infantry was approaching or near Cox's Intersection at that time. The only non-forested ground from the East Ridge's crest to Moser Road was Lambert's Field on the northeast corner of Cox's Intersection. Cannon must have some clearance immediately in front before they can be operational. The Lambert Field location thus supports the speculated position of the cannon referenced by Cox.

Two Hills Identified by Cox

In his *Military Reminiscences*, Cox told us that the Confederates, before their night retreat, held two strategic hills between Old Sharpsburg Road and Old National Pike. Cox implied that both hills were, or could become, Union objectives, if not on September 14, then on September 15:

> On the left [west], Longstreet's men were pushed down the mountainside beyond the Rohrersville and Sharpsburg roads, and the contest there was ended. The two hills between the latter road

and the turnpike were still held by the enemy, and the further one could not be reached till the Mountain House should be in our hands.[27]

The two hills Cox identified between Old National Pike and Old Sharpsburg Road were Hill #1 and Hill #2 on the modified *Atlas Map* (Map 15). According to Cox, the "further" hill, Hill #1, could not be taken successfully until the Mountain House was under Union control. The capture of the ground near the Mountain House depended upon the Union First Corps under Major General Hooker at Turner's Gap.

Pelham's two artillery pieces and Rosser's dismounted 5th VA cavalry were near the Ridge-Loop Intersection about a half-mile south of Fox's Gap when the battle began at 9:00 am. Pelham and Rosser retreated from the Ridge-Loop Intersection at about 11:00 am. Soon after, the Confederate cannon on Hill #1 started lobbing shells into Fox's Gap. Cox told us that by noon, Pelham and Rosser probably relocated to Hill #1. However, according to Ripley, Pelham and Rosser were near Cox's Intersection, probably in or near Lambert's open field in the immediate northeast quadrant of that intersection, between 3:00 and 5:00 pm.

The Confederates probably learned of the Hill #1 location and its suitability for artillery before the battle. Indeed, Zittlestown, where Bondurant's Battery reportedly spent the night of September 13, was near the Moser Road and Old National Pike

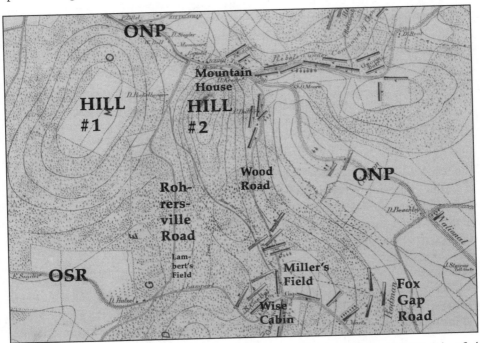

Map 15: Cox's Hill #1 and Hill #2, Adjacent Cox's Rohrersville Road, September 14, 1862. (Identified on *Atlas Map* by Curtis Older)

intersection. Perhaps Bondurant and Pelham encamped with their artillery at Hill #1 the night before the battle.

According to Cox:

> The dismounted cavalry and their battery retreated across the Sharpsburg Road [Old Sharpsburg Road] on the mountain's west side. They took a new position on a separate hill in the rear of the heights at the Mountain House. There was considerable open ground at this new position, from which their battery had a full play at a range of about twelve hundred yards upon the ridge held by us. But the 11th [OH] and 23rd [OH] stuck stoutly to the hill which [Lieutenant Colonel Rutherford B.] Hayes had first carried, and their line [along the Lower Ridge Road] was nearly parallel to the Sharpsburg Road [Old Sharpsburg Road], facing north.[28]

However, Brigadier General Roswell S. Ripley told us that Pelham's artillery section, along with Colonel Rosser and his 5th VA cavalry, was along Old Sharpsburg Road before 5:00 pm:

> The enemy forced his way to the Braddock Road [Old Sharpsburg Road] between General Drayton's force and my own and sent a column of troops down the road as if to cut off the troops forming our right [west]. In this object, he was thwarted by two pieces of artillery belonging to Colonel Rosser's cavalry, which was speedily placed in position a short distance in our rear on the Braddock Road.[29]

Unfortunately, very little information about the operation of Rosser and his cavalry unit during the battle is available. Old Sharpsburg Road was called Braddock Road by people living outside the local area as it was the road General Braddock and George Washington took in their failed attempt to capture Fort Duquesne in 1755.

Strengthening Ripley's statement was the following narrative found in Edward O. Lord's *History of the Ninth Regiment New Hampshire Volunteers*:

> After firing that one volley, we moved forward in a charge across the field and down the mountain on the other side, where we received the fire of a rebel battery, which checked the regiment's advance. We moved by the right flank a short distance and got the order to cover as we lay flat on the ground. Then there came two or three loud reports from the cannon, which seemed to shake the mountain, and we fell back to the summit, where we reformed.[30]

The 9th New Hampshire was in Sturgis's 2nd Division.

Lord's statement indicated the ability of a Union regiment to move quickly over a large area of ground and that it might move down the mountain and then back up again. Later in the day, the nearness of Union infantry under Sturgis or Union cannon drove Rosser and Pelham away from their location near Cox's Intersection. The Confederate guns between two mountain ridges magnified and reverberated the sound.

It was reasonable to assume that the advance of Sturgis's entire division down the west slope of the East Ridge must have driven away Rosser's Cavalry and Pelham's artillery from near Cox's Intersection and Lambert's Field. Sturgis's Division then occupied Cox's Intersection with the 1st Brigade under Brigadier

General James Nagle along Park Hall Road south of the intersection and the 2nd Brigade under Brigadier General Edward Ferrero occupying Old Sharpsburg Road east of the corner.

Of significance was Ripley's statement that "the enemy forced his way to the Braddock Road [Old Sharpsburg Road] between General Drayton's force and my own and sent a column of troops down the road as if to cut off the troops forming our right [west]." Some Union troops attempted to open a greater separation between Ripley's Brigade and Drayton's Brigade along Old Sharpsburg Road, probably within 900 feet west of the Wise Cabin.

Ripley also indicated that a column of Union troops tried to cut off some soldiers on Ripley's right (west). Those Confederate troops on Ripley's right (west) probably were part of his brigade. Ripley's statement thus indicated some Union troops at the time must have been at least a quarter-mile or more west of Fox's Gap along Old Sharpsburg Road. Ripley's Brigade front probably was about 1,150 feet in length, slightly less than a quarter-mile.

Civil War battles were usually fought by "lines of troops." The line of battle could extend for hundreds of feet. The experience of part of a regiment at one end of the line might be completely different from the experience at the other.

Private Daniel Hurd of the 9th New Hampshire complained:

> No doubt, some of our regiment saw someone to fire at, but I didn't. You must remember that 900 men strung out in double file would reach some distance; the enemy was not in sight of where our part of the regiment was.[31]

Hurd clarified why reporting troops' various actions and movements during a battle was so complex.

At an elevation of about 1,201 feet, Hill #1 provided ample opportunity for Confederate artillery to shell the Union positions at Fox's Gap, at least 130 feet lower in elevation. Cox indicated the Confederate guns' wrath focused on the 11th and 23rd Ohio infantry that occupied the Lower Ridge Road and part of the trail that led down the mountain to J. Slifer's property along Park Hall Road.[32]

Hill #1 presented the Confederates with a solid defensive position should they choose to use it. Cox intended to push his Ninth Corps north along Moser Road and attack any Confederates occupying Hill #1 should the opportunity present itself. It was unlikely that Cox intended to mount an attack along Wood Road towards Turner's Gap. The terrain along Wood Road was too challenging to overcome.

According to Cox:

> Reno had followed Rodman's division up the mountain and came to me a little before sunset, anxious to know why the right [east] could not get forward quite to the summit. I explained that the ground there was very rough and rocky, a fortress in itself and evidently very strongly held.[33]

One cannot take this statement by Cox to signify a possible Union advance along Wood Road. Cox probably indicated to Reno that Union troops had not taken possession of the north part of Miller's Field.

Before Cox made the above quote in his *Military Reminiscences*, he stated, "Sturgis and Willcox, supported by Rodman, again pushed forward, but while they made progress, they were baffled by a stubborn and concentrated resistance." It was challenging to determine what Cox meant by this statement. It most likely referred to the situation when Sturgis's Division first arrived at Fox's Gap and before Cox's Kanawha Division occupied Old Sharpsburg Road east of Sturgis's troops at Cox's Intersection.

Brian Jordan, the author of *Unholy Sabbath: The Battle of South Mountain in History and Memory*, quoted a Union soldier in the 8th Pennsylvania Reserves who fought at Turner's Gap:

> The place where the reserve fought at South Mountain was the worst looking place to take ever I seen.[34]

The ground along the East Ridge and Wood Road presented no place for an infantry line of battle to form.

Cox's after-battle report of September 20 and his *Military Reminiscences* are consistent and present a solid case that the Union Army occupied Cox's Intersection when the fighting ended on September 14.

Cox disclosed the following in his *Military Reminiscences*:

> Though my private memoranda are full enough to give me reasonable confidence in the accuracy of these reminiscences, I have made it a duty to test my memory. I constantly referenced the original contemporaneous material so abundantly preserved in the government publication of the *Official Records of the Union and Confederate Armies*.[35]

Cox thus attempted to refute his critics who claimed he wrote his *Military Reminiscences* too long after the war.

The Diary of Private John F. Holahan

Private John F. Holahan in the 45th Pennsylvania Infantry recorded in his diary the following on Monday, September 15:

> We fell in as rearguard to the wagon train at 3:00 pm and had a slow, tiresome march. All the way down the mountain, the enemy's dead lay strewn thickly in the woods and at the roadside where they had been thrown to make way for the wagons. Putrefaction had already begun as the hot sun poured down upon the unprotected bodies. The stench was almost insufferable![36]

Holahan confirmed that numerous dead Confederates were in the woods and along Old Sharpsburg Road "all the way down the mountain." Holahan described the distance from the Wise Cabin to Cox's Intersection, which marked the bottom of the mountain as one came down Old Sharpsburg Road from Fox's Gap.

Holahan confirmed many Confederates died along Old Sharpsburg Road on the west side of Fox's Gap. His account reinforced the statement of Cox, "On the left [west], Longstreet's men were pushed down the mountainside beyond the Rohrersville and Sharpsburg Roads [Cox's Intersection], and the contest there was ended."

Holahan also noted in his Sunday, September 14 diary entry:

> South Mountain! How, as I sit tonight on the field of battle, surrounded by the dying and the dead, writing our doings of the day—how from one end of our proud land to other, millions are reading, or hearing read the telegrams telling of

<u>O U R V I C T O R Y</u>

Holahan considered the battle a tremendous and decisive Union victory.[37]

The Letter of Lieutenant George W. Whitman

Another primary Union source was Lieutenant George W. Whitman of the 51st New York, 2nd Brigade under Brigadier General Edward Ferrero, 2nd Division of Sturgis. Whitman wrote a letter to his mother, Louisa Van Velsor Whitman, on September 21, 1862. In the letter, Whitman described the following:

> General Cox, who commands a Division of our Army Corps, somehow got around the enemy's left [south] and drove him from his best position on the crown of the mountain.
>
> Our division was then brought up and took the advance. The enemy, falling back slowly until night, when we found ourselves, on the opposite side of the mountains and about a mile from where the fight commenced, with all the best positions on the field in our possession. As it was now dark, our division formed in line of battle to hold all the ground we had gained during the day and lay down to await the enemy's movements.
>
> Our regiment lay in an open field near the edge of a wood the enemy had been driven into. We had just got our position and laid down when the enemy opened fire on us from the woods directly in front of us. Our regiment was ordered to lie close and not fire a shot until the enemy advanced out of the woods and into the field where we lay. The regiments on our right [east] and left [west] had a regular crossfire on the enemy and kept pouring the lead into them like rain.
>
> I had command of our Company (as the Captain was not well although he was on the field), and I had mighty hard work to keep some of them from getting up and blazing away as they said they did not like to lay there like a lot of old women and be shot without fighting back. I thought it was mighty singular, but when I saw how things were situated the next morning, I saw that their fire could not harm us much as long as we lay down. At the same time, if they had come out to the open field, we would have got up and given them a volley that would have done terrible execution.
>
> The enemy kept up a sharp fire for about half an hour (and it was about the toughest half-hour that I ever experienced as I could hear the bullets whiz all around me, and some of them seemed to graze me) when the enemy's fire began to slacken. It was evident that he did not intend to come out of the woods so that we could get a fair chance at him. The order was given for us to open fire, and you never saw men go to work with a better relish.
>
> In about 15 minutes, the enemy's fire ceased altogether, and we knew he had fallen back out of range, so we ceased firing and lay down again until daylight when we found no enemy in sight; they skedaddled during the night. After assuring ourselves that they were gone for good, we stacked arms, and I took a walk over our part of the battlefield. In some parts of the field, the enemy's dead lay in heaps, and in a road for nearly a quarter of a mile, they lay so thick

that I had to pick my way carefully to avoid stepping on them, I think judging from what I saw that the enemy's loss was fully eight times as great as ours. I am told that the slaughter was equally as great on our right [east].[38]

Whitman, a brother of the famous poet Walt Whitman, found himself in an open field on the west side of the mountain about one mile from where his unit's fight began. The men of the 51st NY began taking incoming shells from the Confederate artillery north of Old National Pike when the regiment approached Fox's Gap. Whitman's unit was along Old Sharpsburg Road about four-tenths of a mile east of the Wise Cabin or about halfway between the Wise Cabin and the Fox Gap Road and Old Sharpsburg Road intersection. The 51st NY initially was near the PA Light Artillery, Battery D, of Captain George Durell on the east side of Fox's Gap.

Where was Whitman on the battlefield when the fighting ended the night of the 14th? Whitman stated, "the enemy, falling back slowly until night when we found ourselves on the opposite side of the mountains and about a mile from where the fight commenced." He indicated, "with all the best positions on the field in our possession. As it was now dark, our division formed in line of battle to hold all the ground we had gained during the day." Whitman indicated he was one mile from where the fight commenced.

What did Whitman mean by "a mile from where the fight commenced?" Did he imply where the battle began with Lieutenant Colonel Rutherford B. Hayes about one half-mile south of Fox's Gap at 9:00 am? The problem with this interpretation was that Whitman had no way of knowing when this battle began: he arrived at the battlefield much later in the day with Sturgis's Division. The best comprehension we can attribute to Whitman's statement was "where the battle started for him upon his arrival at the battlefield." If we interpreted Whitman to mean a mile from where the battle began at 9:00 am in the morning, it would place him even farther west than Cox's Intersection.

What accuracy did Whitman have regarding his use of the term "mile"? Given that infantry movement during the war involved extensive marching and travel by foot, it seemed fair to say that a typical soldier's estimate of the distance of a mile probably was entirely accurate.

If we calculated Ferrero's brigade front for his 2nd Brigade of 1,500 men (his 2nd Brigade had 2,285 men on September 2) using a conservative estimate, his brigade front extended 1,275 feet or approximately one-quarter of a mile.[39] Steven R. Stotelmyer, an Antietam authority, suggested using the following method to calculate a brigade front. First, subtract 15 percent for officers and file closers (officers posted at the rear of a line or on the flank of a column of soldiers to rectify mistakes and ensure steadiness and promptness in the ranks). Next, place the men in two ranks, the standard line of battle, and allocate 24 inches per man per file. For example, a 1,000-man brigade would yield a brigade front of 850 feet.

Whitman also indicated, "the regiments on our right and left had a regular crossfire on the enemy and kept pouring the lead into them like rain." Thus, if Whitman was near Lambert's Field in the immediate northeast quadrant of Cox's Intersection, at least one Union regiment was west of Moser Road or south along Park Hall Road.

Whitman indicated, "our division formed in line of battle." Could Whitman be more unambiguous regarding what he meant? Where could his division be in a battle line other than in or near a road? Sturgis's Division of 3,411 men (4,815 men on September 2) was in line along Park Hall Road and Old Sharpsburg Road.[40] For this reason, the intersection will bear the name Cox's Intersection throughout the remainder of this book. The division's battle line was probably at least 2,000 feet long or about two-fifths of a mile.

The distance from Fox's Gap to Cox's Intersection was about one half-mile. Sturgis's Division's battle line extended along Park Hall Road for at least 1,000 feet and along Old Sharpsburg Road for 1,000 feet. Cox's Kanawha Division occupied part of Old Sharpsburg Road between Sturgis and the Wise Cabin. Some of Rodman's men also were near those roads.

According to Willcox, "Sturgis opened with his artillery on the enemy's battery and troops across the central pike, and night came on."[41] Under Sturgis, Durell's battery began to shell the Confederates north of Old National Pike from about halfway between the Wise Cabin and Fox Gap Road. The distance between the Wise Cabin and the Fox Gap Road corner was eight-tenths of a mile. Thus, half that distance would be about four-tenths of a mile. The distance from the Wise Cabin to Cox's Intersection was approximately .54 miles. If we add the interval from where Sturgis's Division began their fight, we arrive at about .94 mile, very near one mile.

Whitman indicated, "our Regt lay in an open field near the edge of a wood into which the enemy had been driven." The *Atlas Map* showed that the first open area west of Wood Road was near the Lambert property at Cox's Intersection. The conclusion must be that Whitman was near Cox's Intersection. Whitman told us that the objective of Sturgis's division was "to hold all the ground we had gained during the day." At the beginning of the battle, the Confederates possessed Ridge Road, which ran about one half-mile south-southwest from the Wise Cabin. Therefore, the Confederates had lost all the ground south of Old Sharpsburg Road during the day. Whitman also told us that:

> I thought it was mighty singular, but when I saw how things were situated the next morning, I saw that their fire could not harm us much as long as we lay down. At the same time, if they had come out to the open field, we would have got up and given them a volley that would have done terrible execution.[42]

The image below, taken just north of Cox's Intersection, provides the view of a possible location where Whitman's 51st NY sheltered while they were in a line of battle along Old Sharpsburg Road.

Moser Road and Old Sharpsburg Road. (Photo by Ted Ellis, March 2022)

The Diary of Captain James Wren

Union Captain James Wren was a member of Company B, 48th PA Volunteers, 1st Brigade commanded by Brigadier General James Nagle, 2nd Division under Sturgis.[43] Wren found himself and his regiment "in a cornfield" at the end of the day:

> At 5:00 pm, I was ordered to the front with my Company to form a line of skirmishers with the 51st New York in front of their Brigade & we were all extended in splendid order and advanced & my men [were] perfectly cool & determined. When about [in] 150 yards advance from the battle line, in front, we met the enemy's skirmish line & we opened fire on them & they opened on us & their ammunition reaching the battle line, the old troops lay quiet.
>
> So, Company B was in the eyes of all the troops. So, we advanced in line of skirmish & got out in the woods about 125 yards [probably relative to Park Hall Road, Old Sharpsburg Road, or an open field] & met the enemy's skirmish line. We opened fire on them & fell back, loading at the same time, & the enemy yelled & followed us up. We faced & stood again & gave them another volley & being within 75 or 80 yards of our battle line I ordered the Company to "rally to the right & left, double-quick to the rear," which was done very quick & we took our position on the left of our regiment in the battle line.
>
> I reported to Lieutenant Colonel Sigfried that the enemy was within 75 yards of us, coming up in the woods in front of us & that the 51st New York skirmishers were also driven in. While I was delivering the condition of things to Sigfried, the rebel flag made its appearance & [they were] yelling, thinking that they had got us on a retreat when the whole Brigade opened fire from the battle line. Our Regiment remained in the battle until they had expended all their ammunition & we fell back & the 2nd Maryland relieved us, they being in the 2nd line of battle. The line of troops was three lines deep—all lying down. We then rested in a cornfield. [We] had nothing to eat & was not allowed to build a fire, being in range of the enemy. It was very cold & I then had roll call, and we found Alfred E. Bendley, John Howells, and Johnathan Leffler [all B Co.] missing.[44]

Records on ancestry.com and fold3.com indicated that Alfred E. Bendley, John Howells, and Jonathan C. Leffler probably were captured by the Rebels at South Mountain but survived the war.

Wren informed us that his 48th PA Regiment was near Lieutenant George W. Whitman's 51st New York regiment. Thus, we know that the 1st and 2nd Brigades of the 2nd Division under Sturgis were together. Wren indicated Nagle's 1st Brigade, consisting of perhaps 1,500 men, was in a three-deep battle line, while Whitman disclosed Sturgis's Division was in a division line of battle.

Sturgis's 2nd Division was at Cox's Intersection. Like the Confederates had done when preparing for their afternoon counterattack, Sturgis's men occupied both Old Sharpsburg Road and Park Hall Road. Some regiments occupied Park Hall Road to the south, and some units occupied Old Sharpsburg Road east of the intersection.

Sturgis reported that Reno assigned the 2nd MD and 6th New Hampshire to the turnpike for picket duty, probably near Benjamin's Union artillery batteries east of Fox Gap Road. Therefore, we might conclude that Nagle only had the 9th NH and 48th PA in the fight at Cox's Intersection. However, according to Wren, there were three regiments on the battle line: the 48th PA, the 2nd MD, and one unnamed unit. Captain Oliver C. Bosbyshell of Company G, 48th PA, clarified the situation:

> The 6th New Hampshire and the 2nd Maryland from Welsh's brigade finally arrived, following a couple of hours of duty along the National Pike.[45]

The other regiment aiding Wren's 48th PA might have been the 6th NH. Again, we see how easily troops might move around a battlefield and the difficulty of identifying the location of a particular regiment at any point in time.

Park Hall Road became somewhat parallel to Old Sharpsburg Road as they met. Wren's regiment probably was along Park Hall Road, extending about 1,000 feet south of the intersection. The ground on the immediate west side of Park Hall Road tapered off considerably and made any Federal troops on the road challenging for the Confederates to attack from the west or north.

The 51st NY skirmishers probably were near the crossroads and perhaps along Old Sharpsburg Road at Lambert's Field. Advancing north towards the approaching brigades under Hood, skirmishers in the 48th PA and 51st NY left their respective roads or open fields and marched through woods to the north.

When Wren and his fellow skirmishers advanced about 450 feet from the Union battle line, they confronted the Rebel skirmishers, and the Rebel battle flag appeared. The Union skirmishers' advance was less than a tenth of a mile north of the Park Hall Road and Old Sharpsburg Road intersection. Wren indicated, "we got out in the woods." Thus, his reference point must have been a road or open field.

When the Confederates were about 75 yards from the battle line, "the whole brigade opened fire from the battle line." Much of the brigade was lying down as the Confederates approached. Wren gave no indication his regiment retreated or that it advanced. The most likely scenario was that the 1st Brigade of Nagle remained in or near Park Hall Road. Whitman's 51st NY Regiment probably was in the Lambert's Field area.

After his encounter with the Confederates, Wren and his regiment rested in a cornfield. Wren's use of the term "cornfield" could imply that the corn planted in that field was still standing. The better conclusion was that the corn was no longer standing. In a typical year, Maryland farmers often harvested corn by September 15. The cornfield identified by Wren was south of Old Sharpsburg Road and west of Park Hall Road. Wren was not in a cornfield near the Wise Cabin, as suggested by other authors. As we will find later, Wren's description of his brigade's engagement with the Confederates was similar to that of Brigadier General John Bell Hood when his Confederates fixed bayonets and approached Wren's Union troops.

Cox's Intersection was about 2,850 feet directly west of the Wise Cabin. The crossroads was immediately east of Dog Creek and in the area where the original land tracts for Booker's Resurvey on Well Done, the Resurvey on Security, and Partnership met.[46] Moser Road ran north to Old National Pike through the 685-acre Partnership tract. Dog Creek, in all probability, provided much-needed water for Rosser's cavalry horses during the battle. However, Confederate Major General J. E. B. Stuart attested that cavalry was not very useful in fighting for Turner's and Fox's Gaps.

Wren's Stone Fence and Crossroads

Wren's account of September 15 described the Confederate dead as follows:

> We all went over & took a view & we found [that] in front [of] where our regiment was engaged the enemy lay very thick on the field. I measured the ground & [in] 40 feet square. I counted 16 of the enemy lying dead on it. We also found a number of wounded & we gave them water & covered them with their blankets & just to the right of my skirmish line of yesterday was two crossroads [Park Hall Road and Old Sharpsburg Road] in the shape of an "X," & on our front, there was a stone fence [between Park Hall Road and Dog Creek] & behind that fence & in the "X" road [Cox's Intersection] the enemy lay very thick.[47]

One might interpret Wren's description of "two crossroads" in either of two ways. Ted Ellis indicated Moser Road never aligned with Park Hall Road, where they met Old Sharpsburg Road. Hence, Wren referred to two crossroads. The *Atlas Map* bears out this interpretation. Moser Road did not flow through that intersection in a straight line into Park Hall Road. The other understanding would be that Wren meant where two roads crossed.

The only location on the Fox's Gap battlefield where two roads crossed was at Cox's Intersection. The Wood Road and Ridge Road connections with Old Sharpsburg Road did not create an "X," as did Cox's Intersection. If Wren had meant the Wood Road and Ridge Road intersections along Old Sharpsburg Road, he most likely would have identified it by referencing the Wise Cabin.

Maps 16, 17 and 18 focus on the differences between Cox's Intersection and the Wood Road and Ridge Road junctures with Old Sharpsburg Road. Wood Road

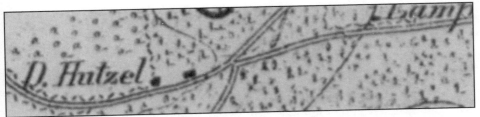

Map 16: Wren's "X" at Cox's Intersection, September 14, 1862. (Image from *Atlas Map*)

Map 17: Wood Road and Ridge Road Intersections. Not an "X" at Old Sharpsburg Road. September 14, 1862. (Image from *Atlas Map*)

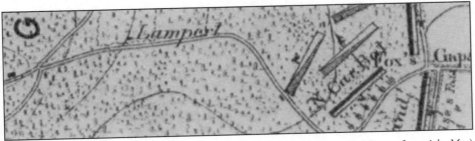

Map 18: Cox's Intersection versus Wood and Ridge Roads, September 14, 1862. (Image from *Atlas Map*)

and Ridge Road did not form an "X" like Cox's Intersection. Wren's statement accurately identified the crossroads about a half-mile west of Fox's Gap along Old Sharpsburg Road.

In my opinion, Maps 19 and 20 identify the most significant discovery on the Battlefield of South Mountain in the past 160 years. On April 25, 2022, Ted Ellis confirmed a stone wall or fence near Cox's Intersection. Captain Wren identified the stone fence in his diary on September 15, 1862. It was the only stone fence found within a half-mile area.

Two structures bordered the north side of Old Sharpsburg Road just west of Cox's Intersection. Farther west, adjacent to the second structure, was a large orchard. The area surrounding Cox's Intersection was wooded. The stretch from Wren's stone fence to Cox's Intersection was along Dog Creek and consisted of trees and undergrowth. The wooded area extended about 150 feet west of the stone fence.

The "stone fence" identified by Captain James Wren during the battle measured 297 feet long, stood approximately 600 feet southwest of Cox's Intersection, and ran from Dog Creek to Park Hall Road. The stone fence stood near a parallel line given in various land records or deeds from as early as 1813 until as recently as 1977. Related land records from Bash to Hutzel in 1813, from Hamilton to O'Neal in 1867, from O'Neal to Poffenberger in 1869, and from Poffenberger to Hans in 1977, all included a line "South 41 degrees east eighteen perches to a stone pile."[48]

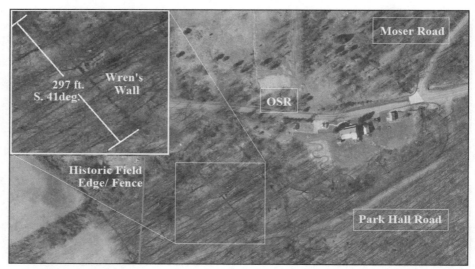

Map 19: Aerial view of Captain James Wren's stone fence. Stone wall southwest of Cox's Intersection. (Image from Maryland state GIS website "Merlin," c.2017, Map by Ted Ellis)

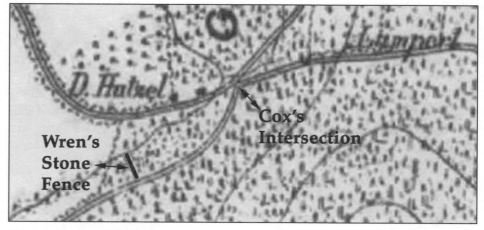

Map 20: Location of Captain James Wren's stone fence between Dog Creek and Park Hall Road, September 14, 1862. (Identified on the *Atlas Map* by Ted Ellis)

View from Park Hall Road of Wren's stone fence, between Park Hall Road and Dog Creek parallel to "South 41 degrees East eighteen perches" line of an 1813 deed. (Photo by Ted Ellis, April 2022)

None of the deeds mentioned the stone fence or stone wall itself, but the fence or wall was identical in length and was perfectly parallel with the south 41 degrees east angle given in the various legal documents. It was reasonable to believe the landowner of the stone fence did not want to use it as a boundary line but rather keep the stone fence on his side of the boundary line and within his property to retain ownership.

The previous images of Cox's Intersection and the photo of the stone fence between Park Hall Road and Dog Creek document that Cox's Intersection and the stone fence matched the descriptions given by Captain Wren:

> Just to the right of my skirmish line of yesterday was two crossroads in the shape of an "X" & on our front, there was a stone fence & behind that fence & in the "X" road, the enemy lay very thick.[49]

Since the battle, all other writers incorrectly placed Wren near Wise's Cabin. Wren confronted the troops under Hood near Cox's Intersection, roughly one half-mile west of Fox's Gap.

Wren also disclosed in his diary on the 15th:

> The Captain said, "Well, Billy, did you see them?" "O truth, I did," said Billy. "But Captain," he said. "Isn't them strange men?" Why? said the Captain. "Be my soul; every man of them has a third eye in his head." The Captain laughed & explained the matter to Billy & said, "Billy, you saw that stone fence?" "Yes, sir." "Well, the enemy was behind it when we were engaged yesterday & in order to fire on us they had to take aim over the stone fence & consequently, they got shot by our men somewhere between the shoulders & head & that is the reason so many of them is shot in the head."[50]

Wren described the stone fence as situated on his front and indicated he must have been along Park Hall Road or perhaps in the open field on the west side of Park Hall Road. Some Rebels died along the north side of the stone fence, while others died at Cox's Intersection. Hood's troops advanced south along Moser Road in a line of battle, moved through the woods, and confronted the Union troops in the area of Cox's Intersection. Some Rebels advanced to the stone fence described by Wren.

Ezra Carman described the intersections where Ridge Road and Wood Road met Old Sharpsburg Road at Fox's Gap:

> On the south side of the Sharpsburg Road, 40 yards east from where the Mountain House Road [Wood Road] comes into it, commences a lane or ridge road [Upper Ridge Road] running southerly. For about 300 yards, this narrow lane was flanked on both sides by stone fences, then a single stone fence ran nearly its entire length, separating the woods from the cleared fields.[51]

Carman confirmed the distance between the Wood Road intersection and the Ridge Road intersection with Old Sharpsburg Road was 40 yards. A stretch of 120 feet and, without a doubt, not the "X" crossroad identified by Wren.

The Society of the Burnside Expedition and the Ninth Army Corps set in place plans to erect a monument to Major General Reno on the battlefield at Fox's Gap. The Society appointed General John Hartranft to head the memorial committee and the President of the Society would appoint other members to the committee.[52] On September 14, 1889, surviving members of the Union Ninth Corps dedicated the elaborate "Reno Monument" on what was then the southeast corner of today's Reno Monument Road and the former Ridge Road.

During the mid-20th century, the Maryland Forest Service erected a forest fire lookout tower a mile and one-half south on Lamb's Knoll. They also built the present road, Lamb's Knoll Road, to access the facilities.

The original 1862-era Ridge Road through private land fell out of use and almost disappeared completely. Map 21, based on a high-resolution satellite image from the Maryland Department of Natural Resources from 2017 showed a faint trace of the original Ridge Road alongside the Reno Monument. The measurement of Old Sharpsburg Road from Wood Road to the remnant of Ridge Road was 40 yards, similar to the distance given by Ezra Carman. The Maryland state GIS website "Merlin" generated the calculation for Map 21 and confirmed Ezra Carman's statement.

Officers Bosbyshell, Pleasants, & Pollock

Captain Oliver C. Bosbyshell of the 48th PA gave the following account to the *Miner's Journal*, a Schuylkill County, Pennsylvania, Civil War-era newspaper, published on September 21, 1862:

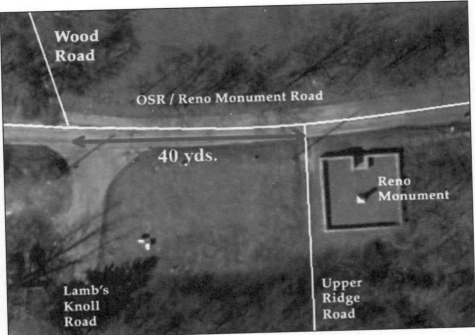

Map 21: Ezra Carman's Measurement at Fox's Gap. Wood and Upper Ridge Roads at Old Sharpsburg Road. (Image from Maryland state GIS website "Merlin", c. 2017, Map by Ted Ellis)

We took up our position behind a small fence in a cleared field, facing a wood—from which the enemy had been driven in the afternoon and where it was feared he would attack again. It was fast growing dark, and appearances seemed to indicate that we would have to remain and watch where we were all night. But no, our skirmishers (Company B, Captain Wren) soon were attacked, and our regiment became engaged shortly. Here, to use a vulgarism, we had the "dead wood" on the enemy and could pop away in grand style. The Rebels' firing was fast and furious, but we returned it as lively until our ammunition became expended when we retired by the left flank, firing all the way. Our place was immediately occupied by the 2nd Maryland of Nagle's Brigade. The enemy "skedaddled" after a few rounds from the 2nd and did not disturb us anymore that night. We remained close to the field all night. Some three or four in the regiment were slightly wounded. The rest of Nagle's Brigade [6th NH and 9th NH] also participated, and the loss in the other regiments was pretty considerable. The next morning, we moved off after the Rebels, passing over the battlefield, where piles and piles of dead Rebels lay, evidence of the accuracy of our firing. They were strewn around thick where we had been firing the night before, and we received the credit of having piled them up so famously.[53]

Bosbyshell's account substantially agreed with Wren's version. Wren identified a "stone fence" used by the Rebels, whereas Bosbyshell referred to "a small fence" that he was behind. The small fence probably was wooden and along the border of an open field. As confirmed by examining the related deeds, the property boundary adjacent to "Wren's wall" always kept the stone wall within the various owner's properties.

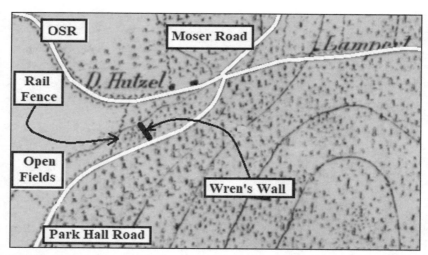

Map 22: Bosbyshell's Rail Fence and Wren's Stone Wall, Southwest of Cox's Intersection, September 14, 1862. (Identified on *Atlas Map* by Ted Ellis)

The *Atlas Map* confirmed the edge of the open fields and woods at approximately 100 yards south of the stone wall and bounded by a rail fence.

Bosbyshell confirmed Nagle's four regiments in his 1st Brigade participated in the engagement. Wren and Bosbyshell agreed the Union skirmishers were from Company B.

Captain Henry Pleasants, soon to be Lieutenant Colonel Pleasants, wrote the following on September 17, 1862, that also appeared in the *Miner's Journal* in Schuylkill County:

> Amidst the din of battle and thunder of artillery, which is echoed again and again by the surrounding mountains, I hasten to inform you of the glorious victory achieved by our forces on Sunday last and of the gallant behavior and slight loss sustained by the 48th Regiment.
>
> We marched to South Mountain on Sunday, where the Rebels were posted in force. The fight lasted from the forenoon until about 10:00 pm that night, resulting in a complete and glorious victory for the Union troops. The Rebels were outflanked and routed by Hooker and repulsed and driven off by Reno. Our regiment was under fire from early afternoon until late that night. It was engaged in a hot contest with the Rebels at short range, from about 7:30 to 10:00 pm, when our ammunition was exhausted. We were relieved by the 4th Rhode Island, and the fire ceased at once. Our loss was very slight because of our fine position behind a rail fence. The next morning, we examined the place from which the Rebels were firing on us and on the 51st New York (which occupied our right). And there lay from 100 to 150 dead bodies. The Union army's loss was slight, but from what we saw, I can state that the Rebels were terribly slaughtered. At no point was the enemy successful, but everywhere defeated. Their retreat continued that night, and our artillery continued in pursuit the next day. (We are ordered to march, so I leave this unfinished.)[54]

Pleasants pointed out that the 4th Rhode Island of Brigadier General Isaac P. Rodman's 3rd Division relieved his 48th PA and not the 2nd MD. If Pleasants was correct, some of Rodman's 3rd Division regiments were along Park Hall Road.

The Union troops in the general vicinity of Cox's Intersection perhaps numbered over 4,000 men.

According to Ezra Carman, the casualties in Hood's two brigades during the battle were extremely low. Carman's casualty numbers directly conflict with the reported numbers by Whitman, Wren, Bosbyshell, and Pleasants.

Union Lieutenant Curtis Clay Pollock, 48th PA, wrote the following letter to his mother the day after the battle:

> On the Field of Battle
> Near Middleton
> September 15, 1862
>
> Dear Ma,
>   We have been in another engagement near Middleton and drove the Rebels from a very strong position in the hills. We fired all our cartridges and then retired in good order to let someone else have a chance. We marched up the mountain at about 5:00 pm but were not engaged until about 7:00 pm. We were lying down behind a fence and peppered the Rebels pretty well. This morning, I went around over the field and found the Rebels lying very thick. We are now about to leave for some other place. I am told that the Rebels are about four miles from here, and our troops are following them up.[55]

Pollock's version of the evening's events agreed with Whitman and Wren. Pollock was in Sturgis's division and the same regiment as Wren.

Pollock's account told us that he was lying down behind a fence and firing at the Rebels. The only fence shown along Park Hall Road began on the north side of the road about 800 feet from Cox's Intersection. An open field was to the north and west of the fence. Pollock went over the area the following day and mentioned no ground characteristics other than dead Confederates. Pollock's account implied that the Confederates charged over the open field on the south side of Old Sharpsburg Road and the west side of Park Hall Road. Perhaps the attacking Confederates came through the orchard on the north side of Old Sharpsburg Road near the property of D. Hutzel.

After Drayton's defeat near the Wise Cabin by 5:00 pm, several Union heavy ammunition wagons ran over the dead and wounded lying in Old Sharpsburg Road. The diary of Private George A. Hitchcock of the 21st Massachusetts of Ferrero's brigade in the Ninth Corps described the horrific scene late in the day:

> We are ordered across the road to the left [south], called Fox's Gap. The sunken road is packed with dead and dying Rebels who had stubbornly held the pass against our troops who have resistlessly swept up over the hill. Here the horrors of war were revealed as we see our heavy ammunition wagons go tearing up, right over the dead and dying, mangling many in their terrible course. The shrieks of the poor fellows were heart-rending.[56]

The Union heavy ammunition wagons described by Hitchcock moved west along Old Sharpsburg Road after Drayton's defeat. Where were the Union heavy ammunition wagons headed? They moved at a reasonable rate of speed, according to Hitchcock. The ammunition wagons supplied Union troops on the west side of Fox's Gap near

Cox's Intersection. Union troops, at that time, must have been in control of Old Sharpsburg Road for some distance west of the Wise Cabin for this event to occur. Hitchcock's account meshed with Wren's statement that his unit used all their ammunition during combat.

The 35th Massachusetts historian gave an account of a section of artillery that passed along Old Sharpsburg Road after dark when the battle ceased:

> When the contest had ceased, General Sturgis sent up a section of artillery. Our men moved the wounded and dead from the road upon the bank to let the guns pass. Sometimes in the darkness, placing several bodies together, which led observers in the morning to report to the newspapers that "the Rebels were piled in heaps as high as the wall."[57]

Captain Bolton, 51st PA, related a somewhat similar account:

> We were all up bright and early this morning [Monday, September 15], going over the field to see what could be seen. In the narrow road that ran through a deep cut near where we had been on picket all night, we found the road itself, and the banks on either side were literally filled with dead and dying. We had heard their moaning the whole night long. The sight was pitiful in the extreme. These were the wounded we had lifted to either side of the roadway late the previous afternoon. Soon after, we commenced driving the enemy from the summit of the mountain when Reno ordered Durell's battery to limber up and go in a gallop up the narrow road to the mountain's crest. With all our care removing them, many were run over by the battery in their haste to reach the crest.[58]

Bolton's casualty numbers for Drayton's Brigade received support from Sergeant Thomas H. Parker, who served under Colonel John F. Hartranft in the 51st PA Infantry:

> The cannonading was terrific, as Durell and the Rebel batteries were having a regular artillery duel, which lasted until near sundown, when it ceased by Durell silencing the enemy's guns, after which, as the Rebels got the worst of it, they had to limber up and leave their position. The 51st was ordered further up the road, toward the mountain's summit. As it was going along a by-road [minor road], it passed a heap of Rebel dead, 47 bodies, piled up in 30 by 10 feet. The wonder was how the dead got there. Going up to the top of the mountain, another pile of 97 lay piled up across each other. The ground in the vicinity was strewn with the dead of the 17th Michigan, telling plainly how the two piles of Rebel dead came to be there.[59]

The Union Ninth Corps numbered over 13,000 men on the Fox's Gap battlefield by early evening on September 14. Besides Hood's two brigades, the only active Confederates on the Fox's Gap battlefield were those along Wood Road near the Saddle, perhaps halfway to the Mountain House, and G. B. Anderson's Brigade, probably west of Park Hall Road or Moser Road.

Hood's two units that made the trek south from Turner's Gap probably numbered no more than 2,000 men. The Confederates had no cannon in the fight south of Old National Pike late in the day. Some Confederate cannon on Hill #1 had the capability of firing toward Old Sharpsburg Road. Just how many guns the Confederates had on Hill #1 and their degree of effectiveness was unknown.

Cox stated that the Confederate guns on the Union right or east flank were no longer troublesome after the arrival of Durell's six-gun battery, part of Sturgis's Division. Confederate guns under Pelham along Moser Road retreated, probably to Hill #1 or perhaps Old National Pike at Turner's Gap.

According to Cox:

> The enemy's battery was found to be across a gorge, beyond the reach of our infantry. Its position was made untenable, and it was hastily removed and not again put in position near us.[60]

Either Union artillery, possibly at the Ridge-Loop Intersection, drove the Confederate battery away from its position near Lambert's Field north of the gorge, or Union infantry was nearby and threatening.

In the late afternoon and early evening fight at Fox's Gap, the Union Ninth Corps possessed many cannon near Miller's Field or along Old Sharpsburg Road. The Union cannon included the two-gun artillery sections under the commands of Lieutenant John Coffin, Lieutenant Asa Cook, Lieutenant Daniel Glassie, and two six-gun batteries under Lieutenant Charles Muhlenberg and Captain George Durell. This Union cannon count did not include the four guns at the Ridge-Loop Intersection under Captain Joseph Clark. It did not have the 16 Union cannon near Fox Gap Road just north of Old Sharpsburg Road that remained there throughout the day.

Union Major General William T. Sherman considered a battery of six guns equivalent to an infantry force of one thousand men.[61] The mathematics of the Fox's Gap battlefield situation gave the Union Ninth Corps overwhelming odds against anything the Confederates could muster late in the day.

Union Brigadier General Ferrero, commanding the 2nd Brigade of the 2nd Division, described the advance of his brigade and told us that his men drove the enemy from the field:

> My command then advanced and, after a long and hard fight lasting until 9:00 pm, drove the enemy from their position and occupied the field. We retained possession of the battlefield during the night, having our whole force on guard, momentarily expecting a renewal of the attack.[62]

Ferrero provided the reader with an unequivocal statement in his after-battle report on September 19. He declared that his men advanced against the enemy and fought until 9:00 pm. His men drove the enemy the entire time and occupied the field at the end of the day. Ferrero could not be more unambiguous.

The Letter of Corporal William Robinson

Confirmation of Ferrero's statement comes from a letter dated September 24, 1862, from Corporal William A. Robinson of the 89th New York, 1st Brigade, 3rd Division of Brigadier General Isaac P. Rodman, to his wife, from near

Sharpsburg, MD. Robinson also described the fighting of the 51st New York and 51st Ohio (actually PA):

> The hottest of the fire was on the left of the regiment. It was my luck to be in the rear guard, and I was just turning the left when the fire opened, and the bullets came with a vengeance. One of the rearguards dropped dead on the spot, and one of Co. K, which was right in front of us, and 18 wounded, all in about one minute. The Rebels then charged bayonets, and our fire opened in their face. About 20 dropped dead and as many more wounded. They broke and fled, and Co. A followed and brought in a dozen prisoners. This was called the Battle of South Mountain.
>
> The right had been fighting all day, and it was about sundown when we were brought in. After they [the Rebels] left us, they formed and went a little farther to the right [north], and the 51st NY went into them [the Rebels] with a vengeance supported by the 51st OH [PA] and piled the Rebels up in heaps. That lasted till about 9:00 pm. Mr. Alpines' son and Charles Waters are in the 51st. They are both well. The next day we marched to near Sharpsburg and were kept in line all day.[63]

Corporal Robinson described his being part of the Union rear guard, which indicated he was at the extreme left flank of the Union line at the Ridge-Loop Intersection, about a half-mile south-southwest of Fox's Gap. Robinson's description of events agrees with Confederate Brigadier General G. B. Anderson's men, who aimed their attack against the extreme Union left or south flank.

Robinson indicated that after the Confederates fled from the area of the Ridge-Loop Intersection, they formed again and went farther to the right or north. The retreat should have taken them along Park Hall Road to Cox's Intersection. Robinson informed us that G. B. Anderson's men soon faced the 51st NY and 51st PA Union infantry. Robinson was not a firsthand witness to this second encounter by G. B. Anderson's troops. Still, we can assume that Robinson had friends in either the 51st NY or 51st PA that communicated information about the fight to him.

Confirming the letter by Robinson to his wife was an article by Private David L. Thompson of Company G, 9th NY Regiment, also in the 3rd Division of Rodman.[64] Thompson recounted his part in the battle as follows:

> The brigade was ordered to the left of the road to support a regular battery posted at the top of a steep slope, with a cornfield on the left and twenty yards or so in front, a thin wood. We formed behind the battery and a little down the slope—the 89th [New York] on the left, the 9th [New York] next, then the 103rd [New York]. We had been in position but a few minutes when a stir in front advised us of something unusual afoot, and the next moment the Confederates burst out of the woods and made a dash at the battery. We had just obeyed a hastily given order to lie down when the bullets whistled over our heads and fell far down the slope behind us. Then the guns opened at short range, full-shotted with grape and canister. The force of the charge was easily broken, for though it was vigorously made, it was not sustained. Perhaps it was not intended to be, as the whole day's battle had been merely an effort of the enemy to check our advance till he could concentrate for a general engagement. As the Confederates came out of the woods, their line touched ours on the extreme left only and was at an acute angle. Their men were nearly treading on those of the 89th, who were on their faces in the cornfield before they discovered them. At that instant, the situation just there was, ideally, cruelly advantageous to us. The Confederates stood before us not 20 feet away, the full intention of destruction on their faces—but helpless, with empty muskets. The 89th simply rose up and shot them down.

Darkness came on rapidly, and it grew very chilly. As little could be done at that hour in the way of burial, we unrolled the blankets of the dead, spread them over the bodies, and then sat down in line, munching a little on our cooked rations in lieu of supper and listening to the firing, which was kept up on the right, persistently. By 9:00 pm, this ceased entirely.[65]

Thompson confirmed Robinson's account regarding G. B. Anderson's attack at the Ridge-Loop Intersection and that the firing on Thompson's right or north, probably near Cox's Intersection, continued until 9:00 pm.

Map 23 demonstrates the known characteristics of the area of Cox's Intersection and Thompson's description of where he fought. Notice the steepness of the East Ridge down to Park Hall Road, the "thin woods" noted by others as thick underbrush, and the open fields on the left.

If we combine the statements of Corporal Robinson, Lieutenant Whitman, and Captain Wren, it is indisputable that the 51st NY Regiment of Whitman was with the 51st PA Regiment and that Wren's 48th PA Regiment was nearby. Whitman was in Ferrero's 2nd Brigade, and Wren was in Nagle's 1st Brigade. Thus, Sturgis's 2nd Division brigades were in the same general area. Sturgis's Division had over 3,000 men. The only large Confederate units these Union troops might face during the late afternoon of September 14 had to be those of either G. B. Anderson or Hood.

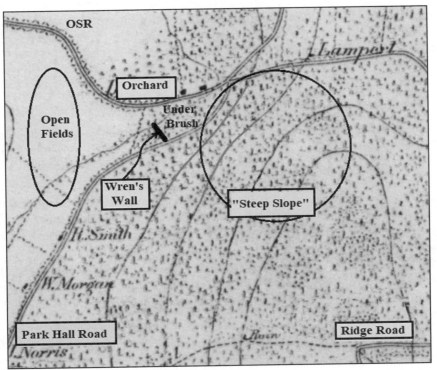

Map 23: Area of Cox's Intersection, September 14, 1862. (Identified on *Atlas Map* by Ted Ellis)

In the case of Captain Wren, there was every reason to believe his 48th PA Infantry faced Hood's two brigades as those units advanced south along Moser Road. Wren told us that his brigade under Nagle, consisting of the 2nd MD, 6th NH, 9th NH, and 48th PA, "opened fire from the battle line." Corporal William Robinson caused us to believe the 51st NY and 51st PA faced G. B. Anderson's Brigade as they retreated north along Park Hall Road to Old Sharpsburg Road.

Lieutenant Whitman, 51st NY, was in an open field with another regiment on his left and another on his right. Whitman informed us that Sturgis's Division was in a line of battle, which must have been along Old Sharpsburg Road and Park Hall Road. Whitman's unit likely was near Lambert's open field. We conclude that Sturgis's 2nd Division brigades under Nagle and Ferrero were along Old Sharpsburg Road and Park Hall Road close to Cox's Intersection.

The difficult question was, "How did G. B. Anderson's Brigade get north beyond Old Sharpsburg Road after they retreated from the Ridge-Loop Intersection and moved north along Park Hall Road?" Ripley informed us that he "found soon afterward that General [G. B.] Anderson's command had been withdrawn at nightfall from the heights to the Braddock Road [Old Sharpsburg Road]." The limited information placed G. B. Anderson's Brigade along Old Sharpsburg Road west of Moser Road.

Major General Burnside, commanding the Union right wing, ordered Major General Jesse L. Reno's Ninth Corps to advance with his entire force against the Confederate position during the late afternoon of September 14. Burnside described his version of events as follows:

> At the same time, I sent orders to General Reno, whose Corps had been sharply engaged all the morning, to move upon the enemy's position with his whole force as soon as I informed him that General Hooker was well advanced up the crest of the mountain on the right [north].
>
> At this time, say 8:00 pm [September 14], the enemy had been driven from their strong positions. The firing ceased, except upon our extreme left [west], where General Reno's division, then under the command of General Cox (General Reno having been killed about 7:00 pm), were partially engaged till 10:00 pm.[66]

Burnside's statement agreed with Cox and McClellan that all the Union forces advanced against the Confederates late in the day. The Union troops at Fox's Gap "were partially engaged till 10 pm." According to the best analysis, Reno was shot about sunset or 6:36 pm, not 7:00 pm, as indicated by Burnside.

We also know that Union artillery near Fox Gap Road directed some of their fire towards Fox's Gap. Lord's *History of the Ninth New Hampshire Regiment* indicated Benjamin's four guns fired at Confederate artillery on the north side of Old National Pike and Confederate artillery at Fox's Gap:

> At the right, Burnside is seen superintending a battery and sighting one of the guns. It is Benjamin's battery of twenty-pound rifles, his pets, and his pride. Some are pointed toward

the mountain pass on the right [Turner's Gap], aimed at a battery beyond the turnpike. It is a mile and a half away and scarcely distinguishable with the naked eye. The others are pointed towards the summit [Fox's Gap], directly in front.

Colonel [Enoch Q.] Fellows, dismounting, goes to General Burnside and converses for a moment. "I want you to take that battery," says the general, pointing to the crest on the left of the road [Fox's Gap] in front, leading directly to the summit.[67]

McClellan testified Sturgis's Division moved to the front beyond Willcox's Division and Cook's Battery was brought into action again:

> Cook's battery now reopened fire. Sturgis's division was moved to the front of Willcox's, occupying the new ground gained on the further side of the slope, and his artillery [Durell] opened on the batteries across the gap. The enemy tried to turn our left about dark but was repulsed by Fairchild's brigade and Clark's battery.[68]

McClellan sent the following message, probably to either the Secretary of War or the president, early on the morning of September 15:

September 15, Monday, 9:30 am, Bolivar

> [I] just sent you a telegram informing you that we yesterday gained a glorious and complete victory; every moment adds to its importance.[69]

Conclusions—Union Perspective

1. A primary objective of the Union Ninth Corps at Fox's Gap on September 14 was a flank attack from the rear or west by way of Moser Road against the Confederates at Turner's Gap.

Union Cavalry Brigadier General Pleasonton, with the concurrence of Brigadier General Jacob D. Cox, identified today's Zittlestown and Moser Roads as the routes for a flank attack against the Confederates at Turner's Gap.

2. Wood Road did not meet the criteria established by Pleasonton and Cox for a flank attack by the Union Ninth Corps against the Confederates at Turner's Gap.

Wood Road met Old National Pike approximately 300 feet *east* of the Mountain House on September 14, 1862. The Moser Road and Old National Pike intersection was 1,300 feet *west* of the Mountain House. Only Moser Road met Pleasonton's and Cox's criteria.

3. Previous authors who wrote about the Battle of South Mountain failed to identify the two ridges of South Mountain between Old National Pike and Old Sharpsburg Road.

Those who wrote about the Fox's Gap battlefield fight failed to identify the West Ridge of South Mountain between Old National Pike and Old Sharpsburg Road. Confederate cannon used Hill #1 along the West Ridge during the battle.

4. Ezra Carman, Antietam historian and author, did not acknowledge the existence of the West Ridge south of Old National Pike.

Carman's assessment was correct; it just was not complete. He did not acknowledge or was unaware of the two ridges south of Old National Pike.

5. By 5:30 pm, Union artillery dominated Fox's Gap, and the Fox's Gap battlefield was clear of Confederate artillery.

The Union cannon included the commands of Coffin, Cook, Glassie, and two six-gun batteries under Muhlenberg and Durell. This Union cannon count did not include the four guns at the Ridge-Loop Intersection under Clark nor the 16 Union cannon near Fox Gap Road.

6. Union Brigadier General Cox stated that he intended to push the enemy troops down the mountain's western slope to what Cox called Rohrersville Road (today's Park Hall Road).

A McClellan staff officer communicated to Cox the whole Union line should advance. To Cox, this meant clearing his front decisively of the enemy from the slopes that went steadily down to Park Hall Road.

7. Union Brigadier General Cox gave the best description of the sequence of events on the Fox's Gap battlefield after the defeat of Drayton's Brigade at Miller's Field by about 5:00 pm.

Cox confirmed that Sturgis's Division then "moved forward in front of General Willcox's position, occupying the new ground gained on the slope's further [west] side." Whitman confirmed Sturgis's Division "was brought up and took the advance."

8. Union Brigadier General Cox identified two hills between Old National Pike and Old Sharpsburg Road.

Cox stated, "The enemy still held the two hills between the latter road and the turnpike, and the further one could not be reached till the Mountain House should be in our hands." It is reasonable to believe Cox intended to move north along Moser Road when the opportunity presented itself.

9. Cox's Intersection, as I have named it, was the intersection of Moser Road and Old Sharpsburg Road about one half-mile west of Fox's Gap.

Cox indicated, "On the left [west], Longstreet's men were pushed down the mountainside beyond the Rohrersville and Sharpsburg Roads, and the contest there was ended."

10. Union Brigadier General Cox described the existence of a gorge near his troops.

According to Cox, "the enemy's battery was across a gorge, beyond the reach of our infantry. Its position was made untenable, and it was hastily removed and not again put in position near us." Evidence indicated this gorge was near Cox's Intersection.

Ted Ellis at Captain Wren's Stone Wall, July 11, 2022. Park Hall Road was approximately 30 feet above Ted. (Photograph by Curtis Older)

11. Union Captain Wren of the 48th PA revealed that "just to the right of my skirmish line of yesterday was two crossroads in the shape of an "X."

Captain Wren was along Park Hall Road, not far from Cox's Intersection. The roads there formed an "X."

12. Ezra Carman, Antietam historian and author, stated the distance between Wood Road and Upper Ridge Road at Fox's Gap was 40 yards.

This measurement confirmed that Wren did not refer to these roads at Fox's Gap as the crossroads where he fought.

13. Union Captain Wren described a stone fence on his front, and the enemy lay very thick behind that fence.

The only stone fence within a half-mile of Cox's Intersection was between Park Hall Road and Dog Creek, about 600 feet southwest of the intersection. The discovery of this stone fence on April 25, 2022, was the most significant discovery on the Fox's Gap battlefield in the past 160 years. Vegetation made the wall difficult to see during the warmer months of the year.

14. Union Captain Wren indicated his 48th PA Regiment was near the 51st NY Regiment when his Union skirmishers approached Hood's skirmishers.

The 51st NY Regiment was under Ferrero, and the 48th PA Regiment was under Nagle. These two brigades made up Sturgis's 2nd Division.

15. Union Lieutenant George W. Whitman disclosed that at the end of the day, he was a mile from where the battle began.

"The enemy, falling back slowly until night when we found ourselves on the opposite side of the mountains and about a mile from where the fight commenced." Whitman was on the west side of Fox's Gap near Cox's Intersection, as Lambert's Field was along Old Sharpsburg Road and was the first open field west of Fox's Gap.

16. Union Lieutenant George W. Whitman confirmed that two other regiments were nearby his 51st NY Regiment.

"The regiments on our right [east] and left [west] had a regular crossfire on the enemy and kept pouring the lead into them like rain."

17. Union troops commanded all the best positions on the Fox's Gap battlefield, according to Lieutenant Whitman.

Union troops dominated "with all the best positions on the field in our possession." It was reasonable to read Whitman's statement to mean that Union troops commanded all roads and crossroads on the Fox's Gap battlefield.

18. Five Union soldiers confirmed they fought near fences and open fields on the west side of Fox's Gap near Cox's Intersection.

Wren, Whitman, Pollock, Pleasants, and Bosbyshell described fighting near fences during the battle. The *Atlas Map* did not show barriers along Old Sharpsburg Road between the Wise Cabin and Cox's Intersection. However, the *Atlas Map* showed railing along Old Sharpsburg Road west of Moser Road and south along Park Hall Road. A fence surrounded Lambert's Field. All barriers shown on the *Atlas Map* were adjacent to open fields.

19. Three members of the 48th PA agreed on several battle details.

Wren, Bosbyshell, and Pleasants agreed that the 48th PA ran out of ammunition, was relieved by another regiment, and the Rebel fire soon ceased. Wren and Bosbyshell identified the 2nd MD as the regiment to replace the 48th PA, while Pleasants identified the 4th Rhode Island, an infantry unit in Rodman's 3rd Division.

20. Union Brigadier General Cox gave a time of 7:00 pm when a persistent Confederate attack began against Sturgis's Division and part of the Kanawha Division.

Pollock acknowledged a Rebel attack came about 7:00 pm, while Pleasants indicated 7:30 pm.

21. Union soldiers Whitman, Bosbyshell, Wren, Pleasants, and Pollock all confirmed many dead Confederates near Cox's Intersection.

Bosbyshell reported, "the next morning, we moved off after the Rebels, passing over the battlefield, where piles and piles of dead Rebels lay, evidence of the accuracy of our firing." "The next morning, we examined the place from which the Rebels were firing on us and on the 51st New York (which occupied our right). And there lay from 100 to 150 dead bodies," according to Pleasants.

22. Union Captain Bolton and Sergeant Parker confirmed large numbers of dead Confederates at Fox's Gap. Private Hitchcock testified about Union ammunition wagons running over dead and wounded Confederates on Old Sharpsburg Road.

These dead Confederates were under Drayton's Brigade.

23. Dead Confederates were along Old Sharpsburg Road from the Wise Cabin to Cox's Intersection.

Private Holahan reported dead Confederates "all the way down the mountain in the woods and at the roadside." Cox's Intersection was the bottom of the mountain coming down Old Sharpsburg Road from the Wise Cabin at the summit.

24. Union Corporal Robinson of the 89th NY indicated that G. B. Anderson's Brigade suffered significant casualties, apparently at Cox's Intersection, after being defeated earlier at the Ridge-Loop Intersection.

Robinson indicated, "the 51st NY went into them [the Rebels] with a vengeance supported by the 51st OH [PA] and piled the Rebels up in heaps."

25. Union Private Thompson confirmed the attack by G. B. Anderson at the Ridge-Loop Intersection and that firing on the right, apparently near Cox's Intersection, continued until 9:00 pm.

Thompson stated that he "sat down in line, munching a little on our cooked rations in place of supper and listening to the firing, which was kept up on the right, persistently. By 9:00 pm, this ceased entirely."

26. Union infantry at Fox's Gap consisted of at least 13,000 men by 6:00 pm.

Given the Union strength in artillery and infantry numbers on the Fox's Gap battlefield, it was not reasonable to believe a Confederate counterattack at Miller's Field could succeed after 6:00 pm.

27. Union Generals McClellan, Burnside, Pleasonton, Ferrero, and Private Holahan praised the Union's success at Fox's Gap.

Private Holahan indicated the North would feel confident of a Union victory at South Mountain. Captain Pleasants agreed. Major General George B. McClellan and Major General Ambrose Burnside testified to the success of the Union Army in the battle. McClellan declared to President Lincoln and Major General Henry Halleck, "God has seldom given an army a greater victory than this."

28. Confederate troops under Brigadier General Garland were confronted at 9:00 am by Union forces under Cox and defeated. Lieutenant Colonel Hayes led the Union attack.

By noon, the Confederates abandoned most of Ridge Road and occupied the area around the Wise Cabin and Miller's Field.

29. Confederate Brigadier General G. B. Anderson's men may have remained along Old Sharpsburg Road west of Cox's Intersection or west of Moser Road before the general Confederate retreat after 10:00 pm.

Upon the death of Confederate Brigadier General Garland between 10:00 am and 10:15 am, Confederate Major General Hill assigned G. B. Anderson command of Old Sharpsburg Road at Fox's Gap. I could not determine the extent of fighting between G. B. Anderson's men and Union forces near Cox's Intersection. Brigadier General Ripley stated, "I found soon afterward that General [G. B.] Anderson's command had been withdrawn at nightfall from the heights to the Braddock Road [Old Sharpsburg Road]." Ezra Carman placed G. B. Anderson along Old Sharpsburg Road at the end of the battle.

30. The Union Ninth Corps did not attempt to advance north along Moser Road on the evening of the 14th.

Captain Wren testified that his brigade neither retreated nor advanced from their battle line as the Confederates approached. Whitman, Pleasants, Pollock, and Bosbyshell gave no indication any Union troops moved north along Moser Road.

32. According to Ezra Carman, Antietam historian and author, the casualties in Hood's two brigades during the battle were extremely low.

Carman's casualty numbers conflicted with the reported numbers by Whitman, Wren, Bosbyshell, and Pleasants.

33. Based on the Union firsthand eyewitness testimony presented, there was no reason to doubt the accuracy of Union Brigadier General Cox's statement:

> On the left [west], Union troops pushed Longstreet's men down the mountainside beyond the Rohrersville [Park Hall Road] and [Old] Sharpsburg Roads, and the contest there was ended. The enemy still held the two hills between the latter route and the turnpike, and the further one could not be reached until the Mountain House was in our hands.[70]

The following chapter will present the Confederate perspective during the battle, and the chapter after it will discuss Hood's advance. These two chapters will dispose of any lingering doubts the reader might have about how events ended on the Fox's Gap battlefield on September 14, 1862.

CHAPTER THREE

Fox's Gap—Confederate Perspective

Hell is empty, and all the devils are here.

WILLIAM SHAKESPEARE[1]

We now turn to the Confederate narrative of events at Fox's Gap on September 14, 1862. We focus on the primary source evidence provided by the Confederate participants in the contest and review the significant developments related to the Confederates on the Fox's Gap battlefield. We set the stage for analyzing the movements of Brigadier General John Bell Hood's two brigades towards Old Sharpsburg Road during the late afternoon at about 5:00 pm.

Ridge Road extended about one half-mile south of the Wise Cabin at Fox's Gap and followed close to the East Ridge crest. Brigadier General Samuel Garland Jr.'s Brigade of Confederates occupied defensive positions along Ridge Road when the battle began at 9:00 am on Sunday.[2] Garland died in the Union infantry attack. His brigade retreated to the north and northeast due to the overwhelming number of Union soldiers in Brigadier General Jacob D. Cox's Kanawha Division. Before noon, the Confederates gradually fell back to the Wise Cabin and Miller's Field areas near Old Sharpsburg Road.

Upon the death of Garland, between 10:00 am and 10:15 am, Major General Hill assigned Brigadier General G. B. Anderson the command of Old Sharpsburg Road at Fox's Gap. Hill placed Colonel Thomas L. Rosser in charge of Ridge Road south of Fox's Gap.[3] The 2nd NC and 4th NC

Confederate Brigadier General Samuel Garland Jr, December 16, 1830 to September 14, 1862. (Artist Paul Martin)

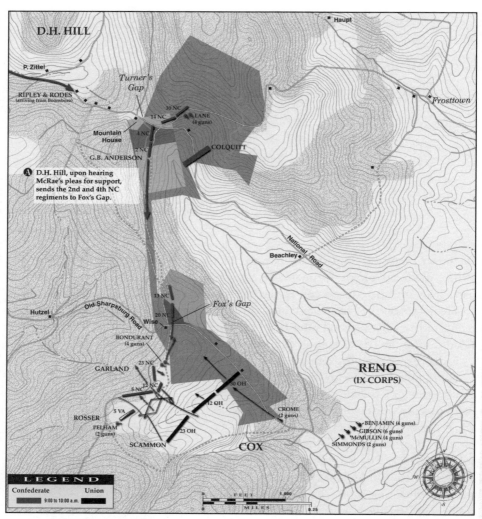

Map 24: Fox's Gap 9:00 am to 10:00 am, September 14, 1862. (Map by Steven Stanley)

from G. B. Anderson's Brigade reinforced Colonel Duncan K. McRae, Garland's replacement, between 10:15 and 11:00 am. The 14th NC and 30th NC Regiments under G. B. Anderson remained at Turner's Gap.

By noon, the Union forces held all the ground along Ridge Road south of Old Sharpsburg Road except the ground near the Wise Cabin and Wise's Field. About noon a two-hour lull in the fighting occurred. Both armies awaited reinforcements. However, Confederate and Union artillery remained active during the infantry lull.

Probably sometime between noon and 2:00 pm, Bondurant found the location of his four cannon near the Wise Cabin indefensible and probably moved his men

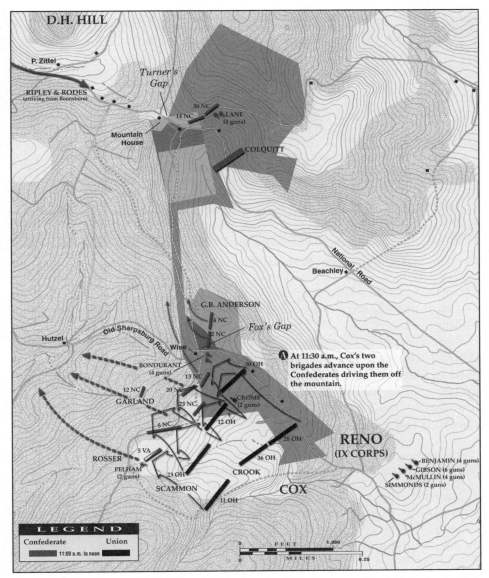

Map 25: Fox's and Turner's Gaps 11:00 am to noon, September 14, 1862. (Map by Steven Stanley)

and guns to the northwest corner of Miller's Field near Wood Road. The new site became Bondurant's position of last resort for him to remain viable on the Fox's Gap battlefield and provided a route of escape to Turner's Gap along Wood Road or possibly along Cut Road (see page 6).

The convex shape of Miller's Field severely restricted Bondurant's guns' usage at this location. The principal effect of his artillery would be against Union troops

Cannon at Fox's Gap. Light 12-pounder Model 1857, September 14, 2012. (Photograph by Curtis Older)

advancing to Miller's Field from the east and perhaps against troops moving along Old Sharpsburg Road between Fox Gap Road or Bolivar Road and the east side of Miller's Field.

Bondurant's situation was similar to the forced eviction of Rosser's Cavalry and Pelham's artillery section from the Ridge-Loop Intersection after 11:00 am to a position near Lambert's Field and Moser Road. The Lambert's Field location was the last resort for Rosser and Pelham to remain viable near the Fox's Gap battlefield. It provided a route of escape along Moser Road and a water source for Rosser's Cavalry at Dog Creek.

Major General Hill's Afternoon Counterattack

The afternoon fight at Fox's Gap revolved around Major General Daniel H. Hill's scheme for a Confederate counterattack to regain possession of Ridge Road, south of Old Sharpsburg Road, lost in the morning fight. Three Confederate infantry brigades assembled along Old Sharpsburg Road and Park Hall Road west of the Wise Cabin. These infantry units sought to function like a swinging door, using the Wise Cabin as the hinge. Under Brigadier General Thomas F. Drayton, a fourth Confederate brigade occupied Miller's Field and advanced south across Old Sharpsburg Road to contest the ground near the Upper Ridge Road and Wise's Field. Captain J. W. Bondurant's four-cannon battery from its position at the north end of Miller's Field was limited in assisting Drayton's advance due to the convex nature of Miller's Field and the cannon positioned behind Drayton's troops.

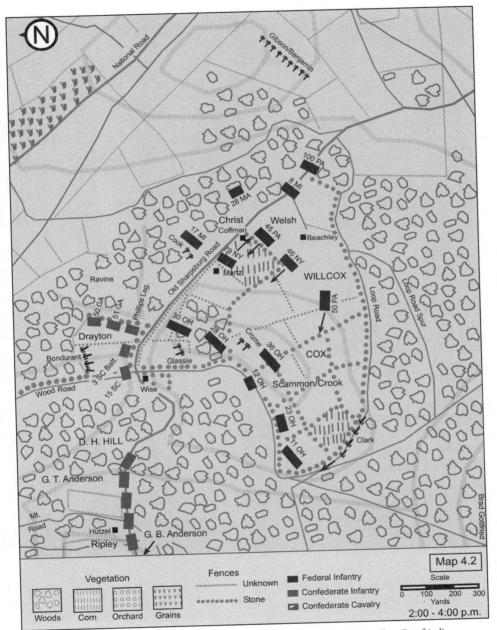

Map 26: Fox's Gap 2:00 pm to 4:00 pm, September 14, 1862. (Map by Bradley Gottfried)

Around 3:00 pm, Confederate brigades under Colonel George T. Anderson, Brigadier General Roswell S. Ripley, and Brigadier General George B. Anderson

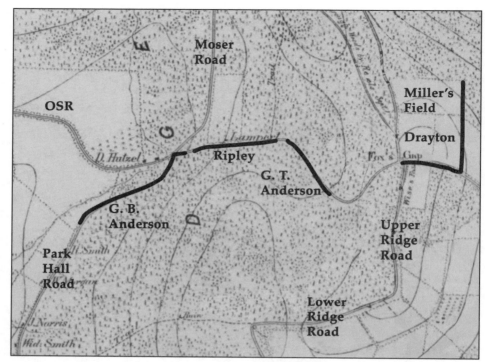

Map 27: Initial Position—Confederate Counterattack, about 3:00 pm, September 14, 1862. Analysis by Steven Stotelmyer. (Identified on the *Atlas Map* by Curtis Older)

began falling in line in Old Sharpsburg Road west of the Wise Cabin. G. T. Anderson's Brigade numbered about 1,000 men, the brigade of Ripley about 1,350 men, and G. B. Anderson's Brigade about 1,750 men. G. T. Anderson's men were supposed to fall in line near the west side of the Wise Cabin and adjacent Drayton's Brigade that occupied Miller's Field. Unfortunately, Confederate misunderstanding resulted in a 900-foot gap in the Confederate line of attack. G. T. Anderson's Brigade's starting position began about 900 feet west of the Wise Cabin and Drayton's Brigade.

Steven Stotelmyer, a student of the Maryland Campaign, calculated a brigade

Confederate Major General Daniel H. Hill. (Courtesy of Archives, Special Collections and Community, Davidson College)

front of 850 feet for G. T. Anderson's Brigade, the approximate distance his brigade extended along the road. Stotelmyer determined a brigade front of 1,150 feet for

Ripley's Brigade and 1,500 feet for G. B. Anderson's. The three extended west approximately 3,500 feet along Old Sharpsburg Road and Park Hall Road.

Following the undulations of Old Sharpsburg Road, the distance to Cox's Intersection was about 3,200 feet west of the Wise Cabin. Ripley's Brigade fell in line after G. T. Anderson's Brigade, which began about 900 feet west of the Wise Cabin. Therefore, the last man of Ripley's Brigade was about 2,900 [900 + 850 + 1,150] feet west of the Wise Cabin. G. B. Anderson's Brigade followed Ripley's Brigade and began about 300 feet east of Cox's Intersection and then followed Park Hall Road south about 1,200 (1,500–300) feet.

A brief review of the movements of the Confederate brigades of G. B. Anderson, Ripley, Drayton, and G. T. Anderson during the afternoon will provide an excellent lead-in to the arrival of Hood's two brigades at Turner's Gap.

Brigadier General George B. Anderson's Brigade

Brigadier General G. B. Anderson's men marched east from Park Hall Road and crossed paths with Ripley's Brigade, who marched south from Old Sharpsburg Road. Ripley's men returned to Old Sharpsburg Road and never fired a shot, or very few, during the battle. G. B. Anderson's men probably returned to Park Hall Road and moved south along the road beyond the property of J. Slifer shown on the *Atlas Map*. Anderson's Brigade possibly moved south through the woods rather than use the road beyond the Union left or south flank at the Ridge-Loop Intersection. Making a correction and expending more time, Anderson's men backtracked and moved to the northeast. They finally initiated an attack against the extreme Union left flank at the Ridge-Loop Intersection, a half-mile south of the Wise Cabin.

Union Major General George B. McClellan disclosed:

> The enemy [G. B. Anderson's Brigade] made an effort to turn our left [south flank] about dark but was repulsed by Fairchild's [1st] Brigade, [Rodman's 3rd Division] and Clark's [4th U.S. Artillery] battery [E].[4]

The 89th NY under Colonel Harrison Fairchild was at the Ridge-Loop Intersection when G. B. Anderson's men attacked.

A September 24, 1862, letter from Corporal William A. Robinson of the 89th NY to his wife described G. B. Anderson's attack against the Union left flank at the Ridge-Loop Intersection. Robinson's letter also alleged an encounter between G. B. Anderson's Brigade and the 51st NY and 51st OH (PA) near Cox's Intersection after the fight at the Ridge-Loop Intersection:

> After they [the Rebels] left us, they formed and went a little farther to the right, and the 51st NY went into them [the Rebels] with a vengeance supported by the 51st OH [PA] and piled the Rebels up in heaps. That lasted till about 9:00 pm. Mr. Alpines' son and Charles Waters are in the 51st and are both well.[5]

Robinson confirmed he was part of the Union rear guard and indicated he was at the extreme left or southernmost flank of the Union line at the Ridge-Loop Intersection. This description of events agreed with G. B. Anderson's men, who aimed their attack against the extreme Union left or southernmost flank.

Robinson indicated that after the Confederates fled from the area of the Ridge-Loop Intersection, they formed again, probably in Park Hall Road, and went farther to the right or north. This movement by Anderson's Brigade put them near Cox's Intersection. According to Robinson, it was there that G. B. Anderson's men faced the 51st NY and 51st PA Union infantry. Robinson indicated the Rebels were "piled up in heaps." Robinson did not personally witness the encounter. We assume he received information about it from friends in the 51st NY or 51st PA.

Unfortunately, G. B. Anderson died from wounds suffered at Antietam, and he did not prepare an after-battle report for South Mountain. A second attack by or against G. B. Anderson's Brigade did not appear in battle accounts. Robinson indicated his regiment entered the contest "about sundown." Thus, when G. B. Anderson's men retreated down the mountain from the Ridge-Loop Intersection and marched north along Park Hall Road, it must have been close to dark, about 6:30 pm.

Several additional Confederate accounts discussed the Confederate attack at the Ridge-Loop Intersection. Benjamin B. Ross, 4th NC, told a slightly different story of the encounter with the Union troops:

> After dinner [lunch], General Ripley came up with his brigade. He made a speech and told us that he and his men were going to stay on the road [Old Sharpsburg Road], and he wanted our brigade ([G. B.] Anderson's Brigade) to go up on the mountain and run the Yankees down, killing as many of them as we could, and his men would stop them as they came down.
>
> We went up, thinking we would have lots of fun driving them down. We saw a little field up there when we reached the top of the mountain. We were tired after climbing the mountain and could hardly clamber over the fence. When we got to the middle of the meadow, the Yankees opened fire on us, about ten thousand firing at one time. We retreated, each one thinking that everybody had been killed but himself. We got to the fence and got over it, hardly knowing it was there. After we crossed the wall, the officers called out "Halt," but everyone, men and officers too, was hurrying down the hill, and not one stopped until we reached the foot of the mountain.[6]

Ross probably referred to Park Hall Road when he stated that "not one stopped until we reached the foot of the mountain."

The report of Colonel Bryan Grimes confirmed the 4th NC, upon reaching the summit (the Ridge-Loop Intersection), made a charge upon a battery, was repulsed, and fell back and reformed. It was then too dark to proceed, according to Grimes.[7]

Captain A. J. Griffith of the 14th North Carolina confirmed that the regiment was on Brigadier General Ripley's right (west or south) side and moved towards the enemy on the mountain (at the Ridge-Loop Intersection). However, it was nearly night before meeting the enemy, and the regiment received orders to fall back to an old road (either Park Hall Road or Old Sharpsburg Road). Receiving no orders from General Ripley, the regiment was not again in action.[8]

Major William W. Sillers of the 30th NC regiment reported that "the regiment, except its skirmishers, was not engaged with any visible portion of the enemy's forces during the battle." The regiment lost one captain and three privates wounded near the area where Garland's Brigade engaged the enemy late morning. Of particular interest, Sillers made the following statement in his report:

> The regiment was under fire from an unseen foe a few minutes before night. The fire was replied to, with what effect is unknown, as it soon became dark, and the brigade moved down the mountain. We changed position several times during the day, marching up and down the mountain. In these movements, made very rapidly and in the heat of the day, some men became exhausted and fell out of the ranks. Others were, no doubt, wounded in the random firing late in the afternoon, causing a loss in missing 15 privates and totaling wounded and missing during the day 19.[9]

Sillers indicated the 30th NC was not in any significant action near the Ridge-Loop Intersection, and as darkness set in, the 30th NC moved back down the mountain. Of most significance, Sillers indicated the 30th NC "changed position several times during the day, marching up and down the mountain. In these movements, made very rapidly and in the heat of the day, some men became exhausted and fell out of the ranks." Again, we see the rapid movement of troops up and down the mountain indicating a very fluid situation during the battle.

Grimes, Griffith, and Sillers did not indicate any significant number of casualties in their respective regiments. The 4th NC, 14th NC, and 30th NC regiments were in G. B. Anderson's Brigade's most notable action late in the day at the Ridge-Loop Intersection. The three regiments had no Confederate artillery assistance.

The *Histories of the Several Regiments and Battalions from North Carolina* described the following events at the Ridge-Loop Intersection:

> We moved toward the south. We swung around gradually toward the east, marching about three-fourths of a mile, when we discovered a heavy force of the enemy in a field on the crest of the ridge, with a battery of field artillery [Clark]. I at once reported this fact to General [G. B.] Anderson, who had now come up with the regiment, quickly returned to the front and was surprised to find the enemy's whole force moving down upon us in line of battle. They opened upon us a heavy fire. Our men received them firmly, returning their fire with spirit. We had the advantage of shelter in the dense woods while the enemy was in the open field and must have suffered severely, but soon night drew on and put a stop to the engagement. We then returned to the road from whence we had started early in the afternoon.[10]

G. B. Anderson's Brigade included four North Carolina regiments. It may be that only the 2nd NC Regiment engaged the Union troops at the Ridge-Loop Intersection. "The road from whence we had started early in the afternoon" probably referred to Park Hall Road, but one cannot conclusively eliminate Old Sharpsburg Road.

Nothing in the Confederate accounts refuted the statements of Robinson of the 89th NY. Ripley stated G. B. Anderson's Brigade returned to Braddock Road (Old Sharpsburg Road) after its encounter at the Ridge-Loop Intersection. Robinson's account also effectively placed G. B. Anderson Brigade at or near Cox's Intersection.

The best conclusion was that G. B. Anderson's Brigade retreated north along Park Hall Road after the encounter at the Ridge-Loop Intersection. One of three events occurred: One. after reaching Cox's Intersection, G. B. Anderson's Brigade attempted to move east along Old Sharpsburg Road and encountered Union troops under Sturgis. Two. G. B. Anderson's Brigade moved north along Park Hall Road and met Union forces under Sturgis near Cox's Intersection. Three. Upon the appearance of Union forces along Park Hall Road or at Cox's Intersection, G. B. Anderson moved his brigade west of Park Hall Road and took up a position west along Old Sharpsburg Road.

Ezra Carman stated that Ripley, returning to the front after the fighting ended, filled the interval between George B. Anderson and Hood. The Confederate line remained in this order until the Confederate retreat. Nothing in the accounts of either Ripley or Thruston indicated that Ripley's Brigade moved south along Moser Road once they reached the area of the Crest of the Heights or Old National Pike earlier in the evening.

Carman also told us that G. B. Anderson had his brigade's 2nd NC, 4th NC, and 30th NC regiments and the 13th NC regiment of Garland's Brigade under his command.[11] Carman stated that the 14th NC regiment became detached from G. B. Anderson's Brigade earlier in the day and fell in with Ripley's Brigade.[12]

Lieutenant George W. Whitman of the 51st NY confirmed many Confederate dead near the area he was in when he arose on the 15th near Lambert's Field. The 51st NY possibly reached the open space of Lambert's Field by moving north along Moser Road. Crossing the gorge between Old Sharpsburg Road and the cleared portion of the field would have been difficult. The open field sloped downward from north to south, and the steepest part of the gorge was along the south end of the area. Men who attempted to cross the ravine would have presented a perfect target for Pelham's cannon if those guns remained at the north end of the field or on Moser Road.

G. B. Anderson knew of Moser Road and its connection to Old National Pike from his previous position at Cox's Intersection. The one difficult question concerning the movement of G. B. Anderson's men was how they got back to the north side of Old Sharpsburg Road after they retreated from the Ridge-Loop Intersection.

I have identified the following casualties in G. B. Anderson's Brigade:

	Killed	Wounded	Missing or Captured
2nd NC	6	19	15
4th NC	0	3	10
13th NC	11	29	1
14th NC	0	4	4
30th NC	1	4	15
Totals	**18**	**59**	**45**

I found these casualties in G. B. Anderson's Brigade, but I am confident these numbers are incomplete. They may represent G. B. Anderson's losses in his attack against the Union forces at the Ridge-Loop Intersection. They do not appear adequate to describe additional losses G. B. Anderson's Brigade might have sustained near Cox's Intersection. John M. Priest listed seven killed, 54 wounded, and 29 missing in G. B. Anderson's Brigade.[13] All Confederate troops captured on the Fox's Gap battlefield were paroled or exchanged by December 1862. Major W. W. Sillers listed 15 missing or caught in the 30th NC Regiment.[14]

Brigadier General Roswell S. Ripley's Brigade

During the Confederate counterattack, Brigadier General Roswell Ripley and his brigade advanced south from Old Sharpsburg Road, hoping to retake Ridge Road south and southwest of Fox's Gap. Ripley's Brigade was in a line of battle along Old Sharpsburg Road, east of Cox's Intersection. His men advanced to the south and crossed paths with G. B. Anderson's Brigade, who marched east from Park Hall Road. Ripley consequently ordered his men to retreat to Old Sharpsburg Road and later took Moser Road north to the Crest of the Heights. According to all the available evidence, Ripley's Brigade never fired a shot, or very few, during the battle.

Reviewing Ripley's Brigade's actions during the day helped identify three significant points. First, Ripley's Brigade came to Fox's Gap via Wood Road:

> At about 9:00 am, I received orders to send forward my artillery and, soon after, to move with the whole force to the main pass east of Boonsborough. Upon arriving, I was directed to follow the road leading to Braddock's Gap and place myself in communication with Brigadier-General Anderson, who had preceded me in that direction.[15]

Ripley's Brigade arrived at Turner's Gap, and Ripley referred to Wood Road as "the road leading to Braddock's Gap." Ripley's statement implied Wood Road was not a "pig path," and he indicated he was accompanied by "my artillery." The artillery unit to which Ripley referred was unclear.

Second, Ripley's Brigade departed from the battlefield by taking Moser Road to the Crest of the Heights, not far from Old National Pike:

> My own brigade had pressed up to within a short distance of the crest of the heights. It held its position under a noisy but comparatively harmless fire, but Anderson's brigade, having extended far to the right, was unsupported by any other troops.[16]

Third, we know that Ripley's Brigade fired very few shots during the Battle of South Mountain.

Major Thruston's Report to Governor Vance

A letter of Confederate Major Stephen D. Thruston, 3rd North Carolina, Ripley's Brigade, dated September 27, 1862, told the following story:

Doing a reconnaissance in person, I discovered the lines of battle occupied by my regiment and General [G. B.] Anderson's Brigade to be so nearly at right angles to each other as to render both inactive. I immediately communicated to Brigadier General Ripley, commanding the brigade, who ordered us to fall back to the base of the mountain [Old Sharpsburg Road], which was done in good order. Here the companies of skirmishers were ordered to their proper positions in line. The regiments again moved by the right flank [west] up the mountain by the steep and narrow road [Moser Road], halting as the right reached the top of the said mountain [near Old National Pike or the Crest of the Heights]. About 9:00 pm, we rested in this position within 200 yards of the enemy [near Old National Pike] until about 11:00 pm, when we took the road to Sharpsburg [Old National Pike to Boonsboro and then to Sharpsburg].[17]

Thruston testified that Ripley ordered the brigade to fall back "to the base of the mountain." Old Sharpsburg Road somewhat followed a gulley on the mountain's west side and the mountain's base was at Cox's Intersection. The most suitable location for Ripley's men to retreat was Old Sharpsburg Road east of Cox's Intersection.

Thruston revealed the 3rd NC and Ripley's Brigade moved by the right (west) flank up the mountain by the steep and narrow road (Moser Road). They halted as the right (the first men) reached the top about 9:00 pm. Thruston indicated the brigade was either at the Crest of the Heights on Moser Road between Hill #1 and Hill #2 or near the Moser Road and Old National Pike intersection.

Thruston's description of the route used by Ripley's men for their retreat could only describe Moser Road. The road ascended from a 740-foot elevation at Cox's Intersection to 1,000 feet at Old National Pike. Moser Road crossed the "Crest of the Heights" between Hill #1 and Hill #2 at 1,120 to 1,130 feet.

Thruston's statement that "we rested in this position within 200 yards of the enemy until about 11:00 pm" is genuinely astounding for those who believed the Confederates were in a strong position at Turner's Gap at the battle's end. Thruston referred to the Union troops who conquered Hartwig's Hill 1500 and who advanced south to within 200 yards of Old National Pike. When the battle ended, Hood and Thruston's statements confirmed that Union troops were within just a couple of hundred yards of Old National Pike and the Mountain House at Turner's Gap.

I did not research this issue nor the battle for Turner's Gap, but the statements of Thruston and Hood gave reason to believe that Hooker's First Corps almost captured Turner's Gap from the Confederates by the end of the day on the 14th. The situation at Turner's Gap presents a matter for further research. Darkness and the Confederate cannon at Turner's Gap probably dissuaded the Union troops from making one last assault.

The statements of Thruston and Hood gave no reason to doubt the words of Chaplain George G. Smith:

If you permit, I will tell you about the afternoon at South Mountain in 1862, when I received a bullet through the neck and when night alone saved General Lee's army from capture.

Hood's division went in as we came out, but the Federals' caution and the cover of the night saved our army from a worse defeat and capture.[18]

The September 21 report of Brigadier General Ripley, who commanded the 1st NC and 3rd NC and the 4th GA and 44th GA regiments, was significant. Ripley referred to two roads and Brigadier General Hood in his report:

> Meantime, General [G. B.] Anderson had extended far to the right and come up with the enemy, with whom he had a short engagement [at the Ridge-Loop Intersection]. My brigade pressed up to within a short distance of the Crest of the Heights [Moser Road between Hill #1 and Hill #2] and held its position under a noisy but comparatively harmless fire. Anderson's Brigade, having extended far to the right [perhaps at least one mile south from Ripley], was unsupported by any other troops for the time. Soon after, Brigadier General Hood's command came from the main pass [Turner's Gap]. Forming upon my left [east], the troops pressed up the road [Moser Road], driving the enemy before them until they [the enemy] occupied their first position [around Cox's Intersection] and darkness put an end to the operations. I found soon afterward that General [G. B.] Anderson's command had been withdrawn at nightfall from the heights to the Braddock Road [Old Sharpsburg Road].[19]

We will analyze Ripley's report in more depth in the next chapter. For now, it was crucial to learn that Ripley confirmed that G. B. Anderson was extended far to the right along Park Hall Road and was unsupported by other Confederate units. Ripley did not indicate that G. B. Anderson entered a fight with any Union troops. However, Ripley stated that he was not aware fully of G. B. Anderson's situation, and it only was later that Ripley learned that G. B. Anderson's Brigade withdrew from the heights to Old Sharpsburg Road. We assume "the heights" Ripley referred to was the Ridge-Loop Intersection.

Brigadier General Thomas F. Drayton's Brigade

As published in a detailed analysis, Brigadier General Thomas F. Drayton's Brigade suffered a terrible loss at Fox's Gap. Kurt Graham researched and constructed an exceptional study of Drayton's Brigade's combat in the vicinity of Miller's Field during the afternoon fight at Fox's Gap.[20] Graham's research disclosed the Phillips Legion's presence as a component of Drayton's Brigade during the battle. Published sources had not listed this unit as a participant in the struggle. Two hundred Confederates in Drayton's Brigade of 1,228 men were killed or mortally wounded at Fox's Gap.

John Miller owned the 13¼-acre field on the immediate northeast quadrant at the Old Sharpsburg Road and Wood Road junction on September 14, 1862.[21] Thus, I have named that area "Miller's Field." Drayton's Brigade began arriving at Miller's Field between 3:00 pm and 4:00 pm and immediately took up positions around the perimeter fences.

The artillery backing for Drayton's men was Bondurant's Battery of four guns positioned along the northwest section of Miller's Field. Bondurant was extremely limited in the support he could provide Drayton from this position. The approximate 900-foot separation between Drayton's Brigade and G. T. Anderson's Brigade along Old Sharpsburg Road resulted in Drayton's men being, in effect, an island unto themselves at Fox's Gap.[22]

About 4:00 pm, Drayton's Brigade received orders to shift to their right and extend farther west along Old Sharpsburg Road. By 4:15 pm, the 3rd South Carolina battalion, 15th South Carolina, and Phillips Legion began their attack south across Old Sharpsburg Road. About the same time, Union forces, occupying the woods near the Upper Ridge Road and to the south, southeast, and southwest of Wise's Field, received the order to advance. Those Confederates near the Wise Cabin, principally the 15th SC, immediately confronted Union troops along and west of the Upper Ridge Road.

According to Cox, Willcox prepared to advance when the Confederates charged out of the woods and across Wise's Field.[23] The advance by three of Drayton's regiments south of Old Sharpsburg Road was met all along the Confederate line by a substantial number of Union troops. Within a period of fewer than 30 minutes, the Confederates retreated. The 3rd SC battalion took the fatal step of occupying the area between the two stone walls along the Upper Ridge Road. It would be here that Confederate Colonel George S. James would make his last stand.[24]

The 17th MI began their advance about 3:30 pm on the north side of Old Sharpsburg Road towards Miller's Field. Their objective was to silence the guns

17th Michigan Marker along Wood Road at Fox's Gap about 1998. (Photograph by Curtis Older)

of Bondurant's Battery. About 4:00 pm, other Union troops were poised south of Miller's Field. Sometime after 4:15 pm and after the 50th Georgia and 51st Georgia infantry abandoned the eastern stone wall at Miller's Field, the 17th MI began their advance, unopposed, to the same stone wall.[25]

The Confederate 50th and 51st Georgia regiments soon occupied Old Sharpsburg Road, focusing on the fight south of the road. They were oblivious to the threat of a flank attack on their left or east. Before 5:00 pm, the Union 17th MI attacked Miller's Field from east to west. They got behind or on the north side of the 50th and 51st Georgia regiments and delivered a devastating blow. Simultaneously, the Union 45th PA attacked the 50th GA from the southeast along Old Sharpsburg Road. Any Confederates in Old Sharpsburg Road were now assaulted from the south, east, and north.

Members of the 50th and 51st GA did their best to escape the death trap they faced. They attempted to flee to the west along Old Sharpsburg Road and northwest of Wood Road. The rout of the other Confederate regiments under Drayton sealed the fate of the 3rd SC battalion, who took up residence between the Upper Ridge Road's stone walls.

Union Brigadier General Orlando Willcox credited Colonel Withington of the 17th MI for driving the Confederates from Miller's Field.[26] The Confederate advance across Old Sharpsburg Road was not without a high cost to the Union troops they fought. The 17th MI lost 132 officers and men while the 45th PA lost 134. Both regiments lost more men than any other regiments in the Ninth Corps.[27]

Bondurant's Battery probably took a toll on the 17th MI as the regiment advanced towards Wood Road. However, the Confederate artillery support was inadequate. With the disappearance of their infantry support, Miller's Field became

Fox's Gap, 1912. Miller's Field to the right. (Photograph from the 45th PA Regimental History)

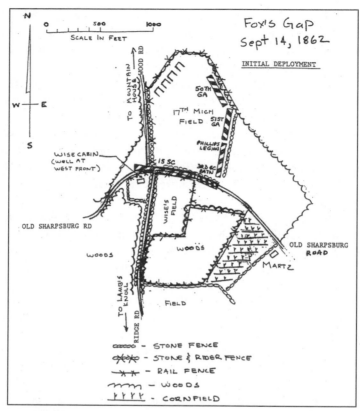

Map 28: Drayton's Deployment of Forces, Approximately 3:00 pm to 4:00 pm, September 14, 1862. (Map by Kurt Graham)

Wise's Field looking north. Wood Road appears at the far left, the Reno Monument appears on the right. (Doug Bast Collection, perhaps about 1930)

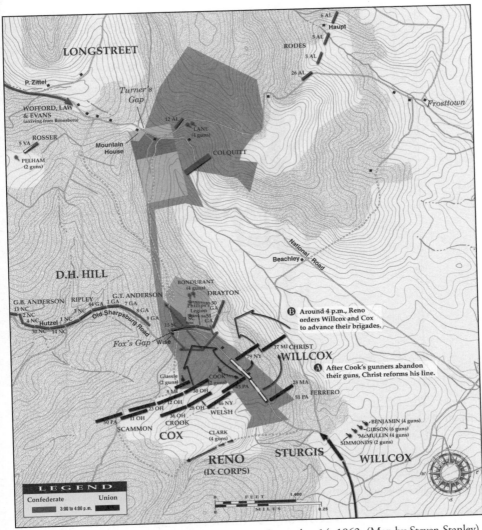

Map 29: Fox's Gap Battlefield 3:00 pm to 4:00 pm, September 14, 1862. (Map by Steven Stanley)

an untenable location, and Bondurant's Battery quickly limbered their guns and retreated north along Wood Road.[28] The Union troops took many prisoners as the situation became desperate for the Confederates. The Confederate counterattack failed, including G. B. Anderson's late attack against the Union left or south flank at the Ridge-Loop Intersection.

Union Brigadier General Cox described the afternoon contest:

> Willcox succeeded in getting a foothold on the other side of the open ground and driving off the artillery there. The enemy was equally repulsed along our center and left where the forest

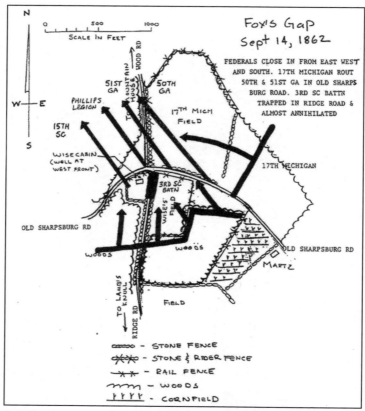

Map 30: Drayton's Forces Overwhelmed by Federals, Approximately 4:45 pm to 5:15 pm, September 14, 1862. (Map Courtesy of Kurt Graham)

was thick. Still, the cover of the timber enabled them to keep a footing nearby. At the same time, they continually tried to extend so as to outflank us, moving their troops along a road that goes diagonally down that side of the mountain from Turner's Gap to Rohrersville.[29]

Cox identified seven Confederate brigades on the Fox's Gap battlefield at one time or another. The Confederate units encompassed Colonel Wofford's and Colonel Evander M. Law's Brigades in Hood's Division, Drayton's and G. T. Anderson's Brigades of Brigadier General David R. Jones' Division, Ripley's and G. B. Anderson's Brigades of Major General Daniel H. Hill's Division, and the remnants of Samuel Garland Jr.'s Brigade, also under Hill.

Cox identified an eighth unit belonging to "Whiting." Cox referred to William H. C. Whiting, whom General Lee replaced with Brigadier General John Bell Hood after the Seven Days Battles. In his report of October 10, Confederate Major General James Longstreet informed us that Whiting's brigade was under Colonel Law at

South Mountain.[30] Therefore, the Confederates had seven brigades at Fox's Gap, not eight, unless we include the 5th VA cavalry under Colonel Thomas L. Rosser and Major John Pelham's horse artillery section as the eighth brigade.

Also occurring about 4:00 pm, Union Brigadier General Isaac P. Rodman's 2nd Brigade under Colonel Edward Harland approached the battlefield near the Fox Gap Road and Old Sharpsburg Road intersection. Union forces soon numbered over 13,000 men at Fox's Gap while the Confederates were broken, scattered, and vastly outnumbered.

According to Cox, the enemy retreated into the woods around Fox's Gap, and Union Brigadier General Samuel D. Sturgis's Division moved forward:

> It was nearly 5:00 pm when the enemy had disappeared in the woods beyond Fox's Gap, and Willcox could reform his shattered lines. As the most accessible mode of getting Sturgis's fresh men into position, Willcox made room on his left [west] for Ferrero's brigade supported by Nagle's, doubling his lines at the extreme right.[31]

Ezra Carman, Antietam historian and author, listed Drayton's Brigade's losses as 49 killed, 164 wounded, and 176 missing in action; in total, 389.[32] In stark contrast, Kurt Graham, author and Fox's Gap researcher, documented 206 men killed or mortally wounded and 227 wounded in Drayton's brigade, an almost unprecedented one-to-one ratio.[33] Graham also listed 210 men unwounded but captured. Thus, Carman's casualty numbers for Drayton's Brigade were deficient.

Captain William J. Bolton of the 51st PA described the scene as his regiment approached the summit of Fox's Gap at about 5:00 pm:

> The artillery having cleared the enemy from the mountain, the 51st was soon ordered to advance towards the summit of the mountain. On our march [we] passed in one pile at least fifty dead Rebels, and on reaching the top of the mountain witnessed the same thing, only there were at least one hundred and twenty-five dead Rebels laying stretched across each other along the stone wall. On the mountain's crest ran a narrow lane protected by a stone fence on either side. The enemy used the position as breastwork. All along this lane, there was a sight to be seen. Along its whole length, the Rebels laid in piles up to the very top of the stone fence. Some were found in a kneeling position in the act of firing. Death to many of them must have been instantaneous. Their arms extended and in position as in the act of firing. And some cases, the bitten cartridges were in their hands.[34]

Most dead Confederates Bolton witnessed must have been in Drayton's Brigade. Bolton's numbers exceed 200 Confederate dead at Fox's Gap. His observations supported Graham's count.

Captain J. Evans Edings, Assistant Adjutant-General to Drayton, recorded the following in his diary entry for September 14, 1862:

> Left Hagerstown and marched back in the direction of Frederick town. At 4:00 pm, engaged the enemy until after night. We got decidedly the worst and were compelled to fall back this morning.[35]

Colonel George T. Anderson's Brigade

Confederate Colonel G. T. Anderson described the movements of his brigade during the late afternoon at Fox's Gap in his after-battle report of September 30:

> Before Drayton had formed his line, Brigadier General Ripley ordered the whole line to move by the right [west] flank, and about this time, the enemy opened a heavy fire on Drayton. By moving to the right [west] under General Ripley's order, I was separated at least 300 yards from General Drayton's right [west]. When General Ripley came by, [he] ordered me to move by the left [east] flank into the wood [out of Old Sharpsburg Road], which I did. My skirmishers (the right-wing of the Georgia Regulars, Captain [R. A.] Wayne commanding), not having the command to change direction, had continued moving by the flank [south] and uncovered my front. Having passed some distance over the mountainside, I halted and sent forward to find Captain Wayne but could not for a reason above given. Seeing that the fire of the enemy was more to my left [east] than front [south], I changed front forward on the left [moved east], and had the left-wing of the Georgia Regulars, under the direction of Colonel (William J.) Magill deployed as skirmishers, and as I was in the act of advancing to find the enemy, Lieutenant Shellman, adjutant 8th Georgia Regiment, reported the enemy as having turned Drayton's right [west] flank and being on our left [east] and rear [north]. A few of them [Union troops] were taken as prisoners. Several of Drayton's men, who had been captured, were released. To prevent the enemy from cutting off my small brigade, being at the time alone (General Ripley's brigade, on my right, being several hundred yards away, as I found by sending Captain (James G.) Montgomery, 1st Georgia Regulars, to report for orders, who reported him at least one-quarter of a mile from my right [west], after a long search). I ordered my brigade to move by the left [east] flank and recross the road [to the north side of Old Sharpsburg Road], in our original rear, and there reformed my line of battle and was advancing to find the right of Drayton's brigade when Captain (Hansford D. D.) Twiggs and Lieutenant (G. B.) Lamar, 1st Georgia Regulars in charge of skirmishers, told me that the enemy was crossing the road in considerable force on my left [east] flank. Seeing this myself and preventing my left [east] from being turned, I moved by the left [east] diagonally to the rear [north] to intercept them and found General Hood's two brigades coming up to support that part of the line. He engaged the enemy and drove him back. I did not know where to find General Ripley or General Drayton, so I reported to General Hood for instructions. He requested me to hold my position to protect his left [east] flank, and [we] remained there until drawn off the field after night. In consequence of being separated from Drayton's right [west] by General Ripley's order and recrossing the road [Old Sharpsburg Road] to avoid being surrounded, my men were not engaged in the fight, except the first line of skirmishers under Captain Wayne.[36]

G. T. Anderson's report was subject to several interpretations regarding his brigade's movements. My analysis of G. T. Anderson's Brigade's movements follows. Given that G. T. Anderson's Brigade's initial formation was along Old Sharpsburg Road facing the southwest, it was reasonable to believe his men initially moved to the southwest as they departed Old Sharpsburg Road.

We know at least six significant facts based on G. T. Anderson's report after his men crossed to the north side of Old Sharpsburg Road: 1) Colonel G. T. Anderson indicated that his men encountered some of Drayton's men who had been defeated at Miller's Field and around the Wise Cabin; 2) G. T. Anderson met with Brigadier General Hood; 3) Colonel Anderson observed at least some of Hood's Brigade's encounter with Union troops; 4) G. T. Anderson's Brigade did not engage in the fight; 5) G. T. Anderson reformed his men into a line of battle. We also know: 6) G. T. Anderson could not locate Brigadier General Ripley or Ripley's Brigade.

Both Ripley's and G. T. Anderson's Brigades retreated north of Old Sharpsburg Road shortly after the Confederate counterattack began. Ripley's Brigade ultimately retreated north along Moser Road, and G. T. Anderson's men moved into the woods north of Old Sharpsburg Road and west of Wood Road.

All the evidence related to Drayton's defeat and subsequent retreat indicated Drayton's surviving men fell back into the woods west of Miller's Field and northwest of the Wise Cabin. Drayton's men retreated to the northwest beyond the northernmost line of Miller's Field due to the 17th Michigan substantially occupying most of Miller's Field.

Union troops were along the Upper Ridge Road and west of the Upper Ridge Road and Wise Cabin during the fight with Drayton. G. T. Anderson indicated many Union troops crossed Old Sharpsburg Road to the east. These Union troops, probably in the Kanawha Division, must have been between the Wise Cabin and Anderson's Brigade's initial starting position 900 feet west of the Wise Cabin. G. T. Anderson indicated Union troops detained some of Drayton's men. Anderson's Brigade overpowered these Union troops and freed Drayton's captured men.

G. T. Anderson indicated that his men were not in the battle and must have been far enough west of the Wise Cabin to avoid contact with the Union troops engaged with Drayton's Brigade. Hood directed G. T. Anderson to keep his brigade on Hood's left or east flank to defend against a Union attack.[37] G. T. Anderson indicated his unit initially formed in line of battle in Old Sharpsburg Road west of Drayton's Brigade by about 300 yards. This location placed Anderson's Brigade about that distance west of Drayton's right (west) near the Wise Cabin.

G. T. Anderson described a mass of Union troops crossing Old Sharpsburg Road to the east. Consequently, Anderson had his brigade recross Old Sharpsburg Road to the north side, continuing to move his men diagonally. This movement took Anderson in a northeasterly direction and kept his men on the west side of Wood Road and far from Miller's Field. Later in the day, his unit remained east of Hood's two brigades, and they retained that position until they retreated. G. T. Anderson noted that his brigade was not engaged in the fight, except for some of his skirmishers.

All the evidence points to G. T. Anderson's Brigade's position west of Wood Road and a substantial distance north from Miller's Field. G. T. Anderson confirmed that Hood "engaged the enemy and drove him back." Can we assume that G. T. Anderson witnessed this event? Anderson gave no indication Hood's men captured or recaptured any ground. If any Confederates were near Wood Road late in the day, they would have been remnants of Garland's Brigade or perhaps Drayton's Brigade and not troops under Hood, G. T. Anderson, G. B. Anderson, or Ripley.

G. T. Anderson's report of September 30 declared that earlier in the day, regarding his and Drayton's brigades, Major General Hill "conducted us in person to the right [south] of our line and, after giving the necessary orders, left for other parts of the field." Thus, Hill, familiar with Wood Road, accompanied both G. T. Anderson and Drayton along that road to arrive near Miller's Field earlier in the day. Therefore, troops under G. T. Anderson were aware of Wood Road and may have retreated along a part of that road during the Confederate night retreat. How close G. T. Anderson's Brigade stayed to Hood's two brigades remains unknown.

G. T. Anderson's Brigade suffered minimal casualties. According to Ezra Carman, a historian of the Maryland Campaign, G. T. Anderson suffered no killed, three wounded, and four missing or captured for seven casualties.[38] G. T. Anderson's Brigade could easily occupy a position on the left or east of Hood's men but remain on the west side of the East Ridge and out of the battle. There was no indication Union forces advanced north of Old Sharpsburg Road to confront G. T. Anderson's Brigade, which remained in the woods west of Wood Road.

Colonel Duncan K. McRae—Garland's Brigade

The report of Colonel Duncan K. McRae of the 5th North Carolina Infantry, October 18, 1862, who commanded Garland's Brigade after Garland's death, concluded with the following statement:

> Notwithstanding, we had the disadvantage of position, the absence of artillery support, and the damaging effect produced by the death of its general, who had possessed in the warmest degree the confidence and affection of the troops, and the great superiority of the enemy's numbers. A prisoner early taken reported the force in our front at sixteen regiments, naming many of them. This brigade maintained its ground for more than three hours. It inflicted heavy loss on the enemy, destroying his cannoneers, compelling him to abandon his guns, killing his general officer, and intimidating him to prevent pursuit. His first intention was the consequent passage of his force into the valley between Sharpsburg and us.[39]

McRae credited Garland's Brigade with the death of General Reno. McRae reinforced the claim made in the *Twenty-Third North Carolina Regimental History* and by Major General Hill that a member of the 23rd NC killed Reno. The 23rd NC was in Garland's Brigade. McRae's statement about the death of Reno was especially significant because he made it about one month after the battle.

Of particular interest was McRae's conclusion about the enemy being so intimidated as to "prevent" pursuit, and the "consequent passage of his force into the valley between us and Sharpsburg," which was "his first intention." McRae believed the Union Army intended to proceed west from Fox's Gap and cut off the Confederate retreat to Sharpsburg. May we conclude that McRae came to this analysis because the Union Ninth Corps advanced to Cox's Intersection by the end of the day on September 14?

Rosser's 5th VA Cavalry and Pelham's Artillery

We know little of Rosser's Cavalry and Pelham's Artillery section after being forced out of the Ridge-Loop Intersection between 11:00 am and noon. However, Ripley confirmed that Pelham's Artillery came to his rescue along the "Braddock Road" when Union troops threatened the westernmost section of Ripley's Brigade about 5:00 pm, perhaps a quarter-mile or more west of the Wise Cabin along Old Sharpsburg Road. It was also reasonable to assume that Rosser's Cavalry occupied an area near Cox's Intersection because of the water availability in Dog Creek for the cavalry horses. Some Confederate dead and wounded near Cox's Intersection perhaps came from Rosser's Cavalry.[40]

Conclusions—Confederate Perspective

1. Confederate Brigadier General Samuel Garland Jr.'s Brigade lost most of Ridge Road south of Old Sharpsburg Road during the morning fight at Fox's Gap to Cox's Kanawha Division. With the death of Garland, his brigade became demoralized and impotent.

Major General Hill considered Garland's Brigade too damaged to continue the fight as a unit. By noon, remnants of Garland's Brigade were along Wood Road and probably in wooded areas north and south of Old Sharpsburg Road on the west side of Fox's Gap.

2. Confederate Brigadier General Garland's death resulted in Major General Hill assigning Rosser command over the Ridge Road and G. B. Anderson command over the Old Sharpsburg Road.

Rosser and Pelham retreated from the Ridge-Loop Intersection after 11:00 am to around Cox's Intersection. The Confederates lost most of Ridge Road to the Union by noon. Perhaps G. B. Anderson attempted to stay along Old Sharpsburg Road because of this assignment from Hill.

3. An approximate two-hour lull in the fighting at Fox's Gap occurred between noon and 2:00 pm.

Although there was little or no infantry activity between noon and 2:00 pm while both sides awaited more support, artillery on both sides continued to exchange rounds.

4. Confederate Major General Hill ordered a Confederate counterattack during the afternoon to recapture the area along Ridge Road south of Old Sharpsburg Road.

Hill assigned four Confederate Brigades to Fox's Gap to recapture Ridge Road south of Old Sharpsburg Road. Three Confederate brigades occupied Old Sharpsburg and Park Hall Roads west of Fox's Gap as the starting point to initiate their attack. At the same time, Drayton commanded his various regiments at Miller's Field.

5. Ezra Carman, Antietam historian and author, told us that G. B. Anderson commanded his brigade's 2nd NC, 4th NC, and 30th NC regiments and the 13th NC of Garland's Brigade. Carman also stated that the 14th NC of G. B. Anderson's Brigade became detached earlier and fell in with Ripley's Brigade.

The rugged terrain confounded the understanding of troop movements and the timing of those movements. Carman's statement confirmed how difficult it was to follow the various Confederate troop movements during the Fox's Gap battle.

6. I could not adequately understand Confederate Brigadier General G. B. Anderson's Brigade's movement.

G. B. Anderson's Brigade moved south along Park Hall Road and through the adjacent woods to attack Union forces at the Ridge-Loop Intersection. Union forces quickly repulsed Anderson's men. Union Corporal Robinson reported that Anderson's men then went north along Park Hall Road, where they were met by the 51st NY and 51st PA Union infantry and sustained heavy losses. I found nothing to confirm this incident.

Brigadier General Ripley reported that Anderson withdrew from the heights, presumably the Ridge-Loop Intersection, and moved to Old Sharpsburg Road. From that point forward, Anderson's Brigade's movement became undetermined.

The 4th NC, 14th NC, and 30th NC regiments initially were in G. B. Anderson's Brigade. Colonel Grimes, Captain Griffith, and Major Sillers indicated no significant number of casualties in their respective regiments. Unfortunately, G. B. Anderson died at Antietam and left no after-battle report on South Mountain.

7. Confederate Brigadier General Ripley's Brigade advanced south of Old Sharpsburg Road as Hill's counterattack commenced. Ripley's Brigade then returned to that road and soon moved north along Moser Road to the Crest of the Heights between Hill #1 and Hill #2.

Ripley's Brigade advanced south from Old Sharpsburg Road late in the afternoon and soon crossed paths with G. B. Anderson's Brigade southeast of Cox's Intersection. Ripley recalled his brigade to Old Sharpsburg Road and retreated north along Moser Road to the Crest of the Heights.

8. Confederate Brigadier General Ripley's critical report informed us that Hood's command came from Turner's Gap and formed in line of battle on Ripley's left or east side.

Ripley's report was a critical primary source document that confirmed his ability to see Hood's two brigades from Ripley's post along the Crest of the Heights on Moser Road.

9. Confederate Brigadier General Ripley stated in his report that he witnessed Hood's "troops press up the road" from a position at the Crest of the Heights along Moser Road.

Ripley could not see Hood's troops if they were along Wood Road. The crest of the East Ridge hid Wood Road from Ripley's sight at the Crest of the Heights.

10. Confederate Brigadier General Ripley reported that Hood's two brigades "drove the Union troops back to their first position."

Ripley's report was adequate to confirm that Hood's troops advanced south along Moser Road. Based on the evidence given by various Union officers and men, Ripley must have meant by "their first position" Cox's Intersection.

11. Confederate Major Thruston in the 3rd NC Regiment in Ripley's Brigade stated that Ripley's Brigade moved "up the mountain by the steep and narrow road" and came to a halt "as the right reached the top of the said mountain."

The steep and narrow road was Moser Road. Cox's Intersection was approximately 700 feet above sea level, and the Moser Road and Old National Pike intersection at roughly 1,000 feet. The Crest of the Heights along Moser Road between Hill #1 and Hill #2 was at an elevation of 1,120 to 1,140 feet.

12. Confederate Major Thruston indicated his regiment rested near the Old National Pike and Moser Road intersection within 200 yards of the enemy at about 9:00 pm.

Thruston's statement is genuinely astounding and worthy of additional research. Union troops under Hooker were close to their goal of flanking the Confederates along the Old National Pike about a quarter-mile west of the Mountain House.

13. Confederate Brigadier General Drayton's Brigade suffered crushing losses at Fox's Gap between 4:00 pm and 5:00 pm. Drayton's Brigade remnants retreated northwest from the area along Old Sharpsburg Road near the Wise Cabin and Miller's Field.

Drayton's regiments suffered enormous casualties, as documented in the research of Kurt Graham and confirmed in the writings of Captain Bolton and Sergeant Parker. Another book of mine, *News from Fox's Gap*, included several research articles by Graham.

Union Brigadier General Cox confirmed the Confederates "disappeared in the woods about 5:00 pm." Drayton's defeat allowed Union artillery and infantry to occupy and dominate the immediate vicinity of Fox's Gap. Captain Edings, Assistant Adjutant-General to Drayton, confirmed that "we got decidedly the worst and were compelled to fall back this morning [September 15]."

14. Kurt Graham, author and researcher, substantiated Drayton's Brigade's decimation at Fox's Gap by about 5:00 pm.

Sergeant Parker and Captain Bolton testified that many dead Rebels were in or near Old Sharpsburg Road as they approached Fox's Gap from the east. The research of Kurt Graham disproved Ezra Carman's count of 49 killed in Drayton's Brigade. Carman listed 176 of Drayton's Brigade as missing, and Kurt Graham proved that most of those men died in the battle.

15. Confederate Colonel G. T. Anderson's men initially advanced south of the Old Sharpsburg Road as part of the Confederate counterattack. Union troops threatened to flank Anderson's troops, so Anderson reversed course and crossed back to the north side of the Old Sharpsburg Road.

G. T. Anderson's Brigade saw little fighting, and the brigade probably took up a position a quarter-mile north of the Old Sharpsburg Road and west of the East Ridge after Drayton's defeat.

16. Confederate Colonel G. T. Anderson's after-battle report disclosed six critical points related to Hood's advance. His report confirmed that Hood's two brigades were west of G. T. Anderson's location.

a) G. T. Anderson's men encountered some of Drayton's defeated men on the north side of Old Sharpsburg Road.

b) G. T. Anderson met with Brigadier General Hood north of Old Sharpsburg Road.

c) G. T. Anderson observed Hood's two brigades encounter Union troops.

d) G. T. Anderson's Brigade did not engage in significant fighting.

e) Hood requested G. T. Anderson to protect Hood's left or east flank.

f) G. T. Anderson reformed his men into a line of battle north of Old Sharpsburg Road.

17. Confederate Colonel McRae reported that his brigade successfully intimidated the enemy to prevent pursuit. McRae also claimed Garland's Brigade prevented the movement by the Federals into the valley between the Confederates and Sharpsburg, which was the Federals' first intention.

McRae believed a Union objective was to stay between the Confederates at South Mountain and Harpers Ferry and beat them to Sharpsburg. McRae's report seemed a bit more boastful than realistic. Did McRae conclude the objective of the Union command was to keep the Confederates split between South Mountain and Harpers Ferry because the Ninth Corps successfully occupied Cox's Intersection?

18. Confederate Colonel McRae's October 18, 1862, report indicated that a 23rd North Carolina Regiment member shot Reno.

The date of McRae's report should indicate a high confidence level in McRae's statement concerning who shot Reno. The 23rd NC was not part of Hood's two brigades.

19. Confederate Colonel Rosser's 5th VA Cavalry probably was along Moser Road near Lambert's Field along with Pelham's Artillery section during the late afternoon.

An unknown element was if there was any coordination or communication between Rosser and Hood as part of Hood's attack along Moser Road. Perhaps some of the dead and wounded Confederates near Cox's Intersection belonged to Rosser's dismounted cavalry.

20. The only Confederate brigade on the Fox's Gap battlefield south of Old Sharpsburg Road after Drayton's defeat about 5:00 pm was G. B. Anderson's Brigade along Park Hall Road.

Other Confederate brigades were north of Old Sharpsburg Road shortly after 5:00 pm. Confederate resistance on the Fox's Gap battlefield after 5:00 pm was non-existent except for G. B. Anderson's and Hood's Brigades.

21. Author and Antietam historian Ezra Carman stated that Ripley, returning to the front after the fighting was over, filled the interval between George B. Anderson and Hood. The Confederates held this line until they retreated.

I have found no evidence to support Carman's claim that Ripley and his brigade filled the space between G. B. Anderson and Hood after the fighting was over. Thruston indicated Ripley's Brigade remained near the Crest of the Heights along Moser Road not far from the Old National Pike intersection between 9:00 pm and 11:00 pm.

22. Confederate Chaplain George G. Smith gave his opinion that the Confederates were near defeat and capture on the night of September 14.

Smith attributed the Confederates' good fortune in escaping capture to the Federals' caution and the cover of night.

23. The stage now was set for the movement of Confederate Brigadier General John Bell Hood's two brigades south from Old National Pike towards Old Sharpsburg Road after 5:00 pm.

Given the location of the other Confederate brigades on the Fox's Gap battlefield after 5:00 pm, the only significant support that Hood might find were the brigades of G. T. Anderson and G. B. Anderson. The possibility existed that Confederate artillery on Hill #1 could be of some benefit, but darkness would soon limit the effectiveness of those guns.

We now turn to the next chapter and analyze Brigadier General John Bell Hood's advance south from Old National Pike to Old Sharpsburg Road. Authors have incorrectly reported the movement of Hood's two brigades during this aspect of the battle for the 160 years since its occurrence.

CHAPTER FOUR

Brigadier General John Bell Hood's Advance

The last march at double time was thinned to skeletons of three or four hundred men to a brigade.

CONFEDERATE MAJOR GENERAL JAMES LONGSTREET[1]

The actions of Confederate Brigadier General John Bell Hood in the Battle of South Mountain are the main subject of discussion and analysis that we now address. During the evening of September 13, General Robert E. Lee decided to defend Turner's Gap on Old National Pike until Major General Thomas "Stonewall" Jackson could achieve the surrender of the Union forces at Harpers Ferry. Accordingly, early on September 14, the troops under Major General James Longstreet's command at Hagerstown began marching south on Old National Pike towards Turner's Gap to reinforce Major General Hill's troops.

Lee relieved Hood from his command after the Battle of Second Manassas due to an argument with Brigadier General Nathan G. Evans over captured federal ambulance wagons. While Lee and Hood proceeded from Hagerstown toward Boonsboro with Longstreet's troops, Lee requested to meet with his banished general. The two men soon reached an agreement that placed Hood in command of two brigades in the upcoming battle, but only until the fight ended.

Hood, in his book *Advance and Retreat*, published in 1880, told us that:

> The division reached the foot of South Mountain at about 3:30 pm, from which point the enemy's shells could be seen as they passed over the rugged peaks in front and burst upon the slope in our proximity.[2]

Hood witnessed Union artillery shells target Confederate artillery near the Mountain House and Hill #1. Historian Ezra Carman placed Hood's two brigades at the Mountain House at 4:00 pm.[3]

Colonel William T. Wofford commanded one brigade under Hood with about 850 men of the 18th GA, the 1st TX, 4th TX, and 5th TX, and the Hampton (South Carolina) Legion. Colonel Evander M. Law oversaw the 2nd brigade with 1,450 men in the 4th AL, the 2nd MS and 11th MS, and the 6th NC.[4] The troop numbers assigned to each of the two units seemed generous given the straggling by the men along the road from Hagerstown.

Upon their arrival at Turner's Gap from Hagerstown, Longstreet's troops took positions along Dahlgren Road.[5] The *Atlas Map* identified the Confederate troops along the road as "Rebels under General Longstreet's command." According to Longstreet, the Confederate troops, numbering about four thousand men, occupied positions along Dahlgren Road from the Old National Pike intersection to about a half-mile east.[6] Hood's two brigades probably took a minimum of 30 minutes after their arrival at Turner's Gap to complete this movement.

Upon his arrival at Turner's Gap, Longstreet described the Confederate situation as follows:

> In riding up the mountain to join General Hill, I discovered that everything was so disjointed that it would be impossible for my troops and Hill's to hold the mountain against such forces as McClellan had there. I wrote a note to General Lee in which I stated that fact and cautioned him to make his arrangement to retire that night.[7]

We briefly return to an examination of the Confederate defensive posture at Turner's Gap. Ted Ellis made the following analysis regarding the location where Dahlgren Road and Old National Pike meet today and where Dahlgren Road met Old National Pike at the time of the battle:

> The location where Dahlgren Road met Old National Pike in 1862 was significant because it moved Confederate operations to the top of the mountain, away from the heralded Wood Road and safely away from the east face of the summit.
>
> The change moved primary Confederate operations behind the bastion created by the semi-circular crest of South Mountain surrounding Turner's Gap from north of Frost Town, across Old National Pike, and beyond the Crest of the Heights on Moser Road! It moved Confederate operations essentially to Old Sharpsburg Road.
>
> The bastion was the Confederates' leading strength and was mentioned repeatedly by the Federals. First, defensive actions would occur on the east face, while functional movements were behind those lines, i.e., Hood's march. Second, maintaining this defensive ring around the Confederate command was a primary goal, hence Hood's urgent engagement at Cox's Intersection and Ripley's position across Moser Road at the Crest of the Heights. This analysis defined the strategy of the whole engagement summed up in the last hours.

Author Brian M. Jordan indicated Longstreet soon ordered Hood's two brigades to proceed south towards Old Sharpsburg Road.[8] Hood's movement supposedly was in reaction to Longstreet learning that Union forces had compelled Drayton's Brigade to retreat from the area of Miller's Field and the Wise Cabin.[9] Perhaps Longstreet also became aware of the movements north of Old Sharpsburg Road by G. T. Anderson's and Ripley's Brigades.

Longstreet may have been mindful of the Confederates' confusing situation south of Old National Pike when he sent Hood and two brigades south towards Old Sharpsburg Road. Longstreet and Hood, both United States Military Academy graduates at West Point, were familiar with military strategy. The "indirect approach"

The Mountain House at Turner's Gap, the Old South Mountain Inn. (Photograph by John Gensor, 2015)

military strategy advised the attacker (Hood) not to renew an attack along the same lines if an assault (Drayton) had failed. There was every reason to believe Hood would not be foolish enough to attack the solid Federal position at Fox's Gap, where Drayton's Brigade suffered a horrendous defeat.

Previously, battle analysts incorrectly assumed Hood's troops went south intending to retake the ground lost by Drayton at Miller's Field. However, two other Confederate brigades, those of G. T. Anderson and Ripley, also failed to meet Hill's objective by this battle stage, and G. B. Anderson's Brigade was the most isolated and problematic of them all. Perhaps Longstreet assigned Hood an undisclosed goal. As a senior general, it would be understandable for Hood to be given discretion in his specific movements and objectives according to the situation encountered as he moved south.

News of Drayton's rout and the dire Confederate situation at Fox's Gap probably did not reach Longstreet before 5:00 pm. A Confederate messenger on horseback who used Wood Road probably communicated the message to Longstreet, who established his command post at the Mountain House. Perhaps a messenger from G. T. Anderson, rather than Drayton, informed Longstreet of the deteriorating Confederate state of affairs near Fox's Gap.

Hood's Account

Hood's men began their advance south from Turner's Gap towards Old Sharpsburg Road no earlier than 5:00 pm. They probably would take over an hour to engage with Union troops near Cox's Intersection. In his book, *Advance and Retreat,* Hood provided essential information about his experience with his two brigades as they advanced south towards Old Sharpsburg Road:

The advance of McClellan's long lines could be seen moving up the slope in our front, evidently to dislodge our forces posted upon the sharp ridge overlooking the valley below. Before long, Major [John W.] Fairfax, of Longstreet's staff, came to me in haste with orders to move to the right of the pike, as our troops on that part of the field had been driven back. He accompanied me to the pike and turned his horse to leave when I naturally asked if he would not guide me. He replied, "No, I can only say, go to the right [south]." The wood and undergrowth were dense, and nothing but a pig path seemed to lead in the direction ordered.

Nevertheless, I conducted my troops obliquely by the right flank [southwest], and while I advanced, I could hear the Federals' shouts as they swept down the mountain upon our side. I then bore still more obliquely to the right [southwest], intending to get as far as possible towards the enemy's left flank [west] before we

Confederate Brigadier General John Bell Hood.

came in contact. We marched through the wood as rapidly as the obstacles in our passage would admit. Each step forward brought nearer and nearer to us the heavy Federal lines as they advanced, cheering over their success and the possession of our dead and wounded. Finally, I gave General Law and Colonel Wofford instructions, directing the two brigades to order their men to fix bayonets. When the enemy came within 75 or 100 yards, I ordered the men to front and charge. They obeyed promptly with a genuine Confederate yell, and the Federals were driven back, pell-mell, over and beyond the mountain at a much quicker pace than they had descended. The night closed in with not only our dead and wounded, together with those of our adversary in our possession, but with the mountain, on the right [west], within our lines.

After the correction of my alignment, I rode, at about 10:00 pm, back to the Gap, where I found General D. H. Hill and other officers on the gallery of a tavern, near the pike, evidently discussing the outlook. As I approached, I inquired about the condition of affairs on our left in an ordinary tone of voice. To my surprise, I was met with a mysterious "Pshe—Pshe," a voice added in an audible whisper, "The enemy is just there in the cornfield; he has forced us back." I suggested that we report the situation to General Lee's headquarters without delay. Accordingly, we rode down to the foot of the mountain, where we found General Lee in council with General Longstreet. After a long debate, it was decided to retire and fall back towards Sharpsburg.[10]

Hood filed his after-action battle report of September 27, 1862, which follows, in part:

On the morning of September 14, we marched back to Boonsborough Gap, a distance of some 13 miles. This division arriving between 3:00 pm and 4:00 pm found the troops of General D. H. Hill engaged with a large enemy force. By direction of the general commanding [Longstreet], I took up my position immediately on the left [north] of the pike [Old National Pike]. Soon, orders came to change over to the right [south], as our troops on that side were giving way to superior numbers. On the march to the right [south], I met General Drayton's brigade coming out, saying the enemy had succeeded in passing to their rear [north]. I ordered the Texas Brigade, Colonel W. T. Wofford commanding, and the 3rd Brigade, Colonel E. M. Law commanding, to move forward with bayonets fixed. They did with their usual gallantry, driving the enemy and regaining all of our lost ground when night came on, and further pursuit ceased. On this field, fell, mortally wounded, Lieutenant Colonel Owen K. McLemore, of the 4th Alabama, a most efficient, gallant, and valuable officer.

Soon after night, orders were received to withdraw and for this division to constitute the army's rearguard.[11]

Hood's after-action report was not as descriptive as the account in his book. In *Advance and Retreat*, Hood did not indicate that he met Drayton's brigade during their retreat from the area of Miller's Field and the Wise Cabin. In neither account did Hood show that he met with Drayton. Nevertheless, both Hood versions testified that his men drove the enemy and regained all of the Confederates' lost ground. Just what "lost ground" Hood referred to will be examined later.

A review of the chain of events described by Hood follows. Hood initially told us that:

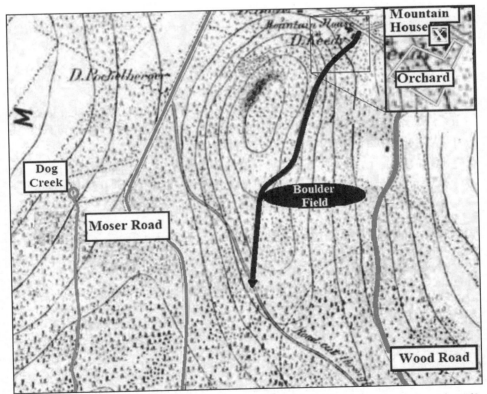

Map 31: Hood's Initial Movement South. Black Line—Hood's Movement, September 14, 1862. (Identified on *Atlas Map* by Ted Ellis)

> Before long, Major Fairfax, of Longstreet's staff, came to me in haste with orders to move to the right [south] of the pike [Old National Pike], as our troops on that part of the field had been driven back.[12]

Fairfax relayed the order to Hood from Longstreet. Fairfax's hurried demeanor indicated his desire to return quickly to Longstreet as the battle at Turner's Gap had become intense.

Nothing in Hood's account indicated he received orders to move south to reclaim Drayton's lost ground. Hood testified, "our troops on that part of the field had been driven back" or "giving way to superior numbers." There was nothing to tell us that Hood received orders to retake the ground in the immediate area of Miller's Field and the Wise Cabin or any other location on the battlefield.

Hood next informed us that he was unaware of Wood Road that led from Turner's Gap to Fox's Gap:

> He [Fairfax] accompanied me to the pike [Old National Pike] and turned his horse to leave when I naturally asked if he would not guide me. He replied, "No, I can only say, go to the right [south]."[13]

Major Fairfax did not come from Fox's Gap, the scene of Drayton's defeat. If Fairfax had come from Fox's Gap, he would have used Wood Road and perhaps directed Hood to that route. It was reasonable to believe that as a member of Longstreet's staff, Fairfax was unfamiliar with the battlefield, having just arrived on the scene with Longstreet.

Major General Hill complained that he should have remained in charge of the battle. From Hill's perspective, he had been engaged all day and was familiar with the terrain and military situation, whereas Longstreet was not:

> Major General Longstreet came up about 4:00 pm with the commands of Brig. Gens. N. G. Evans and D. R. Jones. I became familiar with the ground and knew all the vital points. Had these troops reported to me, the result might have been different. As it was, they took wrong positions, and, in their exhausted condition after a long march, they were broken and scattered.[14]

Longstreet and Hill appeared at odds. Both entertained different opinions about the Confederate situation with the arrival of Longstreet's men at about 4:00 pm. Longstreet thought the Confederates could not salvage their situation at South Mountain, and a retreat was desirable. At the same time, Hill believed the state of affairs still offered hope to the Confederates. Hill disclosed that Longstreet's troops became broken and scattered after arriving at the battle. Hill appeared to blame Longstreet for what he, Hill, considered to be the incorrect positions taken by Longstreet's brigades.

Longstreet's arrival via Old National Pike from the west would have highlighted the peril presented to the entire Confederate army at South Mountain by that sole, isolated escape route, Zittlestown gorge. Learning of the threats north and south to the sides of Zittlestown gorge along Old National Pike west of the Confederate command center at the Mountain House would have been Longstreet's chief concern rather than holding the front as appears to have been Hill's focus.

Hood's Route of Advance South

Hood's orders were to go "south." Wood Road departed Old National Pike in a southeasterly direction for several hundred feet east of the Mountain House. Fairfax probably did not know about Wood Road. Even if Hood saw the first few hundred feet of Wood Road from a position along Dahlgren Road, he probably had no idea where it led.

Using the *Atlas Map*, Ted Ellis estimated the distance from the Mountain House to the intersection of Dahlgren Road and Old National Pike as 100 feet. Ted estimated the distance from the Mountain House to the Wood Road and Old National Pike intersection as 300 feet. Thus, Wood Road met Old National Pike approximately 200 feet east of the Old National Pike intersection with Dahlgren Road during the battle. When Hood and his men departed from their positions along Dahlgren Road and crossed Old National Pike, they were about 200 feet west of Wood Road.

It was understandable that Hood was unaware Wood Road existed. Even if he had noticed it, the entire visible portion of Wood Road led east, countering Hood's ordered direction of right or south. With his only directions coming from the equally unfamiliar Fairfax, Hood would have had no idea Wood Road eventually turned south.

Hood's route of advance was between the East Ridge crest of South Mountain and Wood Road. Map 33 indicates the large boulder field in Hood's path, which probably resulted in his movement to avoid it.

If Hood had the objective to retake Miller's Field, it was impossible to form his troops in a line of battle along Wood Road to initiate an attack at Miller's Field. Wood Road was too narrow and treacherous for that. Hood would need to depart from Wood Road before launching an attack against Union forces occupying Miller's Field. Hood would need to attack Miller's Field from the west.

For Hood and his two brigades, the movement south towards Old Sharpsburg Road only got worse:

> The wood and undergrowth were dense, and nothing but a pig path seemed to lead in the direction in which I was ordered.[15]

On his maps numbers 29 and 30 in *Before Antietam*, John M. Priest showed Bondurant's artillery at the northwest edge of Miller's Field, not far from Wood Road.[16] Therefore, there appeared to be agreement among the various authors that Bondurant's Confederate artillery used Wood Road to move south between Turner's and Fox's Gaps. Then, later in the day, with Drayton's defeat, Bondurant retreated

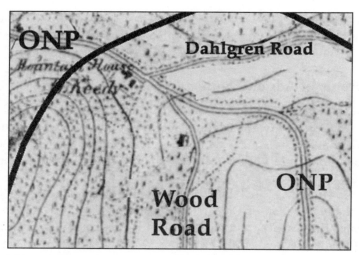

Map 32: Old National Pike Intersections with Dahlgren Road and Wood Road, September 14, 1862. (Identified on *Atlas Map* by Curtis Older)

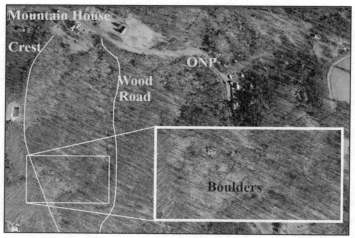

Map 33: Large Boulder Field along the East Ridge, April 2022. (Map by Ted Ellis)

north along Wood Road toward Turner's Gap. Bondurant's artillery's use of Wood Road during the battle refutes the idea that Wood Road was a "pig-path" and unusable by wagons or artillery.

Hood led his troops in their advance by moving "obliquely by the right flank:"

> Nevertheless, I conducted my troops obliquely by the right flank [southwest], and while I advanced, I could hear the Federals' shouts as they swept down the mountain upon our side.[17]

Some confusion resulted in the minds of most battle analysts in their evaluation of this statement. Everyone agreed that Hood moved his two brigades south towards

Old Sharpsburg Road. One can argue Hood's assertion indicated he moved his troops slantwise, diagonally, or sideways as they advanced. Why else would he use the term "obliquely?"

Hood made it clear that he and his men were not on the crest of the East Ridge. Hood indicated Federal troops "swept down the mountain upon our side." Hood's men were on one side of the East Ridge or the other as they moved south.

If Hood's men were on the east side of the East Ridge along Wood Road, Ripley and his men on Moser Road would not be able to see them. Besides, the east side of the East Ridge was too steep to be utilized by foot soldiers, except immediately along Wood Road. Cox ordered his men to advance down the west side of the East Ridge to Park Hall Road and Cox's Intersection. It also was reasonable to believe that any sound, such as a soldier's yell, carried a long way when made between the West Ridge and the East Ridge of South Mountain.

Hood's reference to "the mountain" led battle analysts to assume Hood referred to the mountain's East Crest that ran between Turner's and Fox's Gaps and included Hill #2. The only correct interpretation of this statement was that Hood was at a lower elevation on some mountain, either the West Ridge or East Ridge, than the Union troops who advanced on Hood's side of that ridge.

Were Hood's men moving forward in a battle line, column, or narrow formation? How wide a swath did Hood's men occupy at that time? The statement by Hood was enough to refute the claim that Hood and his men followed Wood Road and moved along the east side of the East Ridge.

Near Old National Pike, the mountain's East Crest between Turner's and Fox's Gap was a few hundred feet west of Wood Road. The East Ridge crest remained west of Wood Road until it merged with Wood Road, near the north side of Miller's Field. The East Ridge crest curved southeast from Turner's Gap to Fox's Gap.

Hood declared his objective as he approached the Union troops and initiated an attack:

> I then bore still more obliquely to the right [southwest], intending to get as far as possible towards the enemy's left flank [west] before we came in contact. We marched on through the wood as rapidly as the obstacles in our passage would admit.[18]

With this statement, Hood was unequivocal. He intended to advance against the Union's left or west flank. He again used the term "more obliquely to the right" to describe his movement towards Old Sharpsburg Road. The repetition emphasized that Hood's route until this point was also "obliquely right." It was doubtful that Hood was aware of Union troops at the Ridge-Loop Intersection far to the south. We also are confident that Hood and his men were not on Wood Road because he mentioned "obstacles in our passage." There were no obstacles along Wood Road.

The following statement by Hood gave rise to several questions:

> Each step forward brought nearer and nearer to us the heavy Federal lines as they advanced, cheering over their success and the possession of our dead and wounded.[19]

The sound of the Union troops indicated they were from a large force, as Hood referred to them as "heavy Federal lines." The sounds suggested at least a brigade rather than a single regiment. Since Hood's objective was to move to the Union left or west, the Union shouts were from the east or south of Hood's position and the west side of the East Ridge. It was doubtful that Hood and his two brigades were along the West Ridge at this point.

Hood's battle line probably did not extend over the west side of Moser Road until it approached Lambert's Field due to the sharp falling off of the ground on the west side of the road. I envision Hood's men advancing down Moser Road and along the east side of Moser Road until they neared Lambert's Field. As Hood's men approached Lambert's Field, most funneled across Moser Road from east to west. Hood's men crossed the West Ridge of South Mountain in this area. Many attempted to advance along the west side of Park Hall Road once they crossed Old Sharpsburg Road west of Cox's Intersection.

The most intriguing part of Hood's statement was his reference to "the possession of our dead and wounded." This statement led most authors to assume Hood referred to the Confederate dead and wounded near Miller's Field or the Wise Cabin. However, we know two things about the Confederate dead west of Wise's Cabin. First, Corporal Robinson of the 89th NY stated that after their attack at the Ridge-Loop Intersection, G. B. Anderson's Brigade retreated north along Park Hall Road. Somewhere to the north, along Park Hall Road or Moser Road, Robinson indicated the 51st NY and 51st PA pummeled Anderson's men. I did not find another participant in the battle who directly corroborated Robinson's statement. However, we might consider the testimony of Lieutenant Whitman to do so. Second, we know that Private Holahan of the 45th PA reported dead Confederates "all the way down the mountain in the woods and at the roadside" along Old Sharpsburg Road.

Where else could Confederate dead be on the battlefield? Dead Confederates were along Ridge Road, running half a mile south of the Wise Cabin, where Garland's Brigade was defeated. However, there was no indication Hood moved south of Old Sharpsburg Road along Ridge Road, so he could not refer to those dead in Garland's Brigade.

All battle analysts failed to consider Confederate dead along Park Hall Road or Moser Road in their analysis of Hood's statement. Hood would not know the location of any Confederate casualties on a battlefield where he had not been. Hood would have to see the dead and injured firsthand. Hood implied the Federal troops were in a battle line, perhaps three or four lines deep.

Unfortunately, battle analysts combined their assumption about Hood's recovery of Confederate dead and wounded with the following statement:

> I met General Drayton's brigade coming out, saying the enemy had succeeded in passing to their rear [north].[20]

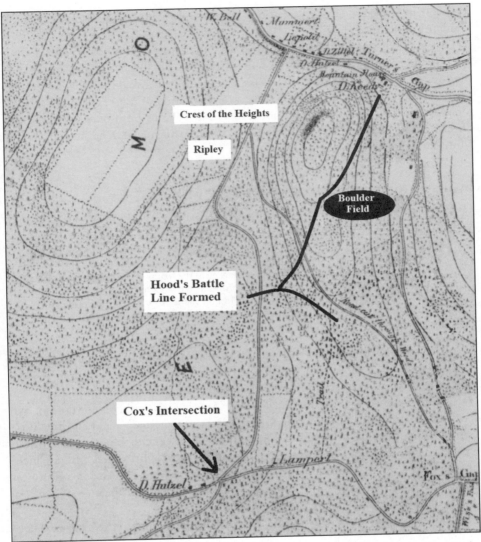

Map 34: Hood's Troops Formed a Line of Battle, September 14, 1862. (Identified on *Atlas Map* by Ted Ellis)

With this statement, battle analysts assumed that Hood sought to recover the ground lost by Drayton near Miller's Field and the Wise Cabin.

However, we remain confronted by Hood's earlier statement that he sought to attack the Union left or west flank and continued to move his two brigades obliquely to the right. Kurt Graham's excellent research regarding Drayton's defeat indicated that Drayton's troops fled to the northwest and not north along Wood Road. If Hood was west of the crest of the East Ridge as contended, Hood's statement supports Graham's conclusion.

Did it make sense for Hood to lead a Confederate attack for a second time against the most heavily defended Union location on the Fox's Gap battlefield, the area of Miller's Field and the Wise Cabin? We can imagine what Drayton's men described to Hood's men: "There are thousands of Yankees up there with lots of cannon." How many cannon did Hood have as he moved south? Zero. Surely Hood could hear Union artillery to the south when he arrived at the Mountain House.

Evidence to Support Hood's Account

Major Bolton told us that Reno directed Durell's Battery to advance to the crest of the East Ridge. The movement by Durell's Battery occurred before 6:30 pm on the 14th:

> These were the wounded we had lifted to either side of the roadway late the previous afternoon. Soon after, we commenced driving the enemy from the mountain's summit when Reno ordered Durell's battery to limber up and go in a gallop up the narrow road to the mountain's crest. With all our care removing them, many were run over by the battery in their haste to reach the crest.[21]

In the opinion of General William T. Sherman, a six-gun Union battery was equivalent to 1,000 infantrymen. Thus, the dozen or more Union cannon at Fox's Gap were equal to at least 2,000 infantry troops, in Sherman's opinion.

It made no sense to contend that Hood's two brigades, probably fewer than two thousand men, could dislodge the Union forces near Miller's Field and the Wise Cabin and recapture any ground Drayton previously held. Hood's men would have been met by overwhelming artillery fire if they approached Miller's Field or the Wise Cabin. Thousands of infantrymen supported the Union cannon at Fox's Gap. Unfortunately, most authors understated the significance of artillery in the battle.

Major Bolton provided us with a measure of the significance of the Union artillery in the fight for Fox's Gap:

> The enemy was well posted on the very top of the mountain. They had to depress their guns to reach us, and we had to elevate ours. The duel lasted until sundown, and General Reno, who commanded the old Ninth Corps, was near his old brigade, directing the artillery fire in person.
>
> The artillery having cleared the mountain of the enemy, the 51st [PA] was soon ordered to advance towards the summit of the mountain.[22]

Bolton described the Union artillery, the guns of Durell's Battery, and perhaps the other Union guns near Wise's and Miller's Fields as having cleared the enemy from the mountain before sundown.

Bolton implied the Confederate cannon and infantry abandoned the eminence at Fox's Gap. The Confederate guns were those of Bondurant's four-gun battery at the northwest corner of Miller's Field or perhaps farther north along Wood Road after Bondurant retreated from Miller's Field towards the Mountain House.

Bolton's description of the effectiveness and the significance of Union artillery reinforced the conclusion that Hood's two infantry brigades, unsupported by artillery, would have found an attack near Wise's and Miller's Fields extremely costly. A Confederate infantry attack near the summit of Fox's Gap after Drayton's defeat and the occupation of the mountaintop by Union cannon would have made it highly unlikely for the Confederates to succeed.

Overwhelming Union artillery and infantry firepower would have doomed any Confederate attack near the summit at Fox's Gap to failure had it been made. Hood must have been aware of the numerous Union cannon near Miller's Field and the Wise Cabin, either by hearing or learning about them from Drayton's men. All the more reason for Hood to decide against a direct attack in the area of Miller's Field and the summit of Fox's Gap.

One source told us that Hood's three artillery batteries did reach the summit of Turner's Gap:

> While the infantry was clearing Boonsborough Gap of Union forces, the Confederate artillery, commanded by Hood's chief of artillery, Major [Bushrod W.] Frobel reached the summit "with his three batteries." Captain [James] Reilly's Rowan artillery, "then consisting of four rifled pieces and two howitzers," joined Frobel in the vicinity of the Mountain House but refrained from firing because of orders.[23]

This statement about Confederate artillery at Turner's Gap further supported Cox's hesitancy to attack Hill #1 until Hooker's Corps possessed the Mountain House.

Unfortunately, where the previous quote appeared, the book's author provided no references or sources that identified where he found the data. Confederate cannon on Hill #1 and along Old National Pike near the Mountain House would have been the only Confederate cannon support Hood's men would have had.

Major Frobel, Hood's Division Chief of Artillery, in his October 1 report, stated:

> In compliance with orders to report the participation of the batteries under my command in the recent engagements before Sharpsburg, I would respectfully submit the following:
> [Frobel reported no activity on his part at South Mountain. He began his report by stating his command brought up the rear from South Mountain down to Boonsboro.]
> After bringing up the rear on the march from Boonsborough, etc.[24]

However, Hood stated in *Advance and Retreat*, "Meantime Major Frobel's batteries had come forward into position on top of the ridge; they opened fire and performed excellent service checking the enemy."[25]

Therefore, we were uncertain if Hood's artillery units, including the German (SC) Artillery and the Palmetto (SC) Light Artillery, were near the Mountain House and were engaged in the battle at Turner's Gap on the 14th. The three artillery units probably consisted of 14 cannon, and they brought up the rearguard of Hood's brigades on the march to Boonsborough and Sharpsburg.

The existence of Hood's three artillery batteries near the Mountain House supported Cox's earlier statement. "The enemy still held the two hills between Old Sharpsburg Road and the turnpike, and the further hill could not be conquered until the Mountain House should be in Union hands." Confederate artillery near the Mountain House would make it difficult for the Union infantry under Cox to attack Hill #1. Cox must have had some awareness of the strength of Confederate artillery at or near Turner's Gap.

We learned next that Hood's skirmishers and Union skirmishers confronted each other:

> Finally, I gave General Law and Colonel Wofford instructions, directing the two brigades to order their men to fix bayonets. When the enemy came within seventy-five or a hundred yards, I ordered the men to front and charge.[26]

Hood's statement agreed with that of Captain Wren of the 48th PA. Wren indicated that skirmishers from the 51st NY also fell back to the Union battle line as the Confederates advanced.

Major General Hill confirmed Hood's movement to the right or south and indicated Hood advanced his skirmishers and drove back the Yankees:

> General Hood, who had gone in on the right [south] with his two noble brigades, pushed forward his skirmishers and drove back the Yankees.[27]

At this point, Hood's troops were in "a line of battle." The width of the area Hood's men covered is open to debate. It also was uncertain how many of Hood's men advanced to this position on the battlefield from Old National Pike.

Ripley stated that his troops were within a short distance of the Crest of the Heights and Hood's troops "forming upon my left, the troops pressed up the road." Ripley viewed Hood's men on his left or east as they came from Turner's Gap. If Hood's men were along Wood Road, Ripley could not have seen them as the East Ridge crest of South Mountain would have blocked his view from the Crest of the Heights on Moser Road.

Ripley seemed to infer that Hood's troops moved some distance south along Moser Road. Hood ordered his men to advance and charge the approaching Union troops. At this time, the Union skirmishers came within the length of a football field:

> When the enemy came within seventy-five or a hundred yards, I ordered the men to front and charge. They obeyed promptly with a genuine Confederate yell, and the Federals were driven back, pell-mell, over and beyond the mountain at a much quicker pace than they had descended.[28]

This aspect of Hood's retelling of his encounter with the Union troops was critical to understanding where this confrontation took place on the battlefield. Most battle analysts assumed that by "over and beyond the mountain," Hood referred to the mountain crest that ran through Turner's and Fox's Gaps, the East Ridge.

The following statement by Hood confused most writers about Hood's movement. Where did Hood's two brigades encounter Union troops? Hood tells us that:

> The Federals were driven back, pell-mell, over and beyond the mountain at a much quicker pace than they had descended.[29]

Most who read the above statement concluded that Hood's two brigades retook Miller's Field along Wood Road and the mountain crest at Fox's Gap. This understanding of Hood's statement was mistaken.

Hood described driving the enemy and regaining "all of our lost ground" when night came on:

> I ordered the Texas Brigade, Colonel W. T. Wofford commanding, and the 3rd Brigade, Colonel E. M. Law commanding, to move forward with bayonets fixed. They did with their usual gallantry, driving the enemy and regaining all of our lost ground when night came on, and further pursuit ceased. On this field fell, mortally wounded, Lieutenant Colonel O. K. McLemore, of the 4th Alabama.[30]

Hood had no way of knowing what ground Drayton's men nor any other Confederates had lost earlier in the battle.

Hood indeed assumed that any ground where Confederate dead or wounded were present was ground previously held by those Confederates. Hood also revealed his location by indicating the shooting of Lieutenant Colonel McLemore.

Hood's most telling statement told of his intent to attack the Union left, or west, flank. Miller's Field and the Wise Cabin were at the Union right (east) flank. It was reasonable to assume that Hood was unaware of the Union troops and cannon at the Ridge-Loop Intersection, the Union's extreme south side.

Most importantly, Hood told us that:

> The night closed in with not only our dead and wounded, together with those of our adversary in our possession, but with the mountain, on the right, within our lines.[31]

Most authors who wrote about Hood at South Mountain assumed he referred to the mountain crest from Turner's Gap to Fox's Gap, the East Ridge. However, Hood identified "the mountain on the right within our lines." As Hood moved south, his right was to the west, not towards the East Ridge that ran through Fox's Gap. Hood did not confuse his right hand and his left!

A Problem with the Maps of Some Authors

A problem with some maps created to depict the battle at Fox's Gap was that G. T. Anderson's Brigade couldn't be so far east of Wood Road. The depiction of G. T. Anderson's Brigade far down the east slope of the East Ridge was unrealistic. The mountain slope was too steep for a soldier to stand upright without holding on to a tree. For the same reason, Union forces never attempted an attack along the east slope of the East Ridge between Turner's and Fox's Gaps.

Kurt Graham wrote an excellent article entitled, "Death of a Brigade at Fox's Gap, September 14, 1862."[32] The reader should compare the placement of the 50th GA infantry of Drayton's Brigade in Miller's Field between 3:00 pm and 4:00 pm to the placement of that same unit between 4:00 pm and 4:15 pm. Drayton shifted the 50th GA from the northeast edge to the east side of Miller's Field. Drayton made the shift because he realized an attack against the northeast edge of Miller's Field was not possible by Union infantry.

One's knowledge of the two mountain ridges significantly alters the interpretation of Hood's statements. For this reason, Ezra Carman and his lack of knowledge about the West Ridge placed Hood's two brigades at Fox's Gap rather than a half-mile west. Carman did not grasp that two mountain crests extended south of Old National Pike. Carman declared:

> The mountain on the north side of the turnpike is divided into two crests or ridges by a narrow valley. Though deep at the gap, the valley becomes a slight depression about a mile to the north.[33]

Perhaps Hood had a chance to discuss the military situation with Longstreet and Hill upon his arrival at Turner's Gap. Most analysts never read Hood's statements about his movement south of Old National Pike, or else they assumed Hood confused his right and left hands. However, Hood described his objective to attack the left or west flank of the Union defense. He reiterated his intent by repeatedly referring to his movements to intercept the enemy's "left" by his own movement "to the right." That was undeniably clear. Flanking movements were a typical military tactic during the war, so Hood's decision was not unusual.

However, one might ask, "Was Hood's objective the defense of Moser Road to prevent a Federal attack from the rear against the Confederates at Turner's Gap?" Did Hood read the minds of Pleasonton and Cox the way J. E. B. Stuart did when Stuart placed Confederate forces at Fox's Gap at least 12 hours before the battle began the following day?

It seemed likely there was at least a 50 percent chance that Hood knew that Moser Road existed before he moved south of Old National Pike. While marching to Turner's Gap on Old National Pike, Hood would have certainly noticed Moser Road intersecting the pike from the south. Any Confederates near the Crest of the Heights on Moser Road would have been visible from the turnpike. Expecting to enter a fight, Hood would have understandably assessed such existing elements he encountered along the way.

Hood's situational awareness would have prompted an assessment of the defensive perimeter offered by the Crest of the Heights between Hill #1 and Hill #2, even if Longstreet or Hill had not explained that strategy to him. Like Longstreet, arriving late in the day by Old National Pike, Hood would have recognized the critical nature of the Crest of the Heights to the survival of the Confederates under the threat of encirclement.

How did the statements of Hood compare to those of Union Captain James Wren of the 48th PA infantry? Wren indicated, "we advanced in line of skirmish & got out in the woods about 125 yards." Wren probably referred to his position relative to Old Sharpsburg Road or an open field along Park Hall Road where it was reasonable to assume the Union line of battle formed. Wren told us that his Union skirmish line "met the enemy's skirmish line." Wren was clear that the only Union troops that Hood's skirmishers drove back were the Union skirmishers.

Hood did not mention a road as he moved south. Ripley, however, indicated Hood's troops "pressed up the road." Ripley inferred that Hood's men moved south along Moser Road, perhaps for some distance. Wren told us his brigade was in a line of battle, and the following morning he identified a crossroads near his location the evening before. Wren asserted there was no retreat by the Union battle line, and he suggested that his skirmishers advanced about 450 feet beyond the Union line of battle.

The Union skirmishers rapidly retreated upon confronting Hood's skirmishers, and possibly they saw Hood's troops in a line of battle. According to Hood, the Union skirmishers were pushed back over and beyond the mountain. Hood implicitly told us that only the Union skirmishers were forced back over the crest. Confederate Major General Hill confirmed this by stating that Hood "pushed forward his skirmishers and drove back the Yankees." Certainly, Confederate skirmishers could not push back a Union brigade.

We also can ask, how far over the West Ridge did Hood's troops extend themselves? Hood intended to attack the Union left flank. The assumption must be that Hood's men moved as far south as possible until being stopped in their attempt to flank the Union troops.

The most significant and thought-provoking statement by Hood was that by his men's actions:

> The Federals were driven back, pell-mell, over and beyond the mountain much quicker than they had descended. The night closed in with not only our dead and wounded, together with those of our adversary in our possession, but with the mountain, on the right [west], within our lines.[34]

Hood did not tell us that the mountain on the left or east was within his lines. He implicitly referred to the existence of two mountain ridges.

Coincident with the actions of Hood's men, Wren told us that "[the Confederates were] yelling, thinking that they had got us on a retreat when the whole brigade opened fire from the battle line." Wren's 48th PA remained in the battle line until they expended their ammunition, and the 2nd MD relieved them. Captain Bosbyshell confirmed that the 2nd MD replaced the 48th PA in the battle line.[35]

Moser Road north of Cox's Intersection about 500 to 1,000 feet north of Old Sharpsburg Road. (Photograph by Ted Ellis, March 2022)

Wren's account informed us that three men from Company B of the 48th PA were missing after his unit's encounter with the Rebels. These three men were captured by the Rebels and survived the war. Wren also indicated the 51st NY Regiment was nearby. Perhaps some skirmishers from the 51st NY also were lost in their advance north of Old Sharpsburg Road against Hood's men.

Hood received orders to withdraw his command to Old National Pike after 10:00 pm. His men retreated from the battlefield using Moser Road. Longstreet's report made Hood's route of retreat unmistakable. If near Miller's Field, Hood's two brigades had no reason to use Moser Road. Indeed, if they were at Miller's Field, as other authors indicated, taking Wood Road one mile north to the Mountain House was more efficient than moving west a half-mile to Moser Road. Cut Road also might have been a possibility.

A terrace of relatively level ground about 800 feet wide south to north extended considerably on both sides of Moser Road near Lambert's Field. The level area formed the north end of Lambert's Field, which was very near Moser Road and probably included an entrance from the road.

Hood's alignment from west to east may have been in this order, entirely my speculation: Law's Brigade—2nd Mississippi, 4th Alabama, 6th North Carolina, 11th Mississippi; Wofford's Brigade—18th Georgia, Hampton's South Carolina Legion, 1st Texas, 4th Texas, 5th Texas; G. T. Anderson's Brigade.

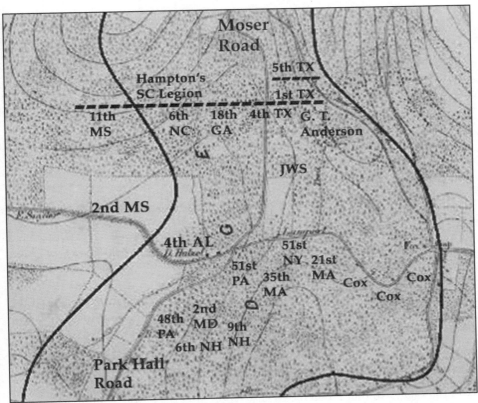

Map 35: Hypothetical Unit Positions, 8:00 pm. JWS = Private John W. Stevens, 5th TX—8:00 pm, September 14, 1862. (Identified on *Atlas Map* by Curtis Older)

Cut Road and Fox Trail

Two paths through the Fox's Gap battlefield on the west side of the East Crest require identification. The first and most noticeable appeared on the *Atlas Map* as "Road Cut Through the Woods by the Enemy," referred to in this book as "Cut Road." The road, as shown on the *Atlas Map*, connected Miller's Field at Fox's Gap to the Crest of the Heights on Moser Road.

Ted Ellis indicated the path Cut Road followed took the best advantage of the rugged geography of South Mountain. Along its path, the only necessary inclines took the best available routes across the gentlest slopes rather than directly up and down the mountainside. The Confederates laying out such a course would have needed a very substantial amount of time. Both Ted Ellis and I believe Cut Road existed before the battle.

One cannot ignore the convenience offered by this route. The Cut Road was still clearly visible in 2022, suggesting its degree of earlier use.

The second path noted on the *Atlas Map* was a trail. It was indicated on the map simply as "Trail" and denoted by a dashed line. Designated "Fox Trail" by me, it followed a gentle slope on the East Ridge's west side. This foot trail provided a shortcut for reaching Turner's Gap from the land perhaps first settled by John Fox near Lambert's Field. "Fox Trail" crossed the East Ridge and met Wood Road southeast of the large boulder field just south of Hill #2.

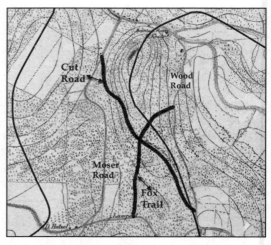

Map 36: Cut Road and Fox Trail, September 14, 1862. (Identified on *Atlas Map* by Ted Ellis)

A spring existed in the gorge Brigadier General Cox referred to that ran from the west side of the East Ridge through Cox's Intersection. John Fox, a tanner, may have used this spring. There was no land record for John Fox near Fox's Gap. However, a land record for Grims Fancy indicated John Fox probably lived near Cox's Intersection.[36]

Reverend Nicholas A. Davis

Nothing suggested that Hood filed a false report after the Battle of South Mountain. There was every reason to believe Hood was truthful and accurate in his description. Was Hood deficient in reporting the number of his troops lost in the charge? Apparently!

A minister of the Gospel corroborated Hood's statements about the struggle. Reverend Nicholas A. Davis restated the account of the battle. In his diary entitled "Chaplain Davis and Hood's Texas Brigade," Davis described the following under the heading of the "Engagement at Boonsboro Gap":

> The contest soon became general and severe. The overpowering numbers, who had forced the brave Drayton to quit his ground, were checked. And the well-directed fire of Hood's men soon taught them that they were advancing over dangerous ground, for, at every turn, they found their numbers lessened and their position growing more critical. Several attempts were made to charge our lines, but they could only utter a few huzzas and move up a few paces when another volley would check and cause them to waver and stagger like drunken men. Finally, the expected "forward" was heard, and then came the full frown shout of success, which always tells what the Texans are doing when they struggle for victory in the presence of mighty foes.
>
> Soon he [Hood] ordered the two Brigades forward with fixed bayonets. The order was promptly obeyed, and our lines were restored upon the ground, which had been lost—night coming on prevented further pursuit. We lost, but very few yet had foiled the enemy in his effort with seventy-five thousand men to relieve Miles at Harpers Ferry.[37]

Davis provided a rather fanciful report on the encounter between Hood's men and their Union counterpart. It was unclear what Davis meant by "general and severe." He seemed to have implied "over a wide area." The name of Drayton appeared in Davis's writing, and the reader, if not careful, can believe the confrontation occurred near Miller's Field over the ground Drayton lost. In contrast to Wren's statement, Davis indicated that the Union troops advanced or charged. Perhaps a Union regiment other than the 48th PA moved against the Rebels. Davis claimed, "our lines were restored upon the ground which had been lost."

It is doubtful that Davis knew of Drayton's defeat when Davis accompanied Hood's troops south towards Old Sharpsburg Road. The most likely scenario was that Davis wrote his statements after the battle and perhaps after reading the report of Hood. Davis would not know what ground Drayton's Brigade lost or where that ground was on the battlefield. It is reasonable to believe that both Hood and Davis assumed the ground where they found dead and wounded Confederates was lost earlier by the Confederates. Perhaps these dead and injured were with G. B. Anderson's Brigade after they headed north from their encounter at the Ridge-Loop Intersection.

Hood's two brigades probably passed over dead and wounded Confederates lying in Moser Road or perhaps in Old Sharpsburg Road, possibly from G. B. Anderson's Brigade that engaged the 51st NY and 51st PA not long before the arrival of Hood's forces. The 48th PA possibly advanced west from Park Hall Road at some point. The two sides held their positions as darkness set in, and neither sought to forge ahead in the dark.

Hood's alignment perhaps encompassed G. T. Anderson's Brigade on the east. However, G. T. Anderson's Brigade might have formed a battle line separate from Hood's two brigades. Hood's troop formation included the West Ridge within its lines. Hood did not indicate the East Ridge was within his lines.

It is difficult to believe that if Hood's alignment was 1,000 feet north of Old Sharpsburg Road, it included some of the dead and wounded Union men. A distance of 1,000 feet north of Old Sharpsburg Road probably was beyond the area where any fighting occurred. As we will learn later, with the 4th Alabama and 2nd Mississippi movement to Old Sharpsburg Road on the west side of Cox's Intersection after dark, Hood probably referred to the dead and wounded in Moser Road or perhaps along Old Sharpsburg Road west of Cox's Intersection.

The size of Hood's force was inadequate to overcome the significant Union presence under Brigadier General Sturgis near Cox's Intersection. Cox did not intend to have Sturgis advance north along Moser Road on the evening of the 14th because Cox could not take Hill #1 until the Mountain House was in Union hands. During the late evening of September 14, Hood probably concluded there would be no Union advance north along Moser Road.

Davis did not indicate the Confederates captured any new ground, only that they restored their lines upon the previously lost terrain. Exactly what Davis meant by that statement is unclear. Perhaps Davis witnessed dead Confederates in Moser Road as Hood's two brigades advanced, and Davis referred to that area as "the ground lost." Both Davis and Hood indicated that darkness resulted in the Confederate troops holding their positions.

Davis's statement about the Union Army attempting to relieve Miles at Harpers Ferry was somewhat fanciful. The only Union troops who endeavored to save Miles were the men under Major General William B. Franklin and Major General Darius N. Couch near Crampton's Gap—far less than 75,000 troops.

Davis's account agreed with Union Captain Wren, Company B, 48th PA Volunteers. The Rebels pushed back the Union skirmishers and continued to advance. However, the "whole [Union] brigade" stopped them. Wren told us the 51st NY Regiment was nearby and that a Union brigade stopped Hood's advance. The 48th PA was in Nagle's 1st Brigade, and the 51st NY was in Ferrero's 2nd Brigade. The number of Union troops around Cox's Intersection to repel Hood's attack was at least an entire division, which was adequate.

Whitman made it abundantly clear that the troops under Sturgis were in a division line of battle. Each of Sturgis's two brigades consisted of four regiments. Wren indicated his line of battle was three units deep. If Sturgis's Division consisted of 3,800 men in eight subdivisions, each averaged about 475 men.

Evidence indicated one brigade of Sturgis's Division was along Park Hall Road south of Cox's Intersection, and the other was east of Cox's Intersection along Old Sharpsburg Road. This formation provided a good defense against a flank attack. Under Sturgis, the two remaining regiments probably occupied a support location near Cox's Intersection.[38]

Lieutenant George W. Whitman, 51st NY, indicated the Union troops had a crossfire on the Confederates. The crossfire may have occurred when Union troops were along Old Sharpsburg Road, Park Hall Road, and along the rail fence west of Park Hall Road and west of Wren's stone fence.

We can add Cox's Kanawha Division, which occupied Old Sharpsburg Road between Sturgis's Division and the Wise Cabin. Sturgis's strength may have been 3,800 men, even without the 2nd MD and 6th NH under Nagle.[39] Cox's Kanawha Division had over 3,000 men, and its division front perhaps extended over 1,500 feet.

Hood had little time to evaluate the battlefield's geography on September 14. He could see the West Ridge and the East Ridge as he advanced, and the shouts of Union troops directed his advance against the Union left flank.

The arrangement of the Union troops, in effect, gave them an east flank at Fox's Gap, a west side at Cox's Intersection, and a south flank at the Ridge-Loop Intersection late in the day at Fox's Gap. The situation had completely reversed itself from the time of the afternoon Confederate counterattack. Union infantry commanded Old Sharpsburg Road from Fox Gap Road on the east to Cox's Intersection on the west and Park Hall Road south of Old Sharpsburg Road.

Major General Longstreet's Compelling Statement

Confederate Major General James Longstreet provided critical information in his book, *From Manassas to Appomattox*, regarding the actions of Hood's two brigades on September 14. "My troops were hurried to his [Hill's] assistance [at Turner's Gap] as rapidly as their exhausted condition would admit of."[40] Longstreet went on to announce:

> General Hill concedes reluctantly that four thousand of my men came to his support in detachments, but does not know how to estimate the loss. Considering the severe forced march, the five brigades that made direct ascent of the mountain were in good order. The three [Drayton, Wofford, Law] that marched south of the turnpike, along a narrow mountain trail part of the way, through woodlands and over boulders, returning, then up the mountain, the last march at double time, were thinned to skeletons of three or four hundred men to a brigade when they reached the Mountain House.[41]

Longstreet revealed that his men came to Major General Hill's support in detachments or separated units. During the long march from Hagerstown to Turner's Gap, the men became spread out.

As regards Hood's two brigades, Longstreet proclaimed they followed "a narrow mountain trail part of the way and then through woodlands and over boulders." Longstreet's description was consistent with that of Hood. Both indicated that Hood's two brigades did not move towards Old Sharpsburg Road using Wood Road.

The most telling part of Longstreet's report was that Hood's two brigades returned "up the mountain" and marched "at double-time." Hood's men had to use an open road to march at double time. They could not march at double time and return the way they came through dense woods and underbrush. Longstreet recounted that Hood's men moved up the mountain. Moser Road rose from an elevation of 740 feet at Cox's Intersection to 1,000 feet at Old National Pike. The only viable route for Hood's men was Moser Road.

We also know from Longstreet that Hood's two brigades dwindled to only three or four hundred men each upon returning to Old National Pike. Many of Hood's men were exhausted from the marching and were in poor physical condition. Less than 2,000 Confederates likely participated in Hood's encounter with the Federals. Due to their lack of sleep, many of Hood's men probably fell asleep after the firing stopped and failed to retreat later during the night.

Longstreet makes no statement regarding Hood's two brigades "driving the enemy and regaining all of our lost ground." Longstreet made no statement about any success on the part of Hood. Hood never regained any of the Confederates' lost ground near the Wise Cabin, Miller's Field, south along Ridge Road, or Old Sharpsburg Road.

The Consequences of Green Corn and Apples

The physical condition of Hood's infantry impacted their movement toward Old Sharpsburg Road. Many, if not most, soldiers under Hood's command were barefoot and hungry, and many were probably ill. Their condition made moving through the brush, woods, and rocks even more challenging and difficult to fight in the mountain terrain south of Old National Pike. The following reports confirmed that the Confederates lacked food and shoes at South Mountain and Antietam.

Confederate Edmund DeWitt Patterson, while himself not at Antietam, described what he learned from his compatriots who were in the Antietam battle:

> The entire regiment numbered only one hundred and thirty men in the battle, and ours was a fair sample of the army. Two-thirds of the men able for duty were barefooted on this [west] side of the Potomac. He [Dolph Owen] tells of the boys' hard times, and I don't doubt it that living on green corn and apples doesn't improve an army's health.[42]

Longstreet helped convince General Lee to venture into Maryland due to the availability of "roasting ears":

> With such a splendid victory behind us, and such bright prospects ahead, the question arose as to whether or not we should go into Maryland. General Lee hesitated a little because of our short supplies, but I reminded him of my experience in Mexico, where sometimes we were obliged to live two or three days on green corn. I told him we could not starve at that season of the year so long as the fields were loaded with "roasting ears." Finally, he determined to go on and cross the river accordingly to Frederick City.[43]

Confederate soldier Randolph A. Shotwell was in Brigadier General Richard B. Garnett's Brigade of D. R. Jones's division north of Old National Pike at Turner's Gap. He described his viewpoint of the events of September 14:

> I had already marched sixteen miles since dawn, including the fatiguing toil up the mountain. As usual, the intense excitement of the battle speedily gave way to extreme relaxation and lassitude, which seemed to deprive me of the last particle of strength, rendering each step more difficult than the previous.
>
> "No time to lose sitting here," thought I, and easing myself over the wall, I threw the whole weight of my body supplemented by 100 pounds of gun and baggage upon my left foot.
>
> Horror! The bare skin and flesh gave way—as if cut by a knife—to the sharp edge of a grey slate rock sticking perpendicularly in the ground or the broken bottom of a large glass bottle. It was too dark to determine which. The leap down from the wall gave a descent of some four feet squarely upon this keen edge, and the result was a terrible gash, two inches in length, diagonally across the hollow of the foot, and fully an inch and a quarter deep![44]

Shotwell departed Turner's Gap and indicated he arrived in Boonsboro by midnight. Shotwell was a member of the 8th VA Regiment. He was not at Antietam, probably due to his cut foot at South Mountain.

David A. Rice, a private in the 108th NY who fought at Antietam, described the capture of 300 Confederates who became ill from eating green corn and apples after partaking of the harvest during the Maryland Campaign.[45]

The *20th North Carolina Regimental History* told of their struggle to obtain food:

> Captain L. T. Hicks of Company E says the enemy came within 15 feet before the regiment retreated down the mountain, which being so steep the enemy fired over our heads. A part of this company, and several from other companies of the Twentieth, were separated from the command. During this time, their rations were green corn from the cob.[46]

Edward O. Lord of the 9th New Hampshire, 2nd Division under Sturgis, commented about the battlefield on September 15:

> The Southern army is very poorly clad. Indeed, a large number of them are barefoot.[47]

Several authors declared that Lee's army had little logistical support; his men subsisted on green corn, apples, and dirty water. The lack of food and supplies prompted an epidemic of dysentery and other illnesses. Some men staggered out of the ranks on the march and died from sunstroke.[48] The physical condition of Hood's men, to some extent, may account for Longstreet's statement that Hood's force, "returning, then up the mountain, the last march at double time, was thinned to skeletons of three or four hundred men to a brigade when they reached the Mountain House."

Private John W. Stevens, 5th TX

Private John W. Stevens, Company K, 5th TX, Wofford's Brigade, found himself and a comrade at a corner of a rail fence not far from Old Sharpsburg Road beyond some open ground at the end of the day. Stevens, who later became a judge, was wounded at Antietam and captured at Gettysburg. Stevens was the most scared in his life on September 14. He made the following statement in his book written many years after the battle:

> Colonel B. [Benjamin] F. Carter carried us down the mountain some 300 or 400 yards from where we lay in line, through a thick brush to a fence on the side of the ridge. We halted at the wall, beyond which was open ground and a line of Federals about 100 yards beyond the wall. Some were standing up with the line officers on horseback, but most were lying down. My comrade and I were placed in the corner of the fence with our guns pointing between the rails. When we were thus posted, Colonel Carter ordered us to remain there, watch the enemy's movements, and keep quiet. If they should advance, wait until their line was within 20 feet of the fence and then fire and fall back in all possible haste to our command.
>
> So we sat there, I suppose, for an hour, or possibly two hours, conversing in a whisper and calculating the chances of escape should they advance upon us and should we wait until they were within 20 feet of us before we fell back. Now, I want to say that I got the biggest scare of the war right there. It seemed to me that I got as large as an ox, and it appeared that the enemy knew we were in that fence corner looking at them and that if they moved up there, we were sure to be killed.
>
> Finally, the Yankee officer called in a low tone, "Attention!" They were all on their feet at once. "Guide center; forward, march!" We thought they were coming toward us. Every hair on my head stood up like a porcupine's quills. We could not tell for the life of us whether they were moving toward or away from us until they had gone some twenty-five or thirty steps. Great, to our relief, we found they were moving in an opposite direction.[49]

Stevens indicated that he and his comrade moved some 300–400 yards down the mountain. He was on the west side of the East Ridge. It was impossible to proceed such a distance down the east side of the East Ridge, and it was doubtful, but not impossible, that he was on the West Ridge. The length of 300–400 yards was a little less than a quarter-mile and was less than half the distance from Cox's Intersection to the Wise Cabin.

Stevens and his comrade were at a fence corner, beyond which there was open ground. On the immediate northeast corner of Cox's Intersection, the land was the first open ground west of Wood Road. According to several records, a Lambert or Lampert occupied it, and the lot will be called Lambert's Field. On the *Atlas Map*, the Lampert name appeared along Old Sharpsburg Road on the east side of an open field on the immediate northeast corner of Cox's Intersection.

Lambert's Field contained approximately 10 acres.[50] The northeast corner of this tract was near the center of the gorge. The open area of the lot was about six acres and north of the chasm. The site included four wooded acres within the ravine and south of it.

No property owned by a Lampert or a Lambert in 1862 appeared in the Washington County land records. Lambert, however, was a commonly encountered name in the area. Ted Ellis, a student of Washington County history, believes the Lampert location was a "tenant house" provided in conjunction with employment. Ted indicated that the Poffenberger family owned this property soon after the war. This family owned much of the farmland in the Park Hall region.

It is reasonable to place Stevens and his comrade at the northeast edge of the fence around Lambert's Field, just beyond the gorge. Stevens's 5th TX unit was about 900 to 1,200 feet north, probably complying with Hood's alignment. Stevens's account does not conflict with the statements of Union Captain Wren and Union Lieutenant Whitman. There also was a large area of open ground surrounded by fencing on both the north and south sides of Old Sharpsburg Road west of Dog Creek.

Hood Received No Credit for Any Success

Several Confederate units took Moser Road north when they departed the battlefield at Fox's Gap. These units included the 5th VA cavalry, Pelham's artillery, Ripley's Brigade, and Hood's two brigades. For this reason alone, it was difficult to conclude that any Confederate units that retreated north along Moser Road occupied a position near Miller's Field during the late afternoon or evening of September 14.

Chaplain George G. Smith was a Phillips (Georgia) Legion member. Smith provided his opinion as to who or what saved General Lee's Army on Sunday, September 14, 1862:

> If you permit, I will tell you about the afternoon at South Mountain in 1862, when I received a bullet through the neck and night alone saved General Lee's army from capture.

Hood's division went in as we came out, but the Federals' caution and the cover of the night saved our army from a worse defeat and capture.[51]

Chaplain Smith gave Hood's two brigades no credit for saving the day for the Confederates on September 14. He did, however, mention, together with darkness and the perceived Union hesitancy, saving "our army from a worse defeat and capture." Davis stated "and capture" as though an otherwise inevitability. Davis may have alluded to the Union's objective of cutting off the Confederate escape route west of Turner's Gap, Zittlestown gorge.

Chaplain Smith and other battle analysts mentioned the caution of the Federals. However, after an extended period of fighting during the afternoon at Fox's Gap, the Union troops were tired and hungry, and many men were low on ammunition. Union canteens may have been empty as well. Cox, or a higher Union commander, set an objective to occupy Cox's Intersection. There does not appear to have been any hesitancy by the Union forces to achieve that objective.

Wofford's Brigade had 864 men present for duty, and Law's Brigade had 1,493 men present for duty on September 14.[52] Another source estimated 1,146 men present for Law's Brigade and 854 men present for Wofford's Brigade on September 16 and 17.[53] Longstreet declared the returning Confederates in Hood's two brigades were "thinned to skeletons of three or four hundred men to a brigade when they reached the Mountain House." So, where did all of Hood's men disappear?

If the number of troops given above was accurate, the difference between the number of men who entered the battle and the number who returned to Old National Pike was substantial. The main difference probably was due to straggling between Hagerstown and Turner's Gap. Some gave out on the advance south from Old National Pike; some fell asleep and woke up after their unit retreated after 10:00 pm.

The other possibility, of course, was that they were killed, wounded, or captured. Union Lieutenant George Whitman indicated, "I think judging from what I saw, the enemy's loss was eight times as great as ours. I am told the slaughter was equally as great on our right [east flank]."[54] Whitman was near Cox's Intersection, and the losses must have come from Confederates engaged in that area.

The terrain east of Wood Road and north of Miller's Field was virtually impassable for humans. The ground 30 to 50 feet east of Wood Road was such that no human being could stand upright without holding onto a tree. The vast extent of the ground between Turner's Gap and Fox's Gap on the east side of Wood Road prohibited any attempt by infantry to launch an attack from Fox Gap Road below. As Cox informed Reno when asked, "the ground there was very rough and rocky, a fortress in itself and evidently very strongly held." The elevation along Wood Road, beside and north of Miller's Field, was about 1,100 feet, while Fox Gap Road, the nearest road 2,000 feet east, was less than 700 feet.

For this reason, the Union hierarchy neither planned nor executed any attack along Wood Road from the area of Fox Gap Road below. There was Union Brigadier General

John Gibbon's attack late in the day on Old National Pike towards Turner's Gap, which proved to be somewhat suicidal.[55] Furthermore, because the ground east of Wood Road and north of Miller's Field was too steep to be used by the Federals, Confederate troops were never committed to defending that area for any length of time.

After Drayton's Brigade's rout by 5:00 pm, Union troops soon controlled the mountain top at Fox's Gap. Union Captain William Bolton of the 51st Pennsylvania confirmed the situation that Durell's Battery cleared the mountain of the enemy, and the 51st PA relocated to the mountain's summit before 6:30 pm, apparently at Reno's direction.[56]

Union Major General Jesse L. Reno, April 20, 1823–September 14, 1862. (Artist Paul Martin)

The shooting of Reno occurred about 6:30 pm immediately south of Miller's Field, but no significant number of Confederate soldiers were nearby. *The Twenty-Third North Carolina Regimental History* stated that Charles W. Bennett, Orderly Sergeant of Company E, killed Reno at long range. Confederate Major General Daniel H. Hill also indicated a member of the 23rd NC regiment, Garland's Brigade, shot Reno.[57]

Hood did not command the 23rd NC.[58] Hood instructed G. T. Anderson's Brigade to remain on Hood's left or east side to protect that flank. The 23rd NC was not in G. T. Anderson's Brigade.

Authors convinced Reno's death came from Hood's men believed that Hood's two brigades were somewhere near Miller's Field. None of Hood's men were near Wood Road or the area near Miller's Field where they could have shot Reno. However, John D. Hoptak, in his book *The Battle of South Mountain*, published in 2011, credited a soldier in Hood's division.[59]

Union Brigadier General Cox believed enemy fire killed Reno, and it is difficult to come to any other conclusion:

> He [Reno] had gone to the skirmish line to examine the situation and had been shot down by the enemy posted among the rocks and trees. There was more or less firing on that part of the field till late evening. When morning dawned, the Confederates had abandoned the last foothold above Turner's Gap and retreated by way of Boonsboro to Sharpsburg.[60]

Cox also told us that enemy fire on that part of the field lasted until late evening on the 14th. The likely scenario was that a remnant of various North Carolina regiments and some of Drayton's men were in the area north of Miller's Field and the dense woods west of Wood Road during the early and late evening hours.

Cox displayed no inclination for a Union attack along Wood Road, believing it was a fortress to itself. It was late in the day, and night had set in, making any venture north along Wood Road difficult. Wood Road did not serve a significant purpose in the Union Army's strategic plans or objectives. McClellan aimed to drive a wedge between Lee's forces at Turner's Gap and the Confederates under Jackson at Harpers Ferry. Union possession of Wood Road would not help achieve McClellan's objective. Control of Cox's Intersection did achieve McClellan's aim.

The Account of Lieutenant Robert Coles, Jr.

Confederate Lieutenant Robert T. Coles, Jr., 4th AL, was part of Colonel Evander M. Law's Brigade. Coles described the movement of his regiment towards Old Sharpsburg Road during the late afternoon:

> After a march of fourteen miles, which taxed the energies of every man in the regiment, we arrived none too soon, between 3:00 pm and 4:00 pm. The 4th AL received orders to attack the enemy on the left [north] of the road [Old National Pike]. Soon afterward, we marched to the right [south] through an orchard, the trees growing among huge boulders luxuriantly, many loaded with tempting fruit and not a minute to spare to eat a single apple. There, we met Drayton's Brigade falling back in confusion, stating they had been flanked. We moved further to the right [west] and secured a position to meet the advancing enemy.
>
> It was now dark. The 4th AL, for better protection, was transferred to a sunken road running obliquely across the gap, the enemy still keeping up a constant firing, inflicting but minor damage, as the road afforded good protection. A fence was next to the enemy on the embankment, a dense laurel thicket on the opposite side. The enemy's bullets striking the laurel leaves caused a loud report and created the impression that the enemy was firing explosive shells. During the heaviest part of this night engagement, Colonel McLemore climbed upon the fence in our front to reconnoiter. He soon fell back into the road, shot through the shoulder.
>
> As the men were awakened, they were ordered to go quietly one at a time down to the main road, which led to Sharpsburg, and reform. We placed Colonel McLemore on a litter and carried him with us. After all the army passed on its way to Sharpsburg, we formed the rear guard of the Corps. We marched the rest of the night until noon on the 15th. [61]

Coles's statements provide invaluable details that help identify Hood's troop movements and the specific locations of various units on the battlefield.

Coles initially received orders to occupy a position north of Old National Pike along Dahlgren Road. The two brigades under Hood selected to trudge south towards Old Sharpsburg Road probably were those along Dahlgren Road nearest Old National Pike:

> We marched to the right [south] through an orchard, the trees growing among huge boulders luxuriantly, many loaded with tempting fruit and not a minute to spare to eat a single apple. [62]

Coles indicated that it was "there [at the orchard], we met Drayton's Brigade falling back in confusion, stating that they had been flanked."[63] Some of Drayton's defeated men reached the orchard when Coles and his men passed through the orchard on their way south. The men of Drayton's Brigade must have taken at least 30 minutes to reach the orchard from the Miller's Field area. It seemed doubtful these men took Wood Road.

We need to ask a crucial question: How did Hood's horse, Jeff Davis, and the horses of Wofford and Law manage to get over the boulders of the East Ridge? Hood told us that he rode to the Mountain House at about 10:00 pm and thus confirmed he had his horse with him. Confederate Major General J. E. B. Stuart previously indicated South Mountain was no place for cavalry.

Did Hood and his two brigades cross over the East Ridge before or after they got to the large boulder field just south of Hill #2? In the opinion of Ted Ellis, the only location where Hood and his horse could cross over the East Ridge from the east side was *just before* they were at the large boulder field about 500 yards south of the Mountain House. Hood and other riders dismounted temporarily to lead their horses through the boulders.

The East Ridge was steep and rocky from the Mountain House for 500 yards south. Near the large boulder field, the elevation difference between Hood's speculated route and the East Ridge crest was only between 20 and 40 feet. It seemed reasonable to believe the large boulder field forced Hood to move to the southwest as he advanced.[64]

After crossing the East Ridge just north of the large boulder field that lay a quarter-mile south of the Mountain House, Hood's troops came within eyesight of Brigadier General Ripley, who was at the Crest of the Heights along Moser Road. Ripley watched Hood's two brigades advance south along Moser Road towards Old Sharpsburg Road.

Fighting probably took place near the area of Lambert's Field, and at least some of Hood's troops moved south of Old Sharpsburg Road to a stone wall that ran from the west side of Park Hall Road to Dog Creek. This wall was the stone fence identified by Captain Wren, about 600 feet southwest of Cox's Intersection.

Hood had no helpful artillery support nearby for his two brigades as they advanced towards Old Sharpsburg Road. How could he have any cannon support nearby? His infantry moved through woods, boulders, and underbrush. The Confederate cannon assigned to Hood's two brigades, consisting of the German (SC) Artillery, the Palmetto (SC) Light Artillery, and the Rowan (NC) Artillery, were not mentioned by other authors who wrote about the battle.

Hood's two brigades passed through the orchard and moved directly south between Hill #2 of the East Crest and Wood Road. Some Confederate troops may have been along Wood Road just south of Old National Pike. If Hood was conscious of their location, he had no reason to suspect it was along a road that led to Fox's Gap. Without knowing Hood's objective as his brigades moved south, we do not know if the use of Wood Road was an appropriate choice for Hood.

Boulders at Coles's Orchard approximately 275 feet south of Old National Pike GPS 39.483895 - 77.620555. (Photograph by Ted Ellis, August 2021)

Three orchards, enclosed by fences, appeared near the Mountain House on the *Atlas Map*. Hood's two brigades passed through the orchard directly south of the Old National Pike and Dahlgren Road intersection. This orchard was halfway between the Mountain House and the Wood Road intersection with Old National Pike and may have been on the property of a D. Keedy shown on the *Atlas Map*. Hood's men were not on Wood Road at this early stage. An August 2021 image of the ground about 275 feet south of Old National Pike in line with the orchard confirmed many large boulders.

Lieutenant Coles, as well as Hood, revealed the situation's urgency. With a fight raging at both Turner's and Fox's Gaps by late afternoon, time was of the essence. Perhaps the adage "haste makes waste" applied to the Confederate decisions made at that moment in the battle.

Coles's unit encountered men from Drayton's Brigade who retreated towards the northwest from the immediate area of Fox's Gap and the Wise Cabin. The East Ridge curved southeast between the Mountain House and Fox's Gap. Hood's stated route "obliquely right" (southwest) from Old National Pike put him on the west side of the East Crest. Hood's location was precisely where Drayton's men retreated. Nonetheless, Hood had to cross the East Crest either due to obstructions or to maintain his original direction.

Given the meeting between Hood's men and Drayton's men, we cannot assume that Hood's objective was to retake the ground lost by Drayton. However, the account of Confederate Lieutenant Robert T. Coles, Jr., 4th AL, does strengthen the assertion that Drayton's men fell back to the northwest from the Wise Cabin and Miller's Field area. Coles stated, like Hood, that his men "moved still further to the right [west] and secured a position to meet the advancing enemy." Hood's and Coles's statements agreed.

Coles indicated that his 4th AL regiment relocated to a sunken road running obliquely across the gap after dark and, later, as the men awakened, they went quietly one at a time down to the main road which led to Sharpsburg. Coles identified two routes; the only sunken road was Old Sharpsburg Road. Moser Road was not below ground level. Only opened as a county road 10 years earlier, Moser Road was still a new road. Old Sharpsburg Road, by 1862, had been extensively used by horse-drawn wagons for at least 135 years.

The sole location where the movement by the 4th AL could occur was near Cox's Intersection. This intersection was the nearest location on the west side of Fox's Gap, near two roads. Coles's statement was critical to identifying the position of the 4th AL.

A review of the *1791 Map of the Road from Swearingen's Ferry to Fox's Gap* found no modifications in the road near Cox's Intersection. The road commissioners plotted the old route and the changes they made in 1791 on their road diagram. The 4th AL moved to Old Sharpsburg Road west of Cox's Intersection.

Coles specifically stated:

> It was now dark. The 4th AL, for better protection, was transferred to a sunken road running obliquely across the gap, the enemy still keeping up a constant firing, inflicting but minor damage, as the road afforded good protection.[65]

We could assume Coles's statement intended that the 4th AL moved south to Old Sharpsburg Road from north of that road and probably on the west side of Moser Road.

However, if the 4th AL was south of Old Sharpsburg Road and west of Park Hall Road, perhaps Coles meant the 4th AL moved north to Old Sharpsburg Road for better protection. Wren indicated dead Confederates were along the stone fence or stone wall near the 48th PA about 600 feet southwest of Cox's Intersection. Perhaps the 4th AL retreated north from the west side of Park Hall Road to Old Sharpsburg Road after they attempted, and failed, to flank the Union troops along Park Hall Road.

Coles stated the 4th AL moved to the Old Sharpsburg Road "for better protection." Coles's reasoning seemed to make more sense if his 4th AL was south of Old Sharpsburg Road and moved north to Old Sharpsburg Road. If one accepted this reasoning, placing Coles's 4th AL at Fox's Gap would be more challenging than locating it at Cox's Intersection.

After moving to the sunken road, Captain Lawrence H. Scruggs of the 4th AL stated:

> [We] went down to our right [west] to the 2nd MS, the nearest regiment, to prevail upon Colonel [John M.] Stone to divide ammunition with us.[66]

This statement placed the 2nd MS on the right, or west side, of the 4th AL. Ted Ellis indicated that between Old Sharpsburg Road and Park Hall Road west of Cox's Intersection was genuinely a "gorge for several hundred feet." We point out that Old Sharpsburg Road at Cox's Intersection could not be lower than Dog Creek.

Coles divulged that "on the embankment next to the enemy was a fence; on the opposite side was a dense laurel thicket." The fence was on the same side of the road as the enemy. The enemy could have been 50 or 100 yards beyond the wall on the far side of the road. Coles's reference indicated which side of the road the fence was on rather than placing the enemy adjacent to the barrier. There was no mention by Coles of an open field or cornfield. However, the existence of a fence would lead one to believe that it surrounded a farm field, pasture, orchard, or road edge.

"During the heaviest part of this night engagement, Colonel McLemore climbed upon the fence in our front to reconnoiter. He soon fell back into the road, shot through the shoulder." [67] According to the *Atlas Map*, a fence ran along both sides of Old Sharpsburg Road west of Cox's Intersection. The railing began about 300 feet west of the intersection on the north side of Old Sharpsburg Road. The barrier started about 600 feet west of the corner on the south side. Accepting the accuracy of the *Atlas Map*, McLemore was in Old Sharpsburg Road, approximately 600 feet west of Cox's Intersection.

Lieutenant Colonel McLemore's wounding was not far from Cox's Intersection. Laurel only grows where there are woods. A laurel thicket was almost impossible to see through. However, laurel only grows at about 8–10 feet in height. It is reasonable to think that McLemore tried to see over the laurel to identify any Union troop activity by climbing up on the fence.

According to moonposition.com, an internet site that reports moon information, there was a full moon on Monday, September 8, 1862.[68] The time for the full moon in New York City was 2:59 (UTC-5, time zone). Another website, nineplanets.org, described the moon phase for September 14, 1862, as the waning gibbous phase:

> The moon's illumination will decrease from 99.0% to 50.1% during this phase. Technically, the change starts as soon as the Full Moon has passed, but with 98–99% of the moon's surface illuminated, it can be tough to calculate and differentiate the first stage of a Waning Gibbous Moon from a Full Moon.[69]

The nineplanets.org website indicated the moon was 69.71% illuminated on the date of the Battle of South Mountain. There was reason to believe that moonlight at Fox's Gap was adequate for a Union soldier to spot McLemore silhouetted above the fence cover and shoot him.

A Washington County Road Survey in 1851 plotted the course of Moser Road from Old Sharpsburg Road to Old National Pike.[70] The road examiners were Frederick Rohrer, Jacob C. Snavely, and Samuel Rinehart. The survey included a line "north forty-four degrees east thirty perches to a bunch of laurels near Lambert's fence."

This road survey gave evidence of laurels near a fence on Lambert's property. The best analysis was that Lieutenant Colonel McLemore was in Old Sharpsburg Road on the west side of Cox's Intersection.

Coles described the capture of a Union soldier who went to fill several canteens with water while the 4th AL remained in Old Sharpsburg Road:

> While talking to Colonel Stone [2nd MS], a Union soldier sent with several canteens for water became lost in the darkness, walked up to them, and was captured. [Lieutenant L. H.] Scruggs [4th AL] brought back two of the filled canteens, and water never tasted sweeter than it did that night, or at least my share of it.[71]

The Union soldier who went for water with empty canteens obtained water from nearby Dog Creek that ran along the west side of Moser Road and crossed Old Sharpsburg Road at Cox's Intersection.

Dog Creek was the closest available water source, as there was no other water source between Bolivar Branch, east of the East Ridge, and Moser Road. This incident with the Union soldier supported the whereabouts of the 4th AL and 2nd MS near Cox's Intersection. The creek crossing was part of the explanation for the misalignment of Cox's Intersection.

Dog Creek was only inches deep and less than two or three feet wide north of Old Sharpsburg Road. The creek carved a gully along its path. However, north of Old Sharpsburg Road, the ravine was not deep enough to prevent a soldier from crossing on foot. Between Old Sharpsburg Road and Park Hall Road, Dog Creek ran in a deep ravine, which was thick underbrush, and possibly accounted for how the Union soldier took the wrong direction back to his lines and into the hands of the enemy. This lost Union soldier episode indicated that some Union troops were west of Park Hall Road.

Coles recounted how the retreat of the 4th AL occurred. "As the men were awakened, they were ordered to go quietly one at a time down to the main road, which led to Sharpsburg." The men of the 4th AL were asleep because they were dead tired from all the marching they endured on the 14th. The men trudged up the west side of the West Ridge and then down the east side of the ridge to Moser Road, where they followed it to Old National Pike. They formed the rearguard for Lee's army near the Mountain House and proceeded to Boonsboro and Antietam Creek.[72]

Coles's men were in Old Sharpsburg Road, and his statement about "the main road, which led to Sharpsburg" implied that the route north along Moser Road ultimately led them to Antietam Creek near Sharpsburg. The 4th AL did not march to Sharpsburg along Old Sharpsburg Road because they were the rearguard for Lee's Army when it departed Turner's Gap.[73]

We learned from Hood that:

> The night closed in with not only our dead and wounded, together with those of our adversary in our possession, but with the mountain, on the right [west], within our lines.[74]

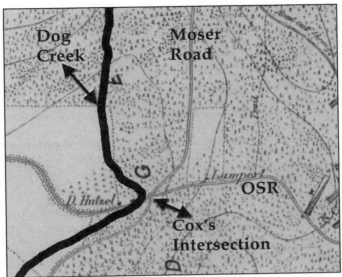

Map 37: Dog Creek at Cox's Intersection, September 14, 1862. (Identified on Atlas Map by Curtis Older)

On Hood's right or west, the mountain was the West Ridge that passed through Hill #1 west of Moser Road and south of Old National Pike. The East Ridge, east of Moser Road, followed the Washington and Frederick County line and passed near the Mountain House and the Wise cabin. Previous assessments that concluded Hood controlled the East Ridge near Wood Road and Miller's Field were in error.

Just as Union Brigadier General Cox indicated his awareness of Hill #1 and Hill #2, Hood recognized their strategic importance as well. According to Cox, Confederate artillery used Hill #1 to bombard Fox's Gap earlier in the day. Cox judged that "the enemy still held the two hills between the latter road and the turnpike, and the further one [Hill #1] could not be reached till the Mountain House should be in our hands."

Hood further indicated that:

> After correcting my alignment, at about 10:00 pm, I rode back to the gap [Turner's], where I found General D. H. Hill and other officers in the gallery [balcony] of a tavern [Mountain House] near the pike, evidently discussing the outlook.[75]

The tipping point of the action was where the momentum for change became unstoppable. The battlefield situation during the night of September 14 was a tipping point for the Confederates.

Hood probably aligned his men from west to east along an area of relatively even elevation north of Lambert's Field. His men occupied both sides of Moser Road, and his alignment probably ran parallel to Old Sharpsburg Road. His alignment placed Hill #1 of the West Ridge on Hood's right, within the Confederate lines. The East Ridge, however, was not within Hood's alignment.

Antietam historian and author Ezra Carman completed his chapter eight on the battle at Fox's Gap with the following two paragraphs:

> On the Confederate side George T. Anderson had come up on Hood's left; George B. Anderson still held ground on the right, and Ripley, returning to the front after the fighting was over, filled the interval between George B. Anderson and Hood. This line was held until the retreat was ordered.
>
> The casualties in the Ninth Corps numbered 157 killed, 691 wounded, and 41 missing, a total of 889. The Confederate loss in killed and injured in front of the Ninth Corps was about 600, and many were captured. The Kanawha Division alone, claiming the capture of 600, however, must include some of the wounded.[76]

I concur that G. T. Anderson's Brigade was on Hood's left or east side and that G. B. Anderson possibly was west of Moser Road and possibly not far from Old Sharpsburg Road.

Can we combine Carman's statement that "George B. Anderson still held ground on the right [west]" with Ripley's statement that he "found soon afterward that General [G. B.] Anderson's command had been withdrawn at nightfall from the heights to the Braddock Road [Old Sharpsburg Road]?" These two statements, taken together, indicate that G. B. Anderson's Brigade fell back from the Ridge-Loop Intersection to Old Sharpsburg Road and did not retreat to Boonsboro until the general Confederate retreat that evening.

By nightfall, we assume Ripley meant no later than 6:30 pm. Therefore, G. B. Anderson's Brigade possibly encountered Sturgis's Division at Cox's Intersection. This encounter between Anderson and Sturgis would confirm the statement of Corporal Robinson that "after they [the Rebels] left us, they formed and went a little farther to the right [north], and the 51st NY went into them [the Rebels] with a vengeance supported by the 51st OH [PA] and piled the Rebels up in heaps."

Back to Major Thruston

Neither Major Thruston nor Ripley corroborated the claim by Carman that Ripley's Brigade, after the fighting ceased, moved south along Moser Road from the Crest of the Heights and took up a position between Hood and G. B. Anderson. Thruston stated that "about 9:00 pm, we rested in this position within 200 yards of the enemy until about 11:00 pm when we took the road to Sharpsburg [Old National Pike to Boonsboro and then to Sharpsburg]". I found no support for Carman's claim that Ripley's Brigade moved south from the Crest of the Heights to a position between G. B. Anderson and Hood on the evening of September 14. There was no reason why Ripley would make such a movement.

Map 38 shows a measurement from Confederate Major Thruston's Moser Road location near Old National Pike to the location of "the enemy" at 200 yards the

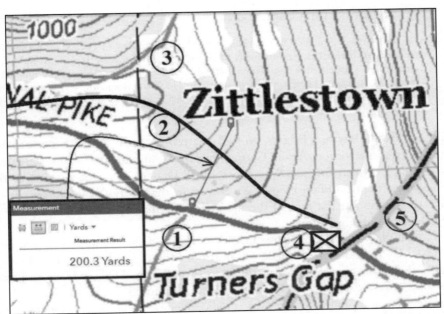

Map 38: Zittlestown Gorge. 1. Thruston's location along Moser Road; 2. Bottom of Zittlestown Gorge; 3. Zittlestown Road; 4. Mountain House; 5. Washington/Frederick County Line, September 14, 1862. (Map by Ted Ellis)

night of September 14. The source of this map was the United States Geological Survey Middletown Quad topographical map. The measurement was made via the Maryland Department of Natural Resources MERLIN GIS mapping software. (Note—each line equals 20 feet elevation.)

Thruston's statement that he was within 200 yards of "the enemy" was significant as the map indicated the critical nature of the Confederate situation at Turner's Gap the night of September 14. Zittlestown gorge, west of the Mountain House, was a possible trap for the Confederates.

Carman later told us in Chapter Ten, *From South Mountain to Antietam*, that:

> The three brigades of Garland, Ripley, and G. B. Anderson, in the order named, moved on byroads from the Old Sharpsburg Road to the vicinity of Boonsboro, then followed [Brigadier General Robert E.] Rodes over the Boonsboro and Sharpsburg pike to Keedysville.[77]

Carman cited no sources for his statement and consistently put virtually all the Confederate brigades on Old Sharpsburg Road.

We learned that units of the 4th AL and 2nd MS were in Old Sharpsburg Road just west of Cox's Intersection and moved north up Moser Road during the retreat. It would make sense that G. B. Anderson's Brigade did the same if it was west of the 4th AL and 2nd MS. Garland's Brigade probably fragmented and scattered amongst the other Confederate brigades on the Fox's Gap battlefield.

We learned further from Carman that:

> Drayton's Brigade, on the Old Sharpsburg Road, near the foot of Fox's Gap, marched in lanes and on byroads and across fields to Boonsboro. After leaving Jenkins to retire last, Kemper and Garnett took the National Road [Old National Pike] down the mountain. George T. Anderson, being ordered to report to Hood for rearguard, was left near Fox's Gap. The brigades of Drayton, Kemper, and Garnett marched by the Boonsboro turnpike to Keedysville.[78]

Carman placed Drayton's Brigade on Old Sharpsburg Road near the foot of Fox's Gap at Cox's Intersection. Again, Carman presented no evidence for this statement concerning Drayton's Brigade. We know some of Drayton's Brigade retreated to the orchard near the Mountain House. We also know that Sturgis's Division occupied Cox's Intersection at the foot of the mountain. Carman's placement of Drayton's Brigade seems highly doubtful.

Carman placed G. T. Anderson's Brigade near Fox's Gap. We must ask, how near is "near"? G. T. Anderson's Brigade was north of Miller's Field and west of the East Ridge. They probably were at least halfway to Turner's Gap. I believe G. T. Anderson probably retreated along Cut Road or moved west to Moser Road. Wood Road near the Mountain House probably was too dangerous for any Confederates to use during their late evening retreat.

Joseph Pierro, in his edition of Carman's *Maryland Campaign*, stated the following:

> The retreat began about ten o'clock. The troops near the Mountain House retired by the National Road and Boonsboro, those confronting Cox generally by the Old Sharpsburg Road to the foot of the mountain and thence to Boonsboro.
> Colonel Rosser, with the 5th Virginia Cavalry, covered the withdrawal of the troops from Fox's Gap.[79]

Major Thruston told us that Ripley's Brigade fell back to Old Sharpsburg Road and moved "up the mountain by the steep and narrow road." The steep and narrow road was Moser Road.

Thruston also told us:

> About 9:00 pm, we rested in this position within 200 yards of the enemy [near Old National Pike] until about 11:00 pm, when we took the road to Sharpsburg.[80]

Thruston's statement indicated Ripley's Brigade moved north along Moser Road to Old National Pike when it withdrew from the battle. That was not to say that a few of Ripley's men did not become lost and took a back route to reach Boonsboro or Sharpsburg. Brigadier General Ripley's report also indicated Ripley was on Moser Road at the Crest of the Heights.

We also mention the statement by Coles that the 2nd MS and 4th AL were in Old Sharpsburg Road just west of Cox's Intersection and just beyond the Union troops at that intersection. Coles's men must have taken Moser Road. It also was evident from the words of Major General Longstreet that Hood's men moved back north along Moser Road to the area of the Mountain House.

G. B. Anderson's men seem to be the most likely to have been forced off Park Hall Road to the west if they encountered Union troops near Cox's Intersection. G. B. Anderson's men must have known Moser Road connected with Old National Pike west of Turner's Gap. Confederate troops near Cox's Intersection also must have been aware of some Confederate cannon on Hill #1.

Carman recorded the following as to the retreat of Drayton's and G. T. Anderson's Brigades:

> Longstreet did not closely follow D. H. Hill. It was necessary to give time for the wagon train and other impedimenta to get on the road, which delayed Longstreet's withdrawal until midnight. On the Old Sharpsburg Road near the foot of Fox's Gap, Drayton's Brigade marched in lanes and on by-roads and across fields to Boonsboro. Kemper and Garnett, leaving Jenkins to retire last, took the National Road down the mountain, and George T. Anderson, being ordered to report to Hood for the rearguard, was left near Fox's Gap.[81]

This statement by Carman confirmed why it is so difficult to write about a military battle. A footnote to this quote from Carman cites G. T. Anderson's report.[82] There was nothing in G. T. Anderson's report to indicate where his brigade was on the battlefield, other than it was likely east of Hood's Brigades.

Carman's statement that G. T. Anderson "was left near Fox's Gap" did not come from Anderson's report. It was doubtful that G. T. Anderson's Brigade was within a quarter-mile of Fox's Gap between the time G. T. Anderson sought to protect Hood's left flank and 10:00 pm that night. This account by Carman was another reason the casual reader might take Carman's statement to support the idea that Hood's attack was near Miller's Field and the Wise Cabin.

Regarding the retreat of Hood and G. T. Anderson, Carman told us:

> General John B. Hood had under his command for his rearguard the two brigades of his division and the brigades of N. G. Evans and George T. Anderson.[83]

I agree with the above statement by Carman. However, Carman goes on to state:

> Hood's two brigades and G. T. Anderson withdrew from Fox's Gap about 1:00 am of the 15th, and by roads [not by-roads] and farm lanes, reached the Keedysville road, a mile south of Boonsboro, and halted until after daylight, when the march was resumed.[84]

We must be cautious in evaluating this statement by Carman. We cannot take Carman to imply that Hood's men did not follow Moser Road to Old National Pike and Boonsboro. However, Hood's two brigades were not within a quarter-mile of Fox's Gap. The paragraph that included the above information by Carman had one footnote, apparently written by Dr. Thomas Clemens, the editor of this version of Carman's work, that stated:

> Much of this is not in official reports, memoirs, or letters examined thus far. Carman may have gotten this from one of Lee's staff members or a letter not yet discovered.[85]

Regarding Hood's two brigades, Longstreet stated:

> Considering the severe forced march, the five brigades that made a direct ascent of the mountain were in good order. The three [Drayton, Wofford, Laws] marched south of the turnpike, along a narrow mountain trail part of the way, through woodlands and over boulders, returning, then up the mountain. The last march at double time was thinned to skeletons of three or four hundred men to a brigade when they reached the Mountain House.[86]

If Hood and his men were near the Mountain House, why would they not march to Boonsboro and then Keedysville and Sharpsburg? When the Confederates got down the mountain on Old National Pike, they already were near Boonsboro.

Hood was clear about his movement towards Old Sharpsburg Road from Old National Pike. He did not confuse his direction of movement when he indicated he moved obliquely to the right. He identified the mountain ridge to the west as within his lines. There was no reason to doubt what Hood told us. Hood intended to attack the Union left or west flank.

Longstreet was clear about Hood's movements and his return to the Mountain House. Hood moved through dense woods and boulders as he moved south and proceeded north up the mountain with his two brigades reduced to mere skeletons upon their return.

The Convincing Report of Brigadier General Ripley

The September 21, 1862, report of Brigadier General Roswell S. Ripley was of great significance. He commanded the 1st NC and 3rd NC and the 4th GA and 44th GA regiments. Ripley referred to two roads and Brigadier General Hood in his report:

> Meantime, General [G. B.] Anderson had extended far to the right and come up with the enemy, with whom he had a short engagement [at the Ridge-Loop Intersection]. My brigade pressed up to within a short distance of the Crest of the Heights and held its position under a noisy but comparatively harmless fire. Anderson's brigade, having extended far to the right [south and probably at least one mile from Ripley], was unsupported by any other troops. Soon after, Brigadier General Hood's command came from the main pass [Turner's Gap]. Forming upon my left [east], the troops pressed up the road [Moser Road], driving the enemy before them until they [the enemy] occupied their first position [east and south of Cox's Intersection] and darkness put an end to the operations. I found soon afterward that General [G. B.] Anderson's command had been withdrawn at nightfall from the heights to the Braddock Road [Old Sharpsburg Road].[87]

In his report, Ripley labeled Braddock Road (Old Sharpsburg Road) as one of two roads, but he did not give a specific name to the second road.

Ripley indicated that Hood's command came from the main pass (Turner's Gap) and formed on Ripley's left [east] side. Hood's troops pressed up the road (Moser Road) and drove the enemy before them until the enemy occupied their first position (Park Hall Road and Old Sharpsburg Road). Ripley did not specifically identify the enemy's "first position."

We recall that Major Thruston of the 3rd NC regiment, Ripley's Brigade, told us that Ripley:

> Ordered us to fall back to the base of the mountain [Old Sharpsburg Road], which was done in good order. Here the companies of skirmishers were ordered to their proper positions in line. The regiments again moved by the right [west] flank up the mountain [north] by the steep and narrow road [Moser Road], halting as the right reached the top of the said mountain [near Old National Pike].[88]

A History of the Third North Carolina Regiment told us:

> On the evening of Saturday, September 13, 1862, the brigade was counter-marched toward the mountain and placed in a line of battle on the north side of the pike, near the foot of the mountain, again in reserve. Next morning, Sunday, Colonel [George Pierce] Doles, with the 4th Georgia, was detached and ordered to take a position in a gap on the north side of the pike [Hamburg Pass northeast of Boonsboro]. The other three regiments [1st NC, 3rd NC, and 44th GA] moved up the mountain. Just to the east of the tavern [Mountain House] on the summit [they] filed to the right [south] and moved along the summit road [Wood Road], having, before leaving the pike, passed the body of General Garland, who died at the head of his command. Leaving this road, they moved by one leading diagonally down the mountain [Old Sharpsburg Road] and, on reaching the foot [Cox's Intersection], were halted half a mile to a mile from the pike, on the south. Here General Ripley concluded that his command and General George B. Anderson's were cut off from the troops on his left [east; consisting of G. T. Anderson's Brigade and Drayton's Brigade]. Assuming command of the division, [Ripley] notified Colonel [William L.] DeRosset to take control of the brigade. General [G, B.] Anderson seemed to have promptly moved up the mountain, and Ripley ordered Colonel DeRosset to do likewise. Lieutenant Colonel [Major] Thruston was ordered to take a company of skirmishers covering the front of the brigade and soon reported that troops were in his front. While remaining at the foot of the mountain [Cox's Intersection], General Ripley was informed of the situation and ordered his brigade to fall back. It was then moved by the left flank up a road leading diagonally up the mountain [Moser Road] and then halted, occupying that position until quietly withdrawn sometime between 9:00 pm and midnight.
>
> General Ripley again assumed command of his brigade and marched by a road leading towards the Boonsboro and Sharpsburg pike.[89]

It was interesting to note that in this discussion of the 3rd NC Regiment, the term "diagonally" was used to mean Old Sharpsburg Road (running east and west) in one instance, and in another referred to Moser Road (running north and south). Also, Thruston indicated, "the regiments again moved by the *right flank* up the mountain by the steep and narrow road." The 3rd NC Regiment history declared the regiment "then moved by the *left flank* up a road leading diagonally up the mountain." Both statements referred to the 3rd NC Regiment advancing up Moser Road to the north.

Our previous estimate for Ripley's Brigade front was approximately 1,150 feet in length or a little more than a fifth of a mile. Both Thruston and Ripley indicated that Ripley's Brigade was along Moser Road and near the area between Hill #1 and Hill #2. Thruston used "the top of the said mountain" to identify the brigade's location, while Ripley fixed the spot by "the crest of the heights." The highest point along Moser Road was approximately 1,120 feet between Hill #1 and Hill #2.

The peaks of Hill #1 and Hill #2 are 1,200 and 1,220 feet, respectively, separated by approximately one half-mile, and Moser Road occupied the low point between them at 1,120 to 1,140 feet elevation. These two separate hills formed a defensive, quasi-buttress surrounding the Confederate command at Turner's Gap. Ripley's description of "the crest of the heights" and Thruston's "top of [the] said mountain" indicated the point along Moser Road and not the crest at Fox's Gap along Old Sharpsburg Road as some authors assumed.

Ted Ellis stated the following about the Crest of the Heights on Moser Road:

> One additional consideration concerning the importance of the "crest of the heights" along Moser Road was the critical nature of the threat to it by Cox and the Union Army upon controlling Cox's Intersection. Zittlestown gorge lay at the north end of the West Ridge at Old National Pike. The turnpike ran through the canyon for three-quarters of a mile. It was the only escape route for all the Confederates north of the crest of the heights on Moser Road and at Turner's Gap. The West Ridge overlooked this chasm, only 300 feet wide and more than 400 feet deep. The entire Confederate Army would be trapped if the Union Army gained the heights on Moser Road.

Ripley revealed that his brigade was in an area of "noisy but comparatively harmless fire." Ripley's description was much the same as that of General Hood, who stated that as his division reached the foot of South Mountain, "from which point could be seen the shells of the enemy, as they passed over the rugged peaks in front, and burst upon the slope in our proximity." Major General Hill indicated that Ripley's Brigade was not in action during the battle. Ripley's Brigade's location along Moser Road not far from Old National Pike put it out of the fight for Fox's Gap. However, Ripley's Brigade held a critical point in the Confederate defense at the Crest of the Heights along Moser Road.

The location of Ripley's Brigade along Moser Road between Hill #1 and Hill #2 clarified another of Ripley's assertions. Ripley told us that Brigadier General Hood's command "forming upon my left, the troops pressed up the road [Moser Road], driving the enemy before them until they occupied their first position [Cox's Intersection] and darkness put an end to the operations." This statement by Ripley solidified the location of Hood's two brigades along Moser Road during the battle.

Ripley's description of the enemy occupying "their first position" was a reference to Union skirmishers before they began their advance north over the West Ridge, or north of Old Sharpsburg Road. Hood confirmed pushing them back, and Wren mentioned his skirmishers being "pushed in." Wren placed where his men were "pushed in" as the area near Cox's Intersection!

We know that Ripley's Brigade was along Moser Road. Hood's Brigade would have been on Ripley's left or east side as it moved south from Turner's Gap. If Hood and his men had been on Wood Road, Ripley could not have seen Hood's two brigades. Wood Road was east beyond Hill #2 and the East Ridge. Ripley could only see Hood's two units as they moved west of the East Ridge. Ripley affirmed that Hood's two brigades formed into a line of battle on the east side of Moser Road and advanced south along the road.

South of the major "S" in Moser Road, the land on the west side dropped off a considerable distance below the road until it approached Cox's Intersection. Hood's men probably advanced down Moser Road and along the east side of Moser Road until they began to come near Cox's Intersection. Closer to the intersection, the ground became much more level on both sides of the road.

A Similarity of Opinions

Ripley declared the respective troop positions at the end of the battle as follows:

> The troops pressed up the road [Moser Road], driving the enemy before them until they occupied their first position [Cox's Intersection], and darkness ended the operations.[90]

Cox declared the respective troop positions at the end of the battle as follows:

> On the left [west], Longstreet's men were pushed down the mountainside beyond the Rohrersville and Sharpsburg Roads [Cox's Intersection], and the contest there was ended.[91]

There was no difference between what Ripley and Cox stated about the respective troop positions at the battle's end. Ripley confirmed Cox's statement.

Ripley confirmed he could see Hood's advance on the west side of the East Ridge. Hood's passage was from the Mountain House at Turner's Gap, crossing to the west side of the East Ridge and toward Cox's Intersection, to flank the Federals already there.

After walking along the mountain crest, Ted Ellis described his inspection of the East Ridge of South Mountain between Turner's and Fox's Gaps. Ted began near Old National Pike and the Mountain House:

> Upon entering the area where the orchard existed in 1862, the ground remained littered with large boulders. The only other orchards south of Old National Pike near the Mountain House, as shown on the official engineers' *Atlas Map* of the battlefield, were along Moser Road. However, the ground was not littered with large boulders as it was southeast of the Mountain House. Thus, the point behind the Mountain House was the only location meeting Coles's description for Hood's starting point.
>
> I arbitrarily selected the 1,080 feet elevation line along the east face of the East Ridge of South Mountain. This line met the parking lot at the Mountain House on the southeast corner and intersected the Saddle of the East Ridge at the south end of the line. Wood Road ran east-southeast away from Old National Pike and undulated to well below the one-thousand-foot elevation for part of its course southward before climbing back up the mountain to the crest at the Saddle.
>
> Following the 1,080-foot line south along the East Ridge was not a challenging walk for the first quarter mile. Beyond that point, the number and size of the boulders littering the ground increased until they eventually became a solid field of individual boulders ranging from

basketball-sized to more than car-sized. This field of boulders reached from near the mountain's crest (exceeding 1,100 feet) to very near Wood Road, several hundred yards east. It was a solid field with no space between rocks, giving the appearance of being emptied from huge dump trucks from the mountain's crest. The slope east of the ridge also became exceedingly steep in the area. I climbed to the top for an inspection as I was closer to the top than the bottom.

I discovered that the ground was flat on the crest. The boulders existed primarily on the east slope, but the top was easily passable. This flat top merged into a "terrace" that sloped away to the south and west at a gradual decline. The public land boundary was at the crest of the East Ridge. According to the USGS topographical map, the width of the ridge top, between the 1,060 feet elevation lines from the east to west, is 275 to 550 feet. While the ground had many exposed rocks, most were ground level, unlike the cluttered boulder field on the east slope.

I think Brigadier General Hood used this route south towards Old Sharpsburg Road from Keedy's orchard near the Mountain House, and he would have climbed to this terrace when he encountered the boulder field.

Determining the number of troops in any military unit at a battle presents a difficult challenge. Hood perhaps had 2,000 men in his command, and many of Hood's men were without shoes. This condition made an arduous march for them, and the boulder field would have been torture. While the soldiers walked, Hood and some of his command were on horseback. The large boulder field was impossible for a horse to cross, even with a dismounted rider.

Upon reaching the large boulder field about a quarter-mile south of the turnpike, Hood moved to his right or west. The west side of the East Ridge was much better for walking as it provided a continuous gentle slope west and south.

Evaluating Some Casualties

Ezra Carman reported the following casualties for Hood's two brigades at South Mountain:

	Killed	Wounded	Missing/Captured/ Not Wounded	Total
Law's Brigade	3	11	5	19[a]
Wofford's Brigade	0	3	2	5[b]

[a] The official reports give three killed and 11 wounded. The muster rolls of the 4th Alabama note five men captured.

[b] The muster rolls of the 18th Georgia give one man wounded; muster rolls of the 1st Texas give one man wounded and one missing, and those of the 4th Texas give one man wounded and one missing.

One source indicated the 2nd MS of Law's Brigade suffered 14 captured, four wounded, and two killed during the battle.[92] Several sources combined disclosed the 6th NC in Law's Brigade suffered one killed, five wounded, and 19 missing or captured.[93] I could not collect casualty information on the other two regiments in Law's Brigade, the 4th AL and the 11th MS.

We know Lieutenant Colonel Owen K. McLemore of the 4th AL was mortally wounded. Sources in fold3.com, a website that provides access to military records, identified one injured and five captured in Company A. These numbers were significantly higher than those of Carman for missing and caught.

The 4th TX had one missing and one wounded soldier in its ranks at South Mountain. Most companies in the 4th TX reported no casualties, although almost all 10 companies indicated they engaged at South Mountain.

I have identified the following casualties in Law's Brigade:

	Killed	Wounded	Missing or Captured
2nd MS	2	4	14
4th AL	4	1	5
6th NC	1	5	19
11th MS	1	Unknown	Unknown
Totals	**8**	**10**	**38**

A 4th AL regimental history told us that "at Boonsboro, the loss was slight."[94] Of the 19 men classified as missing or captured in the 6th NC, only one was missing. Four were arrested on September 15, and the others on September 14. All the captured were paroled or exchanged by the end of December 1862.

After attempting to do some research on casualty numbers for Hood's regiments, I concluded that missing records in fold3.com made it impossible to reconstruct Hood's casualties. Often a single record existed with the name of a soldier and his unit identified. However, no additional documents appeared in the soldier's file.

Might the Confederate dead and wounded divulged by Hood be from an earlier engagement in the same area? Corporal William Robinson of the 89th NY wrote:

> After they [the Rebels] left us, they formed and went a little farther to the right, and the 51st NY went into them [the insurgents] with a vengeance supported by the 51st OH [PA] and piled the Rebels up in heaps.[95]

Perhaps G. B. Anderson's Brigade suffered significant casualties near Cox's Intersection. Besides Robinson, no source found supported this conclusion, but that does not mean Robinson was incorrect.

Lieutenant Whitman of the 51st NY revealed:

> In some parts of the field, the enemy's dead lay in heaps, and in a road for nearly a quarter of a mile, they lay so thick that I had to pick my way carefully to avoid stepping on them.[96]

Which road contained the dead Rebels found by Whitman? Can we assume it was Moser Road and not Old Sharpsburg Road?

Another factor that may account for the discrepancy between the Confederate dead reported by Carman and the number described by Union soldiers and other observers may be the number of Maryland recruits who joined Lee's Army in Maryland.[97]

Randolph A. Shotwell estimated the number to be no more than one thousand.[98] D. Scott Hartwig provided an assessment of 200 Confederate recruits in Maryland, significantly less than the 800 sick Confederates Lee left in Frederick.[99] Ezra Carman indicated the Confederates obtained "less than five hundred recruits. Not enough to compensate for deserters."[100] According to diaries found at Fox's Gap on some of the Confederates the day after the battle, a number only enlisted in the previous three days.[101]

The Confederate dead and wounded identified by Hood, Whitman, and Wren must have been along Moser Road or Old Sharpsburg Road. The statements by Wren indicated that Hood's men did not reach or occupy Park Hall Road in the vicinity of Wren's brigade. Wren's account on September 15 told of dead Confederates behind a stone fence that ran from Park Hall Road to Dog Creek about 600 feet southwest of Cox's Intersection. Wren also described dead Confederates at Cox's Intersection.

Robinson of the 89th NY identified G. B. Anderson's Brigade along Park Hall Road and probably at Cox's Intersection where they were confronted by the 51st NY and 51st PA. Wren indicated his 48th PA was near the 51st NY regiment. Without additional evidence, men from Hood's two brigades and G. B. Anderson's Brigade likely made up the Confederate dead and wounded near Cox's Intersection.

If we look at the casualty lists created by Ezra Carman, G. B. Anderson's Brigade appeared to have taken the brunt of the casualties during the late afternoon and evening hours at Fox's Gap. Carman listed the following Confederate casualties:

	Killed	Wounded	Missing/Captured/ Not Wounded	Total
G. T. Anderson's Brigade	0	3	4	7
G. B. Anderson's Brigade	7	54	29	90
Rosser & Pelham	0	0	0	0
Ripley's Brigade	0	0	0	0

Again, there was no reason to believe that casualty records exist for many Confederate soldiers; thus, the actual number of casualties will probably never be accurately determined.

From the casualty numbers provided by Carman, it is difficult to comprehend how any of the Confederate brigades listed above saw significant fighting on the Fox's Gap battlefield, except the men under G. B. Anderson.[102] G. T. Anderson told us his unit did not engage except for some skirmishers. We know Ripley's Brigade was never committed to action. However, I identified two killed, five wounded, and 21 missing or captured in the 6th NC Regiment in Ripley's Brigade.

Rosser and Pelham did see combat, but their casualty numbers probably were small, although we cannot be sure.[103] According to a regimental history, the 1st NC Regiment of Ripley's Brigade had six companies hotly engaged on the right [south] of Braddock Road with the loss of several men.[104]

The *History of the Sixth New Hampshire Regiment* included the following account, which gave its number of Confederate and Union casualties in the battle for Fox's and Turner's Gap. It also contained yet another rendition of Reno's death:

> Here we made a stand, and on the 14th (Sunday). Our forces fought an intense battle under General Burnside and those of the enemy under Generals D. H. Hill and Longstreet. The latter were pressed steadily back everywhere until late in the evening, when they fled, leaving the field in our possession with about twenty-five hundred dead and wounded and fifteen hundred prisoners. This success, however, was not gained without the loss of about fifteen hundred men on our side. The brave Jesse L. Reno, our corps commander that day, was shot in the forehead just at the close of the battle and died in a few moments.[105]

This regimental history claimed 2,500 Confederate dead and wounded at South Mountain (Fox's and Turner's Gaps). Ezra Carman reported 248 killed and 1,013 wounded Confederates at Fox's and Turner's Gaps, approximately half the number stated by the *History of the Sixth New Hampshire Regiment*. This regimental history also claimed that Reno received a fatal head wound, yet another account of Reno's death.

Some Troublesome Accounts

Other authors gave virtually no evidence to support their case that Hood advanced south near or along Wood Road towards Miller's Field. These authors gave no evidence because there is no evidence to support Hood moving near or along Wood Road to Miller's Field.

What accounts refute Hood's march towards Moser Road and Cox's Intersection? *The History of the Twenty-first Regiment, Massachusetts Volunteers* by Charles F. Walcott presents four confusing statements that need analysis regarding the battle:

> [#1] Longstreet's men had come to retake the summit! [Footnote 1 – The Rebels who made this night attack were two brigades of General J. B. Hood's Division: the Texas Brigade and the other the 3rd Brigade. – Ed.] The veterans of the [2nd] brigade [under Ferrero] behaved with wonderful coolness, and throwing themselves upon the ground, remained in their positions; and now came a succession of fierce Rebel charges, but they all met a bloody repulse at the hands of the two 51sts [NY and PA]. The 21st [MA], being in the second line, could not fire and only hugged the ground while the Rebel bullets hissed over us, except now and then when some poor fellow stopped one with his body. After their final repulse, the Rebels kept up a slow fire till 10:00 pm, when fighting ceased, and the hostile forces posted pickets most amicably.[106]

Walcott's statement was accurate if he described Hood's encounter near Cox's Intersection. Walcott correctly identified the two 51st regiments and stated the Rebels made numerous charges.

Unfortunately, Walcott did not identify the ridge he referred to, the West or East. The statement that "Longstreet's men had come to retake the summit" was an assumption on Walcott's part and was not known by him at the time of the event. Walcott's statements indicated that he consulted other individuals to create his *History of the Twenty-first Regiment.*

> [#2] At the commencement of the attack, our true and loved commander, General Jesse L. Reno, the soldier without spot or blemish, fell mortally wounded by a musket shot in the breast and died in about an hour.[107]

Walcott and other battle analysts associated troops under Hood with the death of Major General Reno. Hood's two brigades were not near Fox's Gap, the location of Reno's death. Walcott may have been correct that Hood attacked near Cox's Intersection at about the time when Reno was shot at Fox's Gap.

Walcott shifted to a discussion of the death of General Reno "at the commencement of the attack." Evidence presented earlier casts significant doubt on Walcott's statement that linked the attack of Hood's two brigades with the death of Reno. Walcott concluded Longstreet's men killed Reno because Walcott assumed Longstreet's men attacked Fox's Gap when Reno died. There was no sizable Confederate attack at Fox's Gap when Reno died. Walcott's statement number two implied that item number one referred to the East Ridge rather than the West.

> [#3] The loss of the 21st [MA] in the battle of South Mountain was slight, being but five enlisted men wounded.[108]

Walcott's statement indicated that the 21st MA did not engage in a significant fight or at least took minimal casualties if it did. Walcott's report that the 21st MA lost few men in the battle tells us nothing about the location of his regiment. His statement about regimental casualties agrees with other eyewitness accounts. We can place Walcott and the 21st MA near Fox's Gap from an account by Private George A. Hitchcock, 21st MA, who testified about Union ammunition wagons running over dead and wounded Confederates in Old Sharpsburg Road. Did Walcott and the 21st MA remain the entire time near the East crest at Fox's Gap? It probably was doubtful that he did.

> [#4] We spent the rest of the night lying on our arms, on the mountain's crest, with no firing between the pickets; the night was very chilly, and our limbs were stiff before morning. I had an interesting conversation with a wounded Rebel officer during the night. About midnight, I heard a call for help and, going to the spot, saw someone moving rapidly away from a man lying on the ground. The prone man told me he was Lieutenant Colonel James of the 15th South Carolina. That he was shot through the body when our men made the last assault and had pretended to be dead, hoping that he should feel able to try to escape before morning, but found himself growing weaker and knew that he should die.[109]

Walcott's statement number four came from personal observation, and there was no reason to suspect it was inaccurate. There was no reason why the 21st MA might not have been at Fox's Gap during some portion of the early night hours and also later during the night. Perhaps the 21st MA altered positions as the night progressed.

Walcott claimed he had a conversation with Lieutenant Colonel James of the 15th SC, who died along the Upper Ridge Road stone walls. However, Walcott indicated the event took place "about midnight." We do not know where the 21st MA was earlier in the evening. Perhaps the 21st MA remained near the Wise Cabin area throughout the evening. Nothing indicated that the regiment received orders to be with the other three units in Ferrero's 2nd Brigade. Perhaps the 51st NY and 51st PA received orders to move to one battlefield area, and the 21st MA and 35th MA received different orders.

Private Stevens of the 5th Texas indicated that a line of Federals he observed during the night moved away from his location, probably at Lambert's Field near Cox's Intersection. Perhaps this group of Federal troops included the 21st MA. Maybe they moved from Cox's Intersection to Miller's Field sometime before midnight, and Walcott was at Fox's Gap about midnight. Nothing could prevent the 21st MA from being near the Upper Ridge Road during the evening.

Walcott indicated the regiment "passed the rest of the night lying on our arms, on the mountain's crest, with no firing between the pickets." Again, we do not know which crest Walcott's regiment occupied. However, it seems clear that he was near the Upper Ridge Road if he spoke with Lieutenant Colonel James at that time.

Walcott's statements do not refute the views of Whitman, Wren, and Pollock nor the utterances of Ferrero, the 2nd Brigade commander. Overall, Walcott's conclusions blend various accounts years after the battle. They do not all reflect the personal knowledge of Walcott at the time the events occurred. Walcott's only statement from intimate knowledge was his interaction with Lieutenant Colonel James of the 15th SC.

It is difficult to conclude that Ferrero's 2nd Brigade, which included Walcott's 21st MA, remained near the summit of Fox's Gap throughout the evening of September 14. Evidence proves that Sturgis's 2nd Division was near Cox's Intersection. Indeed, Walcott's statements contradict the general advance ordered by Cox and the Union command.

During the late afternoon, the Union army approached 13,000 men on the battlefield at Fox's Gap. Hood's two brigades, at best, had no more than 2,000 men, most of whom were tired, hungry, and without shoes. Hood had no artillery support for his troops, while the Union artillery included many cannon late in the day at Fox's Gap. Walcott's account does not refute Hood's attack near Cox's Intersection.

Hood indicated the condition of his men on September 15:

> My troops, at this period, were sorely in need of shoes, clothing, and food. We had issued us no meat for several days and little or no bread; the men had been forced to subsist principally on green corn and green apples.[110]

Allocating 3,000 Union troops to the Ridge-Loop Intersection still provided 10,000 men to occupy Park Hall Road and Old Sharpsburg Road. Most authors who wrote about the battle at Fox's Gap contended that most Union troops remained near the mountain's crest and Wise's Field. As these authors claim, how could it be possible to squeeze 10,000 Union troops into the immediate area of Fox's Gap? It would not be possible. How could it be possible for Hood's 2,000 men (at most) to dislodge those Union troops?

Cox made the following statement in his *Military Reminiscences*, which also may have confused the reader:

> As his [Willcox's] head of column came up, Longstreet's Corps was already forming with its right outflanking my left. I sent two regiments [under Willcox—8th Michigan and 50th Pennsylvania] to extend my left and requested Willcox to form the rest of the division on my right facing the summit.[111]

Willcox's division arrived at Fox's Gap about 2:00 pm, and Hood's two brigades did not reach the Mountain House until around 4:00 pm. Cox referred to Drayton's and G. T. Anderson's Brigades, part of Longstreet's Corps.

Cox also stated that:

> Longstreet's men were now pretty well up and pushed a battery forward to the edge of the timber beyond Wise's farm and opened upon Willcox's line, enfilading it badly. There was a momentary break there, but Willcox was able to check the confusion and reform his lines facing westward as I had initially directed; Welsh's brigade was on my right, closely supporting Cook's battery and Christ's beyond it. The general line of Willcox's division was at the eastern edge of the wood, looking into the open ground at Fox's Gap on the north side of the Sharpsburg Road. A warm skirmishing fight continued along the whole of our line. Our purpose was to hold fast my extreme left, which was well advanced upon and over the mountain crest and swing the right up to the continuation of the same line of hills near the Mountain House.[112]

Again, Cox referred to Drayton's Brigade or G. T. Anderson's Brigade, both under Longstreet.

Cox's previous statement referred to events between 3:00 pm and 4:00 pm. "Our purpose was to hold fast my extreme left, which was well advanced upon and over the mountain crest and swing the right up to the continuation of the same line of hills near the Mountain House." Cox told us first that Union troops had already crossed the mountain's crest at the Ridge-Loop Intersection and along Ridge Road. Second, he referred to "the right" as the same line of hills near the Mountain House, the East Ridge.

Thus, Cox confirmed a constantly pursued objective from beginning to end throughout the day. This statement by Cox indicated that a primary goal of the battle at Fox's Gap was west of the East Ridge. The only road to the enemy's "rear" on Old National Pike in this clearly stated strategy was Moser Road.

Hood's two brigades did not depart Turner's Gap for Old Sharpsburg Road until 5:00 pm. Cox's objective was to position Willcox's Division at Wood Road adjacent to Miller's Field and along the Upper Ridge Road. All the Union troops would be along the mountain's East Ridge, from the north side of Miller's Field to the Ridge-Loop Intersection on the Union left flank. Cox also indicated, "at nearly 4:00 pm, the head of Sturgis's column approached."

Joseph Gould and the 48th PA

Confusion concerning the 48th PA location came about from the publication of *The Story of the Forty-eighth: A Record of the Campaigns of the Forty-eighth Regiment Pennsylvania Veteran Volunteer Infantry During the Four Eventful Years of Its Service in the War for the Preservation of the Union* by Joseph Gould and published by Alfred M. Slocum Company in 1908. We learn about Joseph Gould from the following statement by a descendant:

> My great grandfather, Joseph Gould, who served as a Quartermaster Sergeant of the 48th Regiment, wrote this book. He was designated historian to write about the campaigns and battles of the Regiment during the four years of the war to preserve the Union (1861–5). Joseph Gould accessed many sources such as notes, diaries, Official Records of the War, and the Miners' Journal. The accounts and details are thorough and portray a group of brave men from Schuylkill County, Pennsylvania, dedicated to patriotism and forever abolished human slavery from our borders.[113]

Gould's account of the 48th PA regiment at South Mountain confounded the story of the regiment in the battle:

> After passing Middletown, the army proceeded up the road leading to Fox's Pass. When near the top of the mountain, we turned from the road by the left into a field of growing corn. We advanced in line of battle, in and through a wood, until we reached a low rail fence. Here we became the brigade's right and soon exchanged volleys with the enemy and exhausted our forty rounds of ammunition. Our loss was light, owing to our protected position. The enemy retreated sometime during the night. In passing over the ground the following day, we found that the lane immediately in our front was full of the dead Rebels. They lay, actually two and three deep. One fellow hung upon the fence opposite, an arm and leg on either side, literally riddled with bullets. Another sat in a log house nearby with his eye to a chink between the logs. A bullet through his head. A detail was made to bury the dead, as the hot weather made the bodies unfit to handle in a few hours. Trenches were dug along the side of the hill bordering the road. The earth pulled down upon the bodies after they had been laid therein. A well close to the house was filled with the bodies of those that lay in the lane in front of our line. At Sharpsburg, Md., in 1895, the writer was informed by an eyewitness that forty bodies were taken out of the well and carried south for burial.[114]

Because the 48th PA arrived after Drayton's Brigade suffered a tremendous loss near Miller's Field and the Wise Cabin, Union forces already controlled the Ridge Road south of Fox's Gap. The 48th PA did not take a position along Ridge Road, as Gould seems to indicate.

Gould's account appears to be a compilation of various reports from the battle. Gould's descendant told us that Gould "accessed many sources." Gould did not describe the story of the 48th PA in the struggle from his own words or experience. If the Company B skirmishers advanced from where Gould placed the 48th PA, they would have advanced west of Ridge Road and south of Old Sharpsburg Road and not have found any Confederates led by the Rebel Flag advancing towards them. The only low rail fence west of Ridge Road was near Cox's Intersection. Gould's account does not match the reports of Wren, Bosbyshell, and Pleasants.

Nothing in the accounts of Walcott or Gould refutes the words of Hood, Ripley, Thruston, Coles, Whitman, and Cox. Captain Wren's stone wall and "X crossroads" provides all the physical evidence necessary to place Wren and Hood's advance a half-mile west of Fox's Gap at Cox's Intersection.

One final author, Brit Kimberly Erslev, stated in his PhD dissertation the following:

> Two more brigades under the command of Brigadier General John Bell Hood arrived from Longstreet to help hold the ridge and Sharpsburg roads. By nightfall, Union troops held Fox's Gap but failed to seize the roads descending into Pleasant Valley.[115]

Part of Union Captain Wren's stone wall, July 11, 2022. Perhaps 100 feet west from Park Hall Road. (Photograph by Curtis Older)

Erslev cited in his Footnote 24 the following support for his conclusion about the battle at Fox's Gap: Report of Cox, September 20, 1862, *OR*, 19 (1): 459–460; Report of Hood, September 27, 1862, *OR*, 19 (1):922; Report of Hill, 1862, *OR*, 19 (1): 1020–1021. Perhaps others mistakenly reached the same conclusion as Erslev after reading the above reports.

Conclusions—Hood's Advance

1. Confederate Major General Longstreet confided his thoughts riding up the mountain to Turner's Gap that "everything was so disjointed that it would be impossible for my troops and Hill's to hold the mountain against such forces as McClellan had there."

I agree with Longstreet's assessment based on the material in the preceding chapters. However, Hill thought he should have been left in charge since he knew the geography of the battlefield better than Longstreet.

2. The Confederates' defensive posture or geographical location at Turner's Gap provided them with a solid defensive military position.

Hill 1500 and the mountain peak at the Washington Monument, connected by a crest that ran between the two, provided the Confederates with a military stronghold to the north of the Old National Pike. Cox's Hill #1 and Hill #2, connected by the Crest of the Heights on Moser Road, offered the Confederates a stronghold to the south of the Old National Pike. The area east of Turner's Gap, which included Hill 1280 and Wood Road, provided the Confederates with a solid military location. The negative aspect of the Confederate site at Turner's Gap was that the only escape route was to the west through Zittlestown gorge if Moser Road were unavailable.

3. Confederate Brigadier General Hood's account in his book, *Advance and Retreat*, regarding the movement to the south from Turner's Gap by his two brigades, included the following points:

a. Major Fairfax of Longstreet's staff informed Hood of the need for him to move to the south with two brigades due to Confederate troops on that part of the battlefield driven back.

b. Fairfax indicated to Hood that he was unfamiliar with any route by which to move south.

c. Hood conducted his troops obliquely by the right flank as they advanced south.

d. Hood could hear the Federals' shouts as they swept down the mountain on his side.

e. Hood bore more obliquely to the right.

f. Hood intended to get as far as possible towards the Federals' left flank before contact.

g. Hood identified "heavy Federal lines."

h. Hood described the Federals cheering over their success and possession of Confederate dead and wounded.

i. When the Federals came within 75 to 100 yards, Hood ordered his men to charge.

j. The Federals were driven back beyond the mountain faster than they descended.

k. The night ended with both Confederate and Federal dead in Hood's possession.

l. The mountain on the right (west) was within Hood's lines.

m. Hood aligned his troops and rode his horse to the Mountain House at about 10:00 pm.

n. At the Mountain House, Hood learned that the Federals were nearby.

o. After a discussion with Lee in Boonsboro, the Confederate command decided to fall back to Sharpsburg.

p. In Hood's after-action report on September 27, some of Drayton's Brigade coming out met with Hood and indicated the Union troops at Miller's Field outflanked them.

q. Hood's men drove the Federals and regained all the Confederate lost ground.

r. Lieutenant Colonel McLemore fell mortally wounded in the engagement.

4. I concluded the following from my review of Hood's book and after-action report and additional evidence:

a. There was no indication Major Fairfax directed Hood to Wood Road.

b. There was no indication Longstreet ordered Hood to do any specific action on the Fox's Gap battlefield.

c. Wood Road led southeast from its intersection with Old National Pike.

d. Using Wood Road, it would have been difficult for the Confederates under Hood to form a line of battle as they approached Miller's Field.

e. The wood and undergrowth were dense, and a pig path led south for Hood.

f. There was evidence that Bondurant's artillery used Wood Road, and that road was thus not a pig path.

g. Union troops came down the mountain on Hood's side. The best interpretation was that the Union troops were on the west face of the East Ridge.

h. Hood continued to move to the southwest.

i. Hood intended to attack the Union left or west flank.

j. There was no indication from Hood that his meeting with some of Drayton's men led to his understanding that he was to retake Miller's Field.

k. The amount of moonlight available on the night of September 14, 1862, was adequate to provide a limited ability to see the movement of individual soldiers over a short distance.

5. Union Captain Bolton indicated Durell's Union battery advanced to the crest of the East Ridge before 6:30 pm after the Confederates removed their artillery from the Fox's Gap battlefield.

Union artillery and infantry near Miller's and Wise's Fields were very substantial soon after Drayton's defeat at Fox's Gap.

6. There was no reason to believe any Confederate artillery accompanied Confederate Brigadier General Hood's advance south.

Major Frobel's report did not signal participation in the Battle of South Mountain by Hood's artillery. Hood's movement through woods prohibited the accompaniment by cannon.

7. Confederate Brigadier General Hood's account of the beginning of the battle for his troops was similar to Union Captain Wren's version.

Major General Hill indicated that Hood's skirmishers drove back the Yankees.

8. There was every indication Confederate Brigadier General Hood's men drove the Federals back over the West Ridge of South Mountain rather than the East Ridge.

Hood's men possessed the West Ridge of South Mountain at the end of the battle rather than the East Ridge.

9. Based on the steep terrain along the east side of the East Ridge, Confederate Colonel G. T. Anderson's men were not east of Wood Road.

The East Ridge crest was about 1,000 feet above sea level, while Fox Gap Road was about 700 feet above sea level. Humans could not stand up beyond 60 feet east of Wood Road without holding on to a tree.

10. Confederate Brigadier General Hood did not mention a road during his movement, but Confederate Brigadier General Ripley indicated he witnessed Hood's advance south along a road.

Ripley's report was one of the most confirming primary evidence sources of Hood's location on his movement south.

11. Union Captain Wren witnessed the approach of the Rebel flag and stated his Union battle line was three deep.

There was every reason to believe Captain Wren was near the location of Hood's advance. Wren's regiment was along Park Hall Road, as evidenced by his mention of a stone fence and "X" crossroads.

12. Confederate usage of Cut Road or Fox Trail was unknown.

Cut Road and Fox Trail were part of the Fox's Gap battlefield. I could not determine the use of either of these routes by the Confederates.

13. Confederate Major General Longstreet identified Hood's route of movement south as "through woodlands and over boulders, returning then up the mountain."

Longstreet's description of Hood's movement south coincided with that of Hood. However, Longstreet stated that Hood returned "up the mountain," an apparent reference to Moser Road. To move at "double time," as indicated by Longstreet, required a clear path, similar to Moser Road.

14. Confederate Major General Longstreet confirmed that Hood's two brigades were "thinned to skeletons of three or four hundred men to a brigade when they reached the Mountain House."

Hood's two brigades perhaps consisted of 2,000 men as they moved south from Turner's Gap. Upon their return, Longstreet implied Union troops significantly diminished Hood's troop strength in the attack at Cox's Intersection.

15. Neither Confederate Major General Longstreet nor Major General Hill made any statement regarding Brigadier General Hood regaining any lost ground.

The Union troops at Cox's Intersection did not control any ground north of Old Sharpsburg Road nor west of Park Hall Road other than within the range of their rifles. Hood's men did not recapture any lost ground near Cox's Intersection.

16. In Maryland, Confederate troops existed on green corn and green apples.

Many Confederate soldiers lacked shoes and adequate clothing as well as food. Confederate soldiers Shotwell, Longstreet, and Patterson, as well as Union soldiers Rice and Lord, supported this analysis.

17. Confederate Private John W. Stevens of the 5th Texas testified he was at a fence corner on the side of the mountain beyond open ground and about 100 yards beyond a line of Federal troops.

Lambert's Field was the likely location for Stevens, who would have viewed Federal troops along or near Old Sharpsburg Road.

18. Confederate Chaplain George G. Smith stated that the Federals' caution and the cover of the night saved the Confederate Army.

Chaplain Smith gave no credit to Hood's two brigades for saving the Confederate Army at South Mountain.

19. The Twenty-Third North Carolina Regimental History stated that Charles W. Bennett, Orderly Sergeant of Company E, killed Reno from a long distance.

It made sense that the Confederate side knew who shot Reno.

20. Confederate Lieutenant Robert Coles Jr. of the 4th AL described some significant points about his advance south with Hood's two brigades.
a. His men departed Old National Pike through an orchard.
b. Coles met some of Drayton's men at the orchard adjacent to the Mountain House at Old National Pike.
c. He moved farther to the right or west to meet the advancing Federals.
d. His 4th AL moved to a sunken road that "ran obliquely across the gap."
e. The 2nd MS was west of the 4th AL in the Old Sharpsburg Road on the west side of Cox's Intersection.

e. Lieutenant Colonel McLemore of the 4th AL climbed a fence adjacent to the sunken road and was shot.

f. A Union soldier sent for refilling several canteens was captured by Confederates of the 2nd MS near Lieutenant Coles's location in Old Sharpsburg Road.

g. Coles stated, "as the men were awakened, they went quietly one at a time down to the main road, which led to Sharpsburg."

h. Coles's account strengthened the assertion that Drayton's men fell back to the northwest from the Old Sharpsburg Road, and some soon reached the orchard on the east side of the Mountain House.

21. The only place for the capture of the Union soldier sent for refilling canteens was near Dog Creek and Cox's Intersection.

Dog Creek was the only water supply source west of the East Ridge on the Fox's Gap battlefield. Union troops were near Cox's Intersection, as were the 4th AL and 2nd MS troops.

22. Confederate Brigadier General Hood's horse could only cross from the east side to the west side of the East Ridge just before a large boulder field about a quarter-mile south of the Mountain House.

Ted Ellis, a local authority with knowledge about the area's geography, inspected the ground along the East Ridge and determined, in his opinion, that this location was the only place to cross over the East Ridge coming south from Old National Pike.

23. Antietam historian and author Ezra Carman gave no definitive retreat route for the Confederate troops he placed near Fox's Gap.

At the end of the battle, Carman placed many Confederate troops along or near Old Sharpsburg Road. He did not attempt to identify Moser Road. However, Moser Road did not have an assigned name at the time of the battle.

24. Ezra Carman, Antietam historian, placed Drayton's Brigade on Old Sharpsburg Road near the foot of Fox's Gap at Cox's Intersection.

This location for Drayton's Brigade would have been impossible because Sturgis's and Cox's Divisions occupied the Old Sharpsburg Road between Fox's Gap and Cox's Intersection. Carman's use of the term "by-roads" lacked specificity.

25. Confederate Major Thruston stated that Brigadier General Ripley's Brigade rested along the Crest of the Heights on Moser Road between 9:00 pm and 11:00 pm within 200 yards of Federal troops.

Thruston's statement indicated how close the Federals were to blocking the Confederate retreat route through Zittlestown gorge on September 14.

26. None of Confederate Brigadier General Hood's men killed Reno.

Confederate accounts stated the name of the soldier and his regiment, while Union versions, for the most part, were all over the place. Hood's men did not approach Fox's Gap, and one of them did not kill Reno.

27. Confederate Brigadier General Ripley indicated his brigade was in an area of "noisy but comparatively harmless fire."

Ripley's statement was parallel to that of Brigadier General Hood as Hood approached Turner's Gap about 4:00 pm.

28. Confederate Brigadier General Ripley and Union Brigadier General Cox gave a similar opinion regarding the battle's end near Fox's Gap.

Ripley indicated that Hood's men pressed down Moser Road and the Federals occupied their first position, believed to be Cox's Intersection. Brigadier General Cox stated, "on the left [west], Longstreet's men were pushed down the mountainside beyond the Rohrersville and Sharpsburg Roads (Cox's Intersection), and the contest there was ended." The statements of Ripley and Cox both put the end of the engagement at Cox's Intersection.

29. Primary source evidence to substantiate Confederate Brigadier General Hood's two brigades' attack near Miller's Field at Fox's Gap did not exist.

I have found no credible primary source evidence to support the claim that Hood's two brigades were near Miller's Field or the Wise Cabin. For the most part, the accounts of Charles F. Walcott, the author of *The History of the Twenty-first Regiment, Massachusetts Volunteers,* and Joseph Gould, the author of *The Story of the Forty-eighth: A Record of the Campaigns of the Forty-eighth Regiment Pennsylvania Veteran Volunteer Infantry,* cannot be considered primary source evidence. Ezra Carman, an Antietam historian, was himself not a primary source of evidence.

30. The most likely route of Confederate Brigadier General Hood had him crossing the East Ridge just before a large boulder field.

Upon walking the mountain crest along the East Ridge of South Mountain, Ted Ellis believed Hood's horse, Jeff Davis, and Hood and his men crossed the East Ridge just before the large boulder field about a quarter-mile south of the Mountain House between the East Ridge crest and Wood Road.

31. Previously, all authors significantly understated Confederate casualties on the Fox's Gap battlefield. Ezra Carman, an Antietam historian, gave the Union loss at Fox's Gap as a total of 889 killed and wounded and the Confederate loss as "about 600."

Some Confederate dead near Cox's Intersection could have been men from G. B. Anderson's Brigade or Rosser's 5th VA Cavalry and Pelham's artillery. Some Confederate dead on the Fox's Gap battlefield had joined the Rebel Army within the past few days before the battle. I conclude that missing records in fold3.com, a website that provides access to military records, made it impossible to reconstruct Hood's casualties. The numbers reported of dead Confederates near Cox's Intersection by Union Captain Wren, Union Lieutenant Whitman, and Union Lieutenant Pollock greatly exceeded the numbers given by Ezra Carman.

The *History of the Sixth New Hampshire Regiment* claimed 2,500 Confederate dead and wounded at South Mountain. Ezra Carman reported 248 Confederate killed and 1,013 injured at Fox's and Turner's Gaps.

I estimate the Confederate dead in Garland's Brigade as 100 and 250 wounded. Kurt Graham's numbers for Drayton's Brigade was 206 dead and 227 wounded, while in Hood's two Brigades, I estimate 200 dead and 400 wounded. Recent Maryland recruits possibly were 20 dead and 40 wounded. G. B. Anderson's Brigade, possibly 30 killed and 60 wounded. Private Holahan reported dead Confederates "all the way down the mountain in the woods and at the roadside" along Old Sharpsburg Road, as did Brigadier General Cox.

I estimate the Confederate dead or mortally wounded on the Fox's Gap battlefield as about 500.[116] I estimate the number of Confederate injured on the Fox's Gap Battlefield as 900 to 1,000. Total Confederate killed and wounded at Fox's Gap totaled between 1,400 and 1,500. According to Carman, the Kanawha Division captured 600 Rebels, some of whom were injured.

The Confederates at Turner's Gap could not march to Sharpsburg by way of Old Sharpsburg Road because the Union Ninth Corps defended the Moser Road and Old Sharpsburg Road intersection, i.e., Cox's Intersection. The only retreat route for the Confederates was along Old National Pike to Boonsboro through Zittlestown gorge.

Using primary source evidence obtained from the participants in the events, I conclude that Union Brigadier General Jacob D. Cox's statement was correct:

> On the left [west], Longstreet's men were pushed down the mountainside beyond the Rohrersville [Moser and Park Hall Roads] and Sharpsburg Roads, and the contest ended. The enemy still held the two hills between the latter route and the turnpike, and the further one could not be reached until the Mountain House was in our hands.[117]

The following was the opinion of Ted Ellis regarding the movement of Hood's two brigades:

> All the primary source documentary evidence presented and examined in this investigation came from the theory proposed by Curtis Older. I did not research the battle myself. I merely investigated the plausibility of the evidence against the physical evidence still in existence at South Mountain. I studied the tactical possibility of military decisions that resulted in the movements theorized by Curtis Older.
>
> To that end, I found the theory plausible. I find it the most likely scenario of the events surrounding Fox's Gap late in the day, September 14, 1862. This conclusion became more evident by the on-site examination of the land features of the battlefield.
>
> From a pure common-sense reading of the primary source record and after personal inspection, I find it difficult not to believe Curtis Older's explanation of Hood's actions.[118]

CHAPTER FIVE

The Confederate Dilemma at Turner's Gap

The previous review of the Fox's Gap battlefield events revealed at least two sobering thoughts regarding the Confederates at Turner's Gap on September 14. First, Brigadier General John Bell Hood disclosed the Federals were in a nearby cornfield when he arrived at the Mountain House at about 10:00 pm. Others at the Mountain House told Hood to "Pshe—Pshe" upon his arrival and inquiry about the situation on the Confederate left. Upon learning that the Federals had pushed the Confederates back, Hood immediately suggested that he, Hill, and perhaps others should ride to Boonsboro and meet with General Lee. When Hood and other officers arrived in Boonsboro at Lee's Headquarters, they found Lee meeting with Major General Longstreet.

Randolph A. Shotwell, a Rebel soldier, described the meeting of the Confederate command in Boonsboro on the evening of the 14th.[1] Turning to D. H. Hill, the General merely asked: "Can you hold out another day?" "Not another hour—if pressed by the full weight of troops that the enemy now has upon my flanks." "McClellan," continued General Hill, "has 20,000, or more, men on each of our flanks; he is now on an equality with us, as regards position; and if he tonight shall mass his forces at any given point, he will break our lines and ruin us to a certainty."

Confederate Major Thruston of the 3rd NC told us that Ripley's Brigade fell back to Old Sharpsburg Road and moved "up the mountain by the steep and narrow road." The steep and narrow road was Moser Road. The 3rd NC rested at the Crest of the Heights on Moser Road and near the intersection with Old National Pike. Thruston also told us:

> About 9:00 pm, we rested in this position within 200 yards of the enemy until about 11:00 pm, when we took the road to Sharpsburg.[2]

The Federals were within 200 yards of Old National Pike and near Thruston's men, who were just south of Old National Pike along Moser Road between 9:00 pm and 11:00 pm.

In the fight for Turner's Gap, John M. Priest described numerous Pennsylvania infantry units attacking the Confederates about a half-mile north of Daniel Rent's farm en route to the capture of D. Scott Hartwig's Hill 1500.[3] The loss of Hill 1500 meant the Union forces had outflanked the Confederates at Turner's Gap and that the Federals could now advance south towards Old National Pike. Thruston confirmed that Union troops were 200 yards north of his location between 9:00 pm and 11:00 pm along Moser Road, just south of Old National Pike.

Union Brigadier General Truman Seymour, Brigadier General George G. Meade's Division, 1st Brigade, informed us that not only did the Confederates retreat from Hill 1500, but those sent to reinforce that crucial point turned back before reaching the battle. The Confederates, in effect, conceded Zittlestown Road.

According to Hartwig:

> As the Southern soldiers stumbled down the mountain to the gap above them, exultant Union troops celebrated their capture of Hill 1500 with cheers that "rolled down the mountainside."[4]
>
> His men [Meade's] drove their attack home with great determination until they had captured the position [Hill 1500] that D. H. Hill affirmed was "everything to the Yankees."[5]

Hill 1500, the location Union troops captured during the battle in the early evening, was about three-quarters of a mile directly north of the Mountain House and not far from today's intersection of Washington Monument and Zittlestown roads. According to the *Atlas Map*, Zittlestown Road met Old National Pike one half-mile west of the Mountain House. Today, Zittlestown Road still appears to meet Old National Pike at that exact location.

The threat of Union troops taking up positions near the Old National Pike and Moser Road intersection the night of September 14 was an intriguing subject and one that deserves additional research. I did not research or study the battle at Turner's Gap to any degree. I relied on the reports of Confederate Brigadier General Hood, Confederate Major Thruston, Union Major General McClellan, Union Brigadier General Meade, and Union Brigadier General Seymour related to that aspect of the struggle.

The Confederate escape route to Boonsboro was west along Old National Pike through Zittlestown gorge. Union forces under Meade and Seymour captured Hill 1500 about dark. McClellan reported that:

> General Meade speaks highly of General Seymour's skill in handling his brigade on the extreme right, securing by his maneuvers the great object of the movement—the outflanking of the enemy.[6]

Additional research might confirm Thruston's statement that the Federals advanced south from Hill 1500 and took up positions about 200 yards north of the Moser Road and Old National Pike intersection. Such an advance by the Federals would make sense if the Confederates withdrew back to Old National Pike and conceded the area.

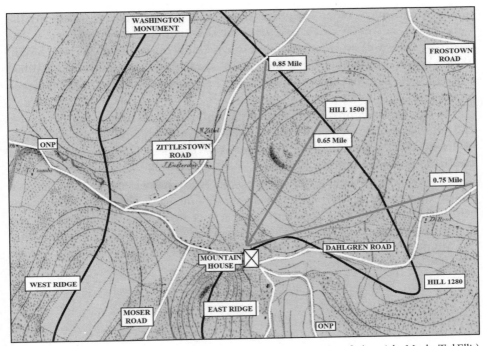

Map 39: Distances from the Mountain House, September 14, 1862. (Identified on *Atlas Map* by Ted Ellis)

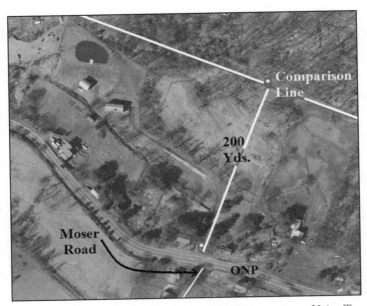

Map 40: Major Thruston's Estimate of 200 Yards. Moser Road Intersection to Union Troops. "Merlin" image c.2017. (Map by Ted Ellis)

The statements of Hood and Thruston are two primary sources that testify the Confederates at Turner's Gap were hard-pressed the night of September 14. The reports of Thruston and Hood gave no reason to doubt the words of Chaplain Smith. There also can be no doubt that the Union advance and attack at Fox's Gap had as its ultimate objective a flank attack along Moser Road to cut off a Confederate retreat from Turner's Gap.

The Confederates probably were near collapse on the night of September 14. They did have many cannon at Turner's Gap and probably on Hill #1 with which to defend themselves. However, the statements of various Confederates indicated they faced possible surrender.

The single escape route for the Confederate Army was west along Old National Pike to Boonsboro through Zittlestown gorge. At the battle's end, the Ninth Corps held Cox's Intersection to the south along Moser Road, and the First Corps was near the Mountain House and the Moser Road and Old National Pike intersection. The Confederate Army was very fortunate to successfully depart Turner's Gap on the night of September 14.

CHAPTER SIX

After South Mountain

I include the following remarks by Major General Burnside and General Lee regarding the Battle of South Mountain.

In his after-battle report of September 30, Burnside told us:

> At the same time, I detached from his [Hooker's First] corps General Gibbon's brigade, with Captain Campbell's battery, to demonstrate upon the enemy's center, up the main pike, as soon as the movements of Generals Hooker and Reno had sufficiently progressed. At the same time, I sent orders to General Reno, whose corps had been sharply engaged all the morning, to move upon the enemy's position with his whole force as soon as I informed him that General Hooker was well advanced up the crest of the mountain on the right.
>
> The general commanding [McClellan] arrived on the ground, and I repeated to him my dispositions, which he thoroughly approved. He remained at my headquarters during the remainder of the engagement, and I reported to him personally all the orders I gave from that time.
>
> The orders given to both Generals Hooker and Reno were most skillfully and successfully executed. General Gibbon was ordered forward just before sunset and succeeded in pushing his command up the main road within a short distance of the main pass's crest. During that movement, he had a brilliant engagement after nightfall, our forces gradually driving the enemy before them.
>
> At this time, say 8:00 pm, the enemy had been driven from their strong positions. The firing ceased, except upon our extreme left, where General Reno's division, then under General Cox's command (General Reno having been killed about 7:00 pm), were partially engaged till 10:00 pm.
>
> Having been engaged for a greater part of the day upon the mountain's crests without water and many without food, my command was very much exhausted. Nevertheless, they maintained their positions and were ready the following morning for an advance on the enemy, who had retreated in the direction of Sharpsburg during the night.
>
> A topographical survey is being made, which will show the country's nature and troops' disposition. I feel sure that history will demonstrate this to have been one of the many brilliant engagements of the war.[1]

Even before learning of the setback at Crampton's Gap, Lee decided not to risk another battle north of the Potomac.[2] On September 14, Lee issued his first order to retreat since assuming command of the Army of Northern Virginia. At 8:00 pm, Lee dictated the following dispatch to Major General McLaws near Harpers Ferry and sent it off at once by courier:

Headquarters Army of Northern Virginia
September 14th, 1862—8:00 pm
Major-General McLaws

Commanding, &c.:

General: The day has gone against us, and this army will go by Sharpsburg and cross the river. It is necessary for you to abandon your position tonight. Send your trains not required on the road to cross the river. Your troops you must have well in hand to unite with this command, which will retire by Sharpsburg. Send forward officers to explore the way, ascertain the best crossing of the Potomac, and if you can find any between you and Shepherdstown, leave the Shepherdstown Ford for this command. Send an officer to report to me on the Sharpsburg Road, where you are, and what crossing you will take. You will, of course, bring Anderson's division with you.[3]

I am, sir, respectfully, your obedient servant,
R. H. Chilton
Assistant Adjutant-General

Then the pendulum swung back. A dispatch from Jackson suddenly brightened the dull prospect of confessing the Maryland expedition a failure.[4] Fresh orders went out to McLaws: he was now to make his best effort to join the army north of the Potomac, at Sharpsburg, whether he had to detour back into Virginia or even find a way across Maryland Heights, to do so. Hill and Longstreet would continue toward Sharpsburg.[5]

On September 17, 1862, the Battle of Antietam became the bloodiest single day in American History. However, the Battle of South Mountain was a truly significant battle. The Confederate Army probably suffered half the number of killed and wounded at South Mountain as it did at Antietam. It certainly did with the inclusion of the Battle at Crampton's Gap.

Some of the misunderstanding of the Battle of South Mountain may fall on various accounts. I must point out that, in his attempt to gain the leadership position in the Army of the Potomac, Major General Hooker, in his report of November 17, 1862, made numerous false and scandalous statements about the Ninth Corps at the Battle of South Mountain.[6] Major General Burnside rebuked Hooker on this account in his report on January 20, 1863.[7] Jacob Dolson Cox learned of Hooker's slanderous report 25 years after the battle.[8]

Reno Monument at Fox's Gap. (Photograph by John Gensor, 2015)

Afterword

He remarked that he had made a vow, a covenant, that if God gave us the victory in the approaching battle, he would consider it an indication of Divine will.[1]

GIDEON WELLES
SECRETARY OF THE NAVY
SEPTEMBER 22, 1862

In the fall of 1862, the Indiana Conference of Wesleyan Methodists requested that its president, Reverend Daniel Worth, address a letter to the president of the United States. Rev. Worth composed the following message, recorded by Aaron Worth, secretary of the Conference.[2]

To his Excellency Abraham Lincoln,

President of the United States of America
Honored Sir:
The Indiana Conference of the Wesleyan Methodists, composed of Ministers and laymen, assembled at Economy, Wayne Co., on September 12, 1862, ordered their president and secretary to address the following epistle to your Excellency. As lovers of our common country, we assure our chief magistrate that we offer our most earnest prayers to Almighty God, that he may be endowed with all wisdom and grace to guide public affairs, as that the Divine blessing may rest upon him and the nation at large.

But to secure the benedictions of Heaven and end the rebellion that is now wickedly raging, allow us to express our firm convictions in all frankness. The confiscation act should be faithfully executed. Freedom should be proclaimed "throughout the land, unto all the inhabitants thereof." And we entertain the firm belief that not only would your Excellency be sustained by the nation, in thus carrying into practical and immediate effect the command of God in giving freedom to the enslaved. But since the nation has become so fully enlightened on the enormity of slavery, we entertain grave fears that no peace can be enjoyed again until this long-delayed act of justice and mercy shall be performed.

We also implore your Excellency to interpose your authority and remove from all commands all officers in our army, who are addicted to habits of intemperance, and the shocking vice of profanity.

We have sent our sons to the field at your and our Country's call, and it seems too dreadful for us to endure that they should be led, not to victory under skillful and God-fearing commanders, but to useless defeat and death, by drunken officers.

As patriots and fathers, as Christians who do not cease to pray for your success in rightly conducting the affairs of this nation, we beg your favorable attention to these points here made.

We are honored sir, your loyal fellow citizens.

D. Worth president
A. Worth secretary

President Lincoln met with Reverends William W. Patton and John Dempster at the White House on September 13, 1862. They presented the president with a memorial in favor of national emancipation:

> The subject presented in the memorial is one upon which I have thought much for weeks past, and I may even say for months. I hope it will not be irreverent for me to say that if it is probable that God would reveal his will to others, on a point so connected with my duty, it might be supposed he would reveal it directly to me. Unless I am more deceived in myself than I often am, it is my earnest desire to know the will of Providence in this matter. And if I can learn what it is, I will do it! These are not, however, the days of miracles, and I suppose it will be granted that I am not to expect a direct revelation. I must study the plain physical facts of the case, ascertain what is possible and learn what appears to be wise and right. The subject is difficult, and good men do not agree. I admit that slavery is the root of the rebellion, or at least its sine qua non. There are fifty thousand bayonets in the Union armies from the Border Slave States. It would be a serious matter if, in consequence of a proclamation such as you desire, they should go over to the Rebels. I have not decided against a proclamation of liberty to the slaves but hold the matter under advisement. And I can assure you that the subject is on my mind, by day and night, more than any other. Whatever shall appear to be God's will, I will do.[3]

Reverend Daniel Worth, in perhaps 1855. Noble J. Tolbert, "Daniel Worth: Tar Heel Abolitionist." (*North Carolina Historical Review* 39 (July 1962): 285)

On September 14, a church in La Moille, Bureau County, Illinois, addressed a letter to Abraham Lincoln as a Memorial and Resolution recommending emancipation.[4]

Did other Northern churches in early September 1862 request Lincoln to free the enslaved people? The answer to that question is unknown to me. However, after Lincoln's meeting at the White House with Reverends William W. Patton and John Dempster on September 13, a fast-approaching battle between the

Union Sergeant William McKinley. (Courtesy Ohio History Connection)

Confederate Army of Northern Virginia and the United States Army of the Potomac was about to begin approximately 55 miles to the northwest.

United States Major General George B. McClellan's Headquarters were between the Fox Inn and Old National Pike.[5] On the evening of the 14th, he telegraphed the following to the General in Chief of the Armies of the United States, Major General Henry W. Halleck:

> Headquarters Army of the Potomac, three miles beyond Middletown, September 14, 9:40 pm.
> To Major General H. W. Halleck:
> After a very severe engagement, the Corps of Hooker and Reno carried the heights commanding the Hagerstown Road.
> The troops behaved magnificently! They never fought better.
> General Franklin has been hotly engaged on the extreme left. I do not yet know with what result, except that the firing indicates progress on his part.
> The action continued until after dark and terminated, leaving us in possession of the entire crest!
> It has been a glorious victory!
> I cannot tell whether the enemy will retreat during the night or appear in increased force in the morning.
> I regret to add that the gallant and able General Reno is killed.
> G. B. McClellan. Major General[6]

At 9:30 am Monday, September 15, at Bolivar, Maryland, McClellan sent a telegraph to Washington, D.C., for Halleck and President Lincoln that contained the following, in part:

> **God has seldom given an army a greater victory than this.**[7]

President Lincoln informed Colonel Jesse K. Dubois in Springfield, Illinois, at 3:00 pm September 15, 1862, of his analysis of the military situation in Maryland:

> I now consider it safe to say that General McClellan has gained a great victory over the great rebel army in Maryland between Fredericktown and Hagerstown. He is now pursuing the flying foe.[8]

Colonel Dubois forwarded Lincoln's message to Illinois Governor Richard Yates, who responded to the president:

> Your dispatch to Col. Dubois has filled our people with the wildest joy. Salutes are being fired & our citizens are relieved from a fearful state of suspense. We thank you for the welcome news.[9]

After the Battle of South Mountain, the roads through Fox's and Turner's Gaps led the Confederate and Union Armies to the banks of Antietam Creek and the village of Sharpsburg. September 17, 1862, became the single bloodiest day in American history.

Major General McClellan wrote Halleck at 1:00 pm on September 17:

> We are in the most terrible battle of the war, perhaps in history. Thus far, it looks well, but I have great odds against me. Hurry up all troops possible. Our loss has been terrific. I hope that God will give us a glorious victory.[10]

Gideon Welles, the Secretary of the Navy, recorded the following notes at the Cabinet meeting held by President Lincoln on September 22, 1862:

> In the course of the discussion on this paper (Emancipation Proclamation), which was long, earnest, and, on the general principle involved, harmonious, he remarked that he had made a vow, a covenant. If God gave us victory in the approaching battle, he would consider it an indication of Divine will and that it was his duty to move forward in the cause of emancipation. It might be thought strange, he said, that he had in this way submitted the disposal of matters when the way was not clear to his mind what he should do. God had decided this question in favor of the slaves. He was satisfied it was right, was confirmed, and strengthened in his action by the vow and the results. His mind was fixed, his decision made, but he wished his paper announcing his course as correct in terms as it could be made without any change in his determination.[11]

President Abraham Lincoln issued his Preliminary Emancipation Proclamation on September 22, 1862, due to the Union victories in the Battles of South Mountain and Antietam, known as Boonsboro and Sharpsburg in the South, on September 14 and 17, 1862. His proclamation included the following:

> That on January 1, in the year of our Lord one thousand eight hundred and sixty-three, all persons held as slaves within any State or designated part of a State, the people whereof shall then be in rebellion against the United States, shall be then, thenceforward, and forever free.[12]

On the evening of September 24, President Lincoln appeared before his fellow citizens outside the White House to acknowledge their support for issuing his Preliminary Emancipation Proclamation.

> On the 14th and 17th days of the present month, there have been battles bravely, skillfully, and successfully fought. We do not yet know the particulars. Let us be sure that in giving praise to particular individuals, we do no injustice to others. I only ask you, after these few remarks, to give three hearty cheers to all good and brave officers and men who fought those successful battles.[13]

President Lincoln visited the various battlefields that were part of the Maryland Campaign during the first five days of October 1862. Major General McClellan accompanied Lincoln in his review of the battlefields of Antietam and South Mountain. Lincoln departed from the fields at South Mountain and returned to Washington, D.C.[14] Lincoln undeniably visited Fox's Gap.

Abraham Lincoln.

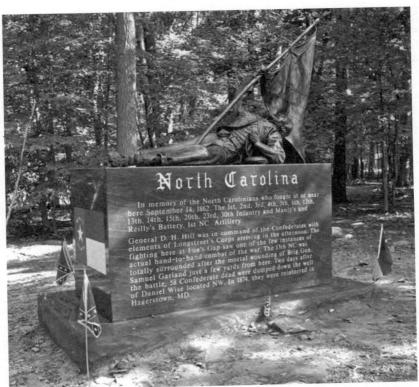

North Carolina South Mountain Memorial. (Photograph by Curtis Older, September 14, 2012)

Allan Powell, Curtis Older, and Doug Bast. (September 14, 2012, Photograph by Mrs. Powell)

Alexander Gardner, a Civil War photographer, confirmed Lincoln's visit to Antietam and South Mountain. Gardner tells us of the president's deep interest in the battles that were fought. Lincoln then proceeded to Frederick and reached Washington, D.C. by special train about 10:00 pm on October 5.[15]

In conclusion, my chief desire was that the battle for Fox's Gap on September 14, 1862, be set in the most accurate light possible. My sincere hope is that the information provided herewith will clarify the events of that momentous day in American history.

Battlefield Features and Locations

Addition to Friendship

A 202-acre tract of land surveyed for Frederick Fox and patented by him in 1805.[1] Approximately 105 acres of the Addition to Friendship tract were near the east side of Turner's Gap. Eighty-five acres of the parcel were near the southeast side of Fox's Gap along Old Sharpsburg Road, and 12 acres were along Wood Road, connecting the two more significant segments.

Much of the Battle of South Mountain took place on this parcel. The Reno Monument stands on this land.[2] This tract was contiguous to the Flonham tract at Turner's Gap.[3] The Addition to Friendship tract was adjacent to the north side of the David's Will tract.[4] The David's Will tract's south side bordered the Loop Road.

Refer to Map 4. The Addition to Friendship, Flonham, and Miller's Field tracts overlay the battlefield map.

Addition to Friendship Woods

The 10-acre densely wooded area was part of Addition to Friendship adjacent to the east and south sides of Wise's Field at the time of the battle. Union Brigadier General Jacob D. Cox showed the area just east of the Addition to Friendship Woods at an elevation of 1,000 feet on his Battlefield of South Mountain map in his *Military Reminiscences*.[5]

Atlas Map

The Map of the Battlefield of South Mountain was included in the *Atlas to Accompany the Official Records*.[6]

Cox's Intersection

I gave this name to the intersection of Moser Road, Park Hall Road, and Old Sharpsburg Road, about half a mile west of Fox's Gap.

Crest of the Heights—Moser Road

The crest was on Moser Road between the peaks of Hill #1 on the West Ridge of South Mountain and Hill #2 on the East Ridge of South Mountain. Confederate Brigadier General Roswell S. Ripley used this term in his September 21, 1862, report.[7] Ted Ellis estimated the crest along Moser Road at approximately 1,120 to 1,130 feet, and the distance from the Mountain House to the Crest of the Heights on Moser Road was 1,500 to 1,600 feet. Ted estimated the distance between Hill #1 and Hill #2 as about one half-mile.

Crest of the Heights—Zittlestown Road

The highest point on Zittlestown Road is between Hartwig's Hill 1500 and the Washington Monument.

Cut Road

(Road Cut Through the Woods by the Confederates.) As shown on the *Atlas Map*, this route connected Miller's Field at Fox's Gap to the Crest of the Heights on Moser Road. The Cut Road also ran near the Saddle of the East Ridge just northwest of Miller's Field. The road was significant because it connected those as mentioned above three high elevation areas.

Ted Ellis and I believe the "Road Cut Through the Woods by the Confederates" existed before the battle and was not created by the Confederates. Cut Road followed a terrace of relatively level ground along the west side of the East Ridge.

David's Will

David Bowser obtained the survey for the 49-acre tract of land.[8] The Addition to Friendship tract was adjacent to the north and east sides of the David's Will tract. The David's Will tract bordered Loop Road, and Loop Road ran along near the David's Will tract's west side.

Flonham

Philip J. Shafer patented the 36-acre tract of land in 1774.[9] The Mountain House, presently the Old South Mountain Inn, stands on this tract of land.

Fox Inn

The two-story stone structure stood along Old Sharpsburg Road about two miles southeast of Fox's Gap before 1777.[10] The building stands on a tract of land surveyed for Daniel Dulaney in 1742 called The Exchange.[11] Dulaney, a land investor, founded the city of Frederick two years later. The building stands at the Marker Road and Bolivar Road intersection.

Fox's Gap

The name of the mountain gap where Old Sharpsburg Road crossed the East Ridge of the South Mountain was approximately four miles northwest of Middletown, MD.[12] John Fox, the man for whom the gap received its name, lived within half a mile west of the mountain crest and probably on the north side of the road.[13] During the battle on September 14, 1862, the Wise Cabin was at the heart of Fox's Gap. The Reno Monument represents the heart of Fox's Gap today.

Hill #1

The highest point along the West Ridge of the South Mountain between Old National Pike and Old Sharpsburg Road, Hill #1 was a 20- or 30-acre cleared field during the battle. A current topographical map shows Hill #1 at an elevation of 1,204 feet. Ted Ellis estimated the distance from the Mountain House to the Hill #1 peak as 3,000 to 3,100 feet.

Hill #2

The highest point on the East Ridge of the South Mountain between Old National Pike and Old Sharpsburg Road and covered by woods during the battle. A current topographical map shows Hill #2 with an elevation of 1,220 feet. Ted Ellis estimated the distance from the Mountain House to the Hill #2 peak as 1,000 feet.

Lambs Knoll Road

The present road not far from the Reno Monument to the top of Lambs Knoll, a 1,758 feet peak on the East Ridge of South Mountain. Referred to as Lamb's Old Field on the *Atlas Map*.

Lambert's Field (Lampert's Field)

The open field on the immediate northeast corner of Cox's Intersection at the battle. Lambert's Field contained approximately 10 acres.[14] The northeast corner of this tract was near the center of the gorge that ran through the tract. The open area of the lot contained approximately six acres north of the chasm. The wooded site included four acres within the ravine and south of it.

Land Depression

A land depression ran west from Old Sharpsburg Road through the lower portion of the Addition to Friendship tract and most of the David's Will tract until it ended a short distance beyond the Loop Road's west side. The depression probably was 100 feet deep near Old Sharpsburg Road and perhaps 40 feet deep near Loop Road.

Loop Road

A farm road that began near the Fox Gap Road and Old Sharpsburg Road intersection on the east side of Fox's Gap, running west until it intersected the Lower Ridge Road about a half-mile south-southwest of Fox's Gap. The road appeared in a 1971 aerial photograph of the Fox's Gap area. The land between Loop Road and Ridge Road was primarily open farmland during the battle, while the areas west of Ridge Road and south and east of Loop Road were dense woods.

Loop Road Spur

The farm road ran south of Loop Road and connected Loop Road and Mountain Road. The road, surrounded by woods, departed Loop Road near line two or three of the David's Will tract and ran southwest uphill to meet Mountain Road on a tract of land called Mt. Pelier.[15] Loop Road Spur vaguely appeared on a 1971 aerial photograph of Fox's Gap, as did Loop Road.

Lower Ridge Road

The portion of Ridge Road that ran west from the NinetyAngle to the Ridge-Loop Intersection.

Miller's Field

A mostly cleared field of 13¼ acres at the time of the battle in the immediate northeast quadrant of the Wood Road and Old Sharpsburg Road intersection. A John Miller owned the land at the time of the fight.[16] Miller may have served as a guide for the Union troops as they approached Fox's Gap. The Miller's Field parcel consisted of 10 acres of a tract named Bowser's Addition and 3¼ acres of the Addition to Friendship tract.

Moser Road

The current name of the road between the East Ridge and the West Ridge of the South Mountain; the route runs north to south between Old National Pike and Reno Monument Road (Old Sharpsburg Road). Ted Ellis estimated the distance from the Mountain House to the Old National Pike and Moser Road intersection on the *Atlas Map* as 1,300 feet. Union Brigadier General Jacob D. Cox labeled this road and Park Hall Road as "the Rohrersville Road" in his *Military Reminiscences*.[17]

Mountain House

The two-story structure at the heart of Turner's Gap. The building stands on a tract of land called Flonham, first surveyed in 1770 by Philip J. Shafer.[18] The building probably dates to after the turnpike construction through Turner's Gap in 1811. Today the building is known as the Old South Mountain Inn. During the battle, the intersection of the road to Daniel Rent's Farm (today Dahlgren Road) and Old National Pike was 100 feet east of the Mountain House.[19] The Old National Pike and Wood Road junction was 300 feet east of the Mountain House on September 14, 1862.

Mountain Road

The road appears on the Battlefield of South Mountain Map in the *Atlas to Accompany the Official Records*. The road ran from near the property of J. Slifer on Park Hall Road to Daniel Castle's property along Old Sharpsburg Road.

NinetyAngle

The 90-degree angle along Ridge Road was about one quarter-mile south of the Reno Monument at Fox's Gap. The NinetyAngle connected Upper Ridge Road and Lower Ridge Road. The location was near lines three and four of the Addition to Friendship tract.

Old National Pike (ONP)

The present road through Turner's Gap.[20] The road is referred to as Old National Pike throughout this book for ease of identification and understanding. Other names for the road have been the National Road, the National Turnpike, and the National Pike. The first road through Turner's Gap was in 1756 and was called the Main Road from Frederick to Fort Frederick.[21]

Old Sharpsburg Road (OSR)

(Today Reno Monument Road.) The sunken wagon road that ran through Fox's Gap during the battle. The road dates to 1727 and initially was the Great Philadelphia Wagon Road.[22] It also was known as the road from Conestoga to Opequon. The road became the Sharpsburg Road with the creation of Sharpsburg in 1763.

Park Hall Road

The current name of the road that runs between the East Ridge and the West Ridge of South Mountain between Reno Monument Road (Old Sharpsburg Road) and the Rohrersville, MD, area. Union Brigadier General Cox labeled this road and Moser Road as the "Rohrersville Road" in his *Military Reminiscences*.[23]

Reno Monument

The monument was built in 1889 to remember Major General Jesse L. Reno, who died at Fox's Gap during the battle. The memorial marks the heart of Fox's Gap today.[24]

Reno Monument Road

The present name of Old Sharpsburg Road.

Ridge Road

Ridge Road ran near the East Crest of South Mountain from Fox's Gap to the southwest for about one half-mile, intersecting Loop Road. At the time of the battle, on the east side of this road were primarily open fields, while dense woods were on the west side.

Ridge-Loop Intersection (RLI)

The Ridge Road and Loop Road intersection was about one half-mile south-southwest of Fox's Gap. Brigadier General Jacob D. Cox showed this area with an elevation of 1,000 feet on his South Mountain map in his *Military Reminiscences*.

Road Cut Through the Woods by the Confederates.

See Cut Road.

Road to Daniel Rent's Farm

(Today Dahlgren Road.) Daniel Rent's Farm was along the road about halfway between the Mountain House and the area known as Frostown.[25] Ted Ellis estimated the distance from the Mountain House to the intersection of Old National Pike and the road to Daniel Rent's Farm as 100 feet at the time of the battle. Today, Dahlgren Road intersects Old National Pike approximately 650 feet east of the Mountain House.

Rohrersville Road

(Today Moser Road and Park Hall Road.) Union Brigadier General Jacob D. Cox's name for the road between the East Ridge and the West Ridge of South Mountain running south from Old National Pike to the Rohrersville, Maryland, area.[26]

Rohrersville Road consisted of today's Moser Road, between Old National Pike and Old Sharpsburg Road, and today's Park Hall Road, between Old Sharpsburg Road and the Rohrersville area. It is the first north-to-south road west of Turner's and Fox's Gaps. Ted Ellis estimated the distance west from the Mountain House to the Old National Pike and Moser Road intersection shown on the *Atlas Map* in 1862 as 1,300 feet.

Saddle

(The Saddle of the East Ridge of South Mountain.) A location along a ridge lower than the adjacent ridge, but not quite a gap. The Saddle of the East Ridge of South Mountain was about halfway between Turner's and Fox's Gaps. It was where the east side of a large gorge that originated near Cox's Intersection met the East Ridge of South Mountain.

Turner's Gap

The name of the mountain gap where Old National Pike crossed the East Ridge of the South Mountain approximately two and four-tenths miles southeast of Boonsboro, Maryland. Robert Turner, the man for whom the gap received its name, patented Nelson's Folly at the present site of Boonsboro in 1750.[27] The first road through the pass, constructed in 1756, provided a more direct route to the newly built Fort Frederick than the Great Road from Frederick to Conococheague (Williamsport) through Fox's Gap. The Mountain House represented the heart of Turner's Gap during the battle and still does today.

Upper Ridge Road

The portion of Ridge Road that ran north from the NinetyAngle to Old Sharpsburg Road.

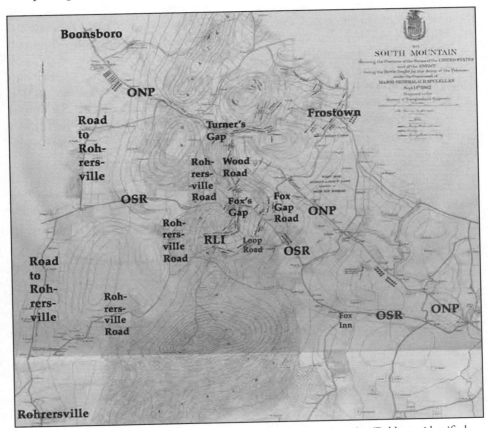

Map 41: Battlefield of South Mountain, *Atlas Map*, September 14, 1862. (Bold text identified on *Atlas Map* by Curtis Older)

Wise Cabin

John and Matilda Wise acquired the small cabin located at the heart of Fox's Gap in 1858.[28] The tiny house sat adjacent to Old Sharpsburg Road (Reno Monument Road today). Today, the apparent site is a parking area for visitors at Fox's Gap and the Appalachian Trail.

Wise's Field

A 4¾-acre cleared field adjacent to the south side of Old Sharpsburg Road and the east side of Upper Ridge Road at the time of the battle.[29] This land was part of the Addition to Friendship tract surveyed for Frederick Fox in 1797. Constructed in 1889, the Reno Monument stands on this tract.

Wood Road

Wood Road began at Fox's Gap along Old Sharpsburg Road and ran north along the near east side of the East Crest of South Mountain until it met Old National Pike. The distance between Wood Road and the East Ridge of South Mountain increased as the road ran north. During the battle dense woods surrounded Wood Road, except on the east side at Miller's Field. Ted Ellis estimated the distance from the Mountain House to the Old National Pike and Wood Road intersection in 1862, as shown on the *Atlas Map*, at 300 feet. Today the Appalachian Trail runs along a significant section of the original Wood Road from Fox's Gap to Turner's Gap. Wood Road, part of the Addition to Friendship tract, laid within the narrow band connecting the two gaps.

Ted Ellis and I prepared numerous maps in this book from a Base Map created from the Map of the Battlefield of South Mountain in the *Atlas to Accompany the Official Records (Atlas Map)*.[30]

Union and Confederate Orders of Battle

Various manpower levels shown below in the following Orders of Battle were from the *Official Records* and authors Ezra Carman, John M. Priest, and D. Scott Hartwig.

Union Order of Battle—Morning
Fox's and Turner's Gaps—September 14, 1862

Ninth Corps commanded by Major General Jesse L. Reno

Union Cavalry, B.G. Pleasanton
   8th IL Cavalry, Maj. Medill
   3rd IN Cavalry, Maj. Chapman
   1st MA Cavalry, Cpt. Crowninshield
Kanawha Division, B.G. Jacob D. Cox
   1st Brigade, Col. Scammon—12th OH, 23rd OH, 30th OH
      Gilmore's Co., WV Cavalry, Lt. Abraham
      Harrison Co., WV Cavalry, Lt. Delaney
   2nd Brigade, Col. Crook—11th OH, 28th OH, 36th OH
      Schambeck's Co., Chicago Dragoons, Cavalry, Cpt. F. Shambeck
   OH Light Artillery, 1st Battery, Cpt. McMullin
      2 × 14-lb James, Lt. Crome
      2 × 14-lb James, near Fox Gap Road
      2 × 14-lb James, near Fox Gap Road
   KY Light Artillery, Cpt. Simmonds
      2 × 20-lb Parrotts, Cpt. Simmonds—near Fox Gap Road
      2 × 10-lb Parrotts, Lt. Glassie
      1 × 10-lb Parrott
      1 × 12-lb Napoleon (howitzer)

1st Division, IX Corps Artillery
  MA Light Artillery, 8th Battery, Cpt. Cook
    2 × 12-lb Napoleons (howitzers), Cpt. Cook
    2 × 12-lb James Rifles, Lt. Coffin
    2 × 12-lb James Rifles
  2nd U.S. Artillery, Battery E, 1st Div., Lt. Benjamin
    2 × 20-lb Parrotts, Lt. Lord
    2 × 20-lb Parrotts, Lt. Graves
Union Reserve Artillery
  3rd U.S. Artillery, Batteries C and G, Pleasonton Cavalry,
    Cpt. Horatio G. Gibson
    2 × 3-inch Ordnance rifles, Cpt. Horatio G. Gibson
    2 × 3-inch Ordnance rifles, Lt. Henry Meinell
    2 × 3-inch Ordnance rifles, Lt. Edmund Pendleton
  3rd U.S. Artillery, Batteries L and M, unattached,
    Cpt. John Edwards Jr.
    2 × 10-lb Parrotts, Lt. William C. Bartlett
    2 × 10-lb Parrotts, Lt. Erskine Gittings

Confederate Order of Battle—Morning
Fox's and Turner's Gaps—September 14, 1862

D. H. Hill's Division, M.G. Daniel H. Hill
  Ripley's Brigade, B.G. Ripley—1st NC, 3rd NC, 4th GA, 44th GA
  G. B. Anderson's Brigade, B.G. G. B. Anderson—2nd NC, 4th NC,
    14th NC, 30th NC
  Garland's Brigade, B.G. Samuel Garland Jr.—5th NC, 12th NC,
    13th NC, 20th NC, 23rd NC
  Colquitt's Brigade, Col. Alfred Colquitt—13th AL, 6th GA,
    23rd GA, 27th GA, 28th GA

Cavalry Division, M.G. J. E. B. Stuart
  Lee's Brigade, B.G. F. H. Lee
  5th Virginia Cavalry, Col. Thomas L. Rosser
  Stuart's (VA) Horse Artillery, Maj. John Pelham
    probably 2 × 3-inch Ordnance Rifles, otherwise, 2 Napoleons

Reserve Artillery, B.G. Pendleton, commanding Cutts's Battalion,
  Lt. Col. Allen S. Cutts
    (During the Maryland Campaign, Cutts's Battalion acted as detached from the
    Reserve Artillery and assigned to Major General Daniel H. Hill's Division.)

Ross's (GA) Battery A, Cpt. Hugh M. Ross
  1 × Napoleon
  3 × 10-lb Parrotts
  1 × 12-lb howitzer (one lost on retreat from S. Mtn.)
Patterson's (GA) Battery B, Cpt. George M. Patterson
  3 × 12-lb howitzers
  3 × 6-lb guns
Blackshear's (GA) Battery D, Cpt. James A Blackshear
    (Note: battery was held in reserve at Boonsboro on the 14th and disbanded
    on October 4.)
  3 × 12-lb howitzers
  3 × 6-pounder guns
Irwin (or Irvin) (GA) Artillery, Battery E, Cpt. John Lane
  2 × 20-lb Parrotts
  3 × 10-lb Parrotts
  2 × 12-lb Whitworth rifle
Jeff Davis (AL) Artillery, Bondurant's Battery, Cpt. Bondurant
  2 × 3-inch Ordnance Rifles
  2 × 12-pound Napoleons or howitzers
Lloyd's NC Battery, Cpt. W. P. Lloyd
  2 × 12-lb howitzers
  2 × 6-pounder guns

Union Order of Battle—Noon to 10:00 pm

Army of the Potomac—Major General George B. McClellan
Turner's Gap: First Corps
Major General Joseph Hooker: 10,122 men

1st Division, B.G. Hatch: 3,682
  1st Brigade, Col. Phelps Jr.: 520 men
    22nd NY, 24th NY, 30th NY, 84th NY, 2nd U.S. Sharpshooters
  2nd Brigade, Col. Wainwright: 968 men
    7th IN, 76th NY, 95th NY, 56th PA
  3rd Brigade, B.G. Patrick: 848 men
    21st NY, 23rd NY, 35th NY, 80th NY
  4th Brigade, B.G. Gibbon: 1,346 men
    19th IN, 2nd WI, 6th WI, 7th WI
Artillery—1st Division, Cpt. Monroe
  NH Light, 1st Battery, Lt. Edgell
    6 Napoleon or howitzers

1st RI Light, Battery D, Cpt. Monroe
  6 Napoleons or howitzers
1st NY Light, Battery L, Cpt. Reynolds
  6 × 3-inch Ordnance rifles
4th U.S., Battery B, Cpt. Campbell
  2 Napoleons, Lt. Stewart
  4 Napoleons
2nd Division, B.G. Ricketts: 3,193 men
  1st Brigade, B.G. Duryea: 1,100 men
    97th NY, 104th NY, 105th NY, 107th PA
  2nd Brigade, Col. Christian: 1,087 men
    26th NY, 94th NY, 88th PA, 90th PA
  3rd Brigade, BG Hartsuff: 1,006 men
    16th ME, 12th MA, 13th MA, 83rd NY, 11th PA
Artillery—2nd Division
  1st PA Light, Battery F, Cpt. Matthews
    4 × 3-inch Ordnance rifles
  1st PA Light, Battery C, Cpt. Thompson
    4 × 10-lb Parrotts
3rd Division, B.G. Meade: 3,247 men
  1st Brigade, B.G. Seymour
    1st PA, 2nd PA, 5th PA, 6th PA, 13th PA
  2nd Brigade, Col. Magilton
    3rd PA, 4th PA, 7th PA, 8th PA
  3rd Brigade, Col. Gallagher
    9th PA, 10th PA, 11th PA, 12th PA
Artillery—3rd Division
  1st PA Light, Battery A, Lt. Simpson
    4 Napoleons or howitzers
  1st PA Light, Battery B, Cpt. Cooper
    4 × 3-inch Ordnance rifles
  5th U.S. Battery C, Cpt. Ransom
    2 guns under Lt. Gansevoort

At Fox's Gap: Ninth Corps
Major General Jesse L. Reno: 13,458 men

Kanawha Division, B.G. Jacob D. Cox: 3,510 men
  1st Brigade, Col. Eliakim Scammon: 1,455 men
    12th Ohio, 23rd Ohio, 30th Ohio

2nd Brigade, Col. George Crook
  11th OH, 28th OH, 36th OH
OH Light Artillery, 1st Battery, Cpt. James R. McMullin
  2 × 14-lb James, Lt. Crome
  2 × 14-lb James, near Fox Gap Road
  2 × 14-lb James, near Fox Gap Road
KY Light Artillery, Kanawha Division, Simmonds Battery,
    Cpt. Seth J. Simmonds
  2 × 20-lb Parrotts, Cpt. Seth J. Simmonds
  2 × 10-lb Parrotts, Lt. Daniel W. Glassie
  1 × 10-lb Parrott
  1 × 12-lb Napoleon (howitzer)
3rd U.S. Artillery, Batteries C and G, Pleasonton Cavalry,
    Cpt. Horatio G. Gibson
  6 × 3-inch Ordnance rifles
1st Division, B.G. Orlando B. Willcox: 3,603 men
  1st Brigade, Col. Benjamin C. Christ
    28th MA, 8th MI, 17th MI, 79th NY, 50th PA
  2nd Brigade, Col. Thomas Welsh
    46th NY, 45th PA, 100th PA
  2nd U.S. Artillery, Battery E, Lt. Samuel N. Benjamin
    4 × 20-lb Parrotts
  MA Light Artillery, 8th Independent Battery, Cpt. Cook
    2 × 12-lb Napoleons or howitzers, Cpt. Asa M. Cook
    2 × 12-lb James Rifles, Lt. John Norton Coffin
    2 × 12-lb James Rifles
2nd Division, B.G. Samuel D. Sturgis: 3,411 men
  1st Brigade, B.G. James Nagle
    2nd MD, 6th NH, 9th NH, 48th PA
  2nd Brigade, B.G. Edward Ferrero
    21st MA, 35th MA, 51st NY, 51st PA
  PA Light Artillery, Battery D, Cpt. George W. Durell
    6 × 10-lb Parrotts
  4th U.S. Artillery, Battery E, Cpt. Joseph C. Clark Jr.
    2 × 10-lb Parrotts, Lt. Dickenson
    2 × 10-lb Parrotts, Lt. Baker
3rd Division, BG Isaac P. Rodman: 2,934 men
  1st Brigade, Col. Harrison Fairchild
    9th NY, 89th NY, 103rd NY

2nd Brigade, Col. Edward Harland
   8th CT, 112th CT, 4th RI
  5th U.S. Artillery, Battery A, Lt. Muhlenberg
   6 × 12-lb Napoleons or howitzers

Confederate Order of Battle—Noon to 10:00 pm

Jackson's Corps
At Turner's Gap: 4,548 estimated present

M.G. Daniel H. Hill's Division
  Colquitt's Brigade, Col. Alfred Colquitt: 1,429 men
   13th AL, 6th GA, 23rd GA, 27th GA, 28th GA
  Rodes' Brigade, B.G. R. E. Rodes
   3rd AL, 5th AL, 6th AL, 12th AL, 26th AL
  Stevens' (Evan's) Brigade
Reserve Artillery, B.G. William Nelson Pendleton
  Cutts's Battalion, Lt. Col. Allen S. Cutts
     (Cutts's Battalion was detached from the Reserve Artillery and assigned to
     Gen. Daniel H. Hill's Division.)
  Ross's (GA) Battery A, Cpt. Hugh M. Ross
   1 Napoleon
   3 × 10-lb Parrotts
   1 × 12-lb howitzer
  Patterson's (GA) Battery B, Cpt. George M. Patterson
   3 × 12-lb howitzers
   3 × 6-lb guns
  Blackshear's (GA) Battery D, Cpt. Blackshear
   1 × 10-lb Parrott
   5 artillery of type unknown
  Irwin (or Irvin) (GA) Artillery, Battery E, Cpt. Lane
   1 × 20-lb Parrott
   3 × 10-lb Parrotts
   1 × 12-lb Whitworth rifle
  Jefferson Davis Artillery, Cpt. Bondurant
   2 × 3-inch Ordnance Rifles
   2 × 12-lb Napoleons or howitzers
  Lloyd's (NC) Battery, Cpt. Lloyd
   2 × 12-lb howitzers
   1 × 6-pounder gun

Major General James Longstreet's Corps

At Turner's Gap:

B.G. David R. Jones' Division
    Kemper's Brigade, B.G. James L. Kemper: 400 men
        1st VA, 7th VA, 11th VA, 17th VA, 24th VA
    Walker's (Jenkins') Brigade, Col. Walker: 562 men
        1st SC, 2nd SC, 4th SC, 5th SC, 6th SC, and
            Palmetto SC Sharpshooters
    Garnett's (Pickett's) Brigade, B.G. R. B. Garnett: 407 men
        8th VA, 18th VA, 19th VA, 28th VA, 56th VA
B.G. John B. Hood's Division:
    Rodes' Brigade, BG Rodes: 1,200 men
        3rd AL, 5th AL, 6th AL, 12th AL, and 26th AL
    Evan's Brigade, Col. Stevens: 550 men
        17th SC, 18th SC, 22nd SC, and 23rd SC, and
            Holcombe SC Legion

At Fox's Gap:

D. H. Hill's Division, M.G. Daniel H. Hill
    Ripley's Brigade, B.G. Roswell Ripley: 1,061 men
        1st NC, 3rd NC, 4th GA, 44th GA
    Garland's Brigade, B.G. Samuel Garland Jr.: 945 men
        5th NC, 12th NC, 13th NC, 20th NC, 23rd NC
    G. B. Anderson's Brigade, B.G. G. B. Anderson: 1,243 men
        2nd NC, 4th NC, 14th NC, 30th NC
B.G. David R. Jones' Division
    Drayton's Brigade, BG Thomas F. Drayton: 1,300 men
        50th GA, 51st GA, 3rd SC battalion, 15th SC, Phillips
        Legion (GA)
    G. T. Anderson's Brigade, Col. G. T. Anderson: 507 men
        1st GA, 7th GA, 8th GA, 9th GA, 11th GA
    Jones's Artillery: 81 men
        Wise (VA) Artillery, Cpt. James S. Brown
           Four guns of unknown type(s)
B.G. John B. Hood's Division
    Hood's Brigade, Col. W. T. Wofford: 864 men
        18th GA, 1st TX, 4th TX, 5th TX, Hampton's (SC) Legion

Law's Brigade, Col. E. M. Law: 1,493 men
   4th AL, 2nd MS, 11th MS, 6th NC
Hood's Artillery: 268 men (16 guns) (Antietam listing)
   German (SC) Artillery, Cpt. Bachman (at MH)
      4 Napoleons
      2 Blakelys (rifled)
   Palmetto (SC) Light Artillery, Cpt. Garden (at MH)
      2 × 12-lb howitzers
      2 × 6-pounder guns
   Rowan (NC) Artillery, Cpt. Reilly (at MH)
      2 × 10-lb Parrotts
      2 × 3-inch Ordnance Rifles
      2 × 24-lb Howitzers
Cavalry Division, Major General James E. B. Stuart
  Lee's Brigade, B.G. Fitzhugh Lee
   5th Virginia Cavalry, Col. Thomas Rosser
  Stuart's (VA) Horse Artillery
      Maj. John Pelham, Battalion Commander
      Cpt. James Breathed (as of August 1862)
   1 Napoleon or howitzer
   2 × 3-inch Ordnance Rifles (captured Aug. 27, 1862, at
     Manassas Junction)
   5 guns of unknown type

Times and Locations—Commanders

Below is a summary of the Confederate and Union commanding officers' movements throughout the day and an overview of the Confederate and Union artillery movements during the battle. The listings below enable the reader to review some of the morning battle's critical elements and provide a reference for understanding the ebb and flow of the fight at Fox's Gap in the afternoon and evening.

Confederate Commanders

Hill	6:00 am	Mountain House
Colquitt	6:00 am	1/8 mile east of the Mountain House on Old National Pike
Hill	7:00 am	along Wood Road near Fox's Gap
G. B. Anderson	7:00 am	Boonsboro area
Longstreet	8:00 am	Hagerstown area
Lee	8:00 am	Hagerstown area
Hood	8:00 am	Hagerstown area
Garland	8:00 am	Turner's Gap east of Mountain House
Rosser	8:00 am	Miller's Field
Garland	8:45 am	along Ridge Road at Fox's Gap
Rosser	8:45 am	near Ridge-Loop Intersection
Ripley	9:00 am	Turner's Gap area
Rodes	9:00 am	Turner's Gap area
G. B. Anderson	9–10 am	Wood Road and Dahlgren Road intersection at Old National Pike
Garland	10:00 am	killed near Wise's Field at Fox's Gap
Rosser	10–10:15 am	Mountain House; Hill gave Rosser command of Ridge Road at Fox's Gap
G. B. Anderson	10–10:15 am	Mountain House; Hill gave G. B. Anderson command of Old Sharpsburg Road at Fox's Gap

Rosser	10:30–noon	near the Ridge-Loop Intersection
G. B. Anderson	10:15–noon	near Miller's Field at Fox's Gap
Hill	10:30 am	with Lt. Col. Ruffin near Miller's Field
Rosser	noon	Cox's Intersection
Rodes	noon	west of Frostown along Dahlgren Road
G. T. Anderson	2:00 pm	Mountain House
Ripley	2:00 pm	Mountain House; in charge of four brigades at Fox's Gap
Hill	3:00 pm	Miller's Field
Longstreet	3:00 pm	Old National Pike near Boonsboro
Jones	3:00 pm	Turner's Gap
Rodes	3:00 pm	Old National Pike west of Mountain House
Stevens	3:00 pm	Old National Pike west of Mountain House
Hood	3:00 pm	Old National Pike near Boonsboro
Law	3:00 pm	Old National Pike near Boonsboro
Wofford	3:00 pm	Old National Pike near Boonsboro
G. B. Anderson	3:00 pm	Cox's Intersection
Drayton	3:00 pm	Mountain House
Rosser	3:00 pm	Cox's Intersection
Lee	3:00 pm	Old National Pike near Boonsboro
Ripley	3:30 pm	Cox's Intersection
Lee	4:00 pm	Boonsboro Headquarters
Drayton	4:00 pm	Miller's Field
Hood	4:00 pm	Mountain House
Longstreet	4:00 pm	Mountain House
Kemper	5:00 pm	Old National Pike west of Mountain House
Hood	5:00 pm	advancing towards Old Sharpsburg Road
Garnett	5:00 pm	Old National Pike west of Mountain House
Walker	5:00 pm	Old National Pike west of Mountain House
G. T. Anderson	5:00 pm	west of the Saddle of the East Ridge
Longstreet	5:00 pm	Mountain House
Hill	5:00 pm	Mountain House
Law	5:30 pm	crossing the East Ridge to west side
Wofford	5:30 pm	crossing the East Ridge to west side
Hood	5:30 pm	crossing the East Ridge to west side
G. B. Anderson	5:30 pm	approaching the Ridge-Loop Intersection
Hood	6:00 pm	Moser Road moving south with two brigades
Walker	6:00 pm	Mountain House
Kemper	6:00 pm	near line 13 of Addition to Friendship tract
Rosser	6:00 pm	near Moser Road or Hill #2
Hood	7:00 pm	Moser Road north of Cox's Intersection

McLemore	9:00 pm	Cox's Intersection
Hill	10:00 pm	Mountain House
Hood	10:00 pm	Mountain House
Hood	10:30 pm	Lee's Headquarters in Boonsboro
Hill	10:30 pm	Lee's Headquarters in Boonsboro
Lee	10:30 pm	Lee's Headquarters in Boonsboro
Longstreet	10:30 pm	Lee's Headquarters in Boonsboro
Hood	midnight	Mountain House

Union Commanders

Cox	6:00 am	west of Middletown, MD
Cox	9:00 am	Loop Road with 1st Brigade, Kanawha Division
Cox	10:00 am	Fox Gap Road at Old Sharpsburg Road[1]
Sturgis	1:00 pm	near Middletown
Willcox	2:00 pm	reports to Cox near Fox's Gap[1]
Willcox	3:00 pm	Loop Road at Old Sharpsburg Road
Sturgis	3:30 pm	Fox's Gap on Old Sharpsburg Road
McClellan	4:00 pm	Pleasonton's knoll in the valley[2]
Burnside	4:00 pm	Pleasonton's knoll in the valley[2]
Reno	4:00 pm	Pleasonton's knoll in the valley[2]
Pleasonton	4:00 pm	Pleasonton's knoll in the valley[2]
Sturgis	4:45 pm	Fox Gap Road at Old Sharpsburg Road[1]
Doubleday	5:00 pm	between Frostown and McClellan's Headquarters
Meade	5:00 pm	between Frostown and McClellan's Headquarters
Hatch	5:00 pm	south of Frostown
Ricketts	5:00 pm	approaching Frostown
Gibbon	5:00 pm	west of Bolivar on Old National Pike
Hooker	5:00 pm	between Frostown and McClellan's Headquarters
Reno	6:30 pm	site of Reno Monument at Fox's Gap
Sturgis	6:30 pm	site of Reno Monument at Fox's Gap
Cox	6:30 pm	Fox Gap Road at Old Sharpsburg Road

---

[1] I believe Cox's Headquarters were near the intersection of Fox Gap Road and Old Sharpsburg Road.
[2] The main knoll was the location of the 16 Union cannon. The *Atlas Map* showed McClellan's Headquarters and perhaps that was the location of Pleasonton.

Times and Locations—Artillery

Confederate Artillery

8:00 am	Lane's two 20-lb Parrotts at the Mountain house; three 10-lb Parrotts and one 12-lb Whitworth east of the Mountain House on Hill #1280
8:00 am	Bondurant's four guns move from Zittlestown to the Mountain House
8:00 am	Breathed's section of artillery at Hill #1 until nighttime
8:00 am	Pelham's two-gun battery in Miller's Field at Fox's Gap
8:00 am	Rosser's 5th VA Cavalry positioned along Old Sharpsburg Road east of the Wise Cabin
9:00 am	Bondurant's four guns east of the NinetyAngle of Ridge Road
9:00 am	Pelham's artillery section and Rosser's 5th VA Cavalry at the Ridge-Loop Intersection
9:00 am	Ross's and Patterson's batteries ordered to Turner's Gap
10:00 am	Bondurant's four guns near the Wise Cabin
11:00 am	Pelham's artillery section and Rosser's 5th VA Cavalry retreat to near Cox's Intersection
11:00 am	Lane's four guns retreat from Hartwig's Hill #1280 to the Mountain House
12–2:00 pm	Bondurant's four guns repositioned to the northwest side of Miller's Field
12–2:00 pm	Infantry lull in battle; Confederate and Union artillery continue bombardment
3:00 pm	Pelham's artillery section and Rosser's 5th VA cavalry remain near Cox's Intersection
3:00 pm	Ross's Battery 1,500 feet east of the Mountain House along Dahlgren Road
3:00 pm	Patterson's Battery 1,500 feet east of the Mountain House along Dahlgren Road
4:00 pm	Hood's Artillery consisting of 14 guns at Mountain House: German (SC) Artillery, Palmetto (SC) Light Artillery; Rowan (NC) Artillery

5:00 pm	Ross's and Patterson's Batteries withdrawn from action
5:30 pm	Pelham's two guns near Cox's Intersection retreat north, probably to Hill #1 or the Mountain House area
5–6:00 pm	Bondurant's four guns abandon Miller's Field and move north along Wood Road or Cut Road

Union Artillery

8:00 am	Benjamin's four cannon near Fox Gap Road and Old Sharpsburg Road intersection
8:00 am	Gibson's six cannon near Fox Gap Road and Old Sharpsburg Road intersection
9:00 am	McMullin's two 20-lb Parrotts and two unknown types of guns near Fox Gap Road and Old Sharpsburg Road intersection where they remain throughout the day
9:00 am	Simmonds' section of two 20-lb Parrott guns near Fox Gap Road and Old Sharpsburg Road intersection where they remain throughout the day
9:00 am	Crome's artillery section of McMullin's Battery at Old Sharpsburg Road and Loop Road intersection
11:00 am	Crome's artillery section moved 1,200 feet southeast of the Wise Cabin
12–2:00 pm	Confederate and Union artillery continue bombardment
12–2:00 pm	Glassie moves two guns near the NinetyAngle
3:00 pm	Cook's and Coffin's guns positioned an eighth of a mile southeast of the Wise Cabin just south of the Addition to Friendship Woods
3:00 pm	Clark's four 10-lb Parrotts in motion along Loop Road moving towards the Ridge-Loop intersection
3:30 pm	Cooper's four 3-inch Ordnance Rifles near Frostown
4:00 pm	Durell's six 10-lb Parrotts reposition near Cook's abandoned guns along the Old Sharpsburg Road
4:00 pm	Clark's four cannon at the Ridge-Loop Intersection
4:00 pm	Cook's two guns move 1,000 feet east of the Wise Cabin to near the Jacob Martz property
5:00 pm	Cook's two pieces of artillery abandoned near Jacob Martz property
5:30 pm	Glassie's two guns positioned at the south side of the Addition to Friendship Woods
5:30 pm	Clark's four guns remain at the Ridge-Loop intersection
5:30 pm	Crome's two guns remain east of the NinetyAngle of Ridge Road
5:30 pm	Durell's six 10-lb Parrott guns remain along Old Sharpsburg Road halfway between the Wise Cabin and Fox Gap Road
6:00 pm	Durell's Battery ordered by Reno to advance to the crest of Old Sharpsburg Road at Fox's Gap

Approximate GPS Coordinates

	Latitude	Longitude
Dahlgren Road and Old National Pike Intersection	39.484315	−77.618432
Moser Road and Old National Pike Intersection	39.485491	−77.623997
Fox Gap Road and Old National Pike Intersection	39.475859	−77.607987
Cox's Intersection	39.471157	−77.626968
Fox Gap Road at Old Sharpsburg Road	39.463596	−77605314
Hill #1	39.482669	−77.627149
Hill #2	39.483645	−77.620437
Reno Monument	39.470588	−77617005
Mountain House	39.484611	−77595178
Moser Road and NW corner of Lambert's Field	39.473922	−77625755
Hill 1500	39.491323	−77.614546
Hill 1280	39.483742	−77.608497
Daniel Rent's Farm on Dahlgren Road	39.486488	−77.609078
Crest of the Heights on Moser Road	39.482942	−77.625464
Wood Road at Old Sharpsburg Road	39.470677	−77.617482
Center of Miller's Field	39.471530	−77.617171
Wren's Stone Fence at Park Hall Road	39.469982	−77.628564

Distances Between Battlefield Locations

Reno Monument to the North Edge of Miller's Field	436 feet
Reno Monument to Cox's Intersection	.54 miles
Reno Monument to intersection of Old Sharpsburg Road and Fox Gap Road	.79 miles
Reno Monument to Dahlgren Chapel	.91 miles
Reno Monument to Hayes's location along Loop Road	.60 miles
Ridge-Loop Intersection to Hill #1	1.07 miles
Ridge-Loop Intersection to Reno Monument	.42 miles
Old Sharpsburg Road and Fox Gap Road Intersection to Dahlgren Chapel	1.57 miles
Hayes's location along Loop Road to Cox's Intersection	.75 miles

Stone Wall along Upper Ridge Road, Near North Carolina South Mountain Monument. (Photograph by Curtis Older, September 14, 2012)

Author at grave of Frederick Fox, 1998, Gebhart or St. John Cemetery, Miamisburg, Ohio. (Photograph by Rachael Older)

Fox Inn. (Photograph by John Gensor, 2015)

The Fox Inn still stands at the corner of Marker Road and Bolivar Road. George Fox, a three-times-great grandfather of mine, owned the Fox Inn from October 7, 1805, until July 25, 1807.[1]

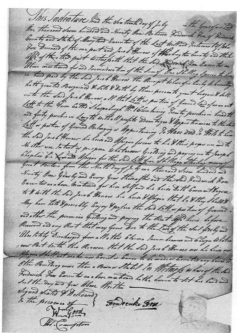

Page two of Deed—signed by Frederick Fox, Thomas Crampton, and William Good. Sale of Lot in Sharpsburg in 1791. (John Fox Estate)

Deed signed by Frederick Fox, executor for John Fox Estate—Sale of Lot in Sharpsburg in 1791. (Gift of Doug Bast to the author)

Daniel Booker Fox, a son of Frederick Fox, perhaps about 1860. (Photograph courtesy of Alan Sentman)

Endnotes

Reference to material in the *Official Records* (U.S. War Department, *The War of the Rebellion: A Compilation of the Official Records of the Union and Confederate Armies*) is abbreviated *OR*. Unless otherwise noted, all references are to Series One.

Chapter 1: The Approaching Battle

1. See Afterword in this book.
2. Stephen W. Sears, *Landscape Turned Red: the Battle of Antietam* (Norwalk, Conn.: Easton Press, 1988), 334–5.
3. Timothy J. Reese, *Sealed with Their Lives* (Baltimore: Butternut and Blue, 1998), Introduction, viii.
4. Sears, *Landscape Turned Red*, 66.
5. Wikipedia. Confiscation Acts.
6. Roy P. Basler, ed., *The Collected Works of Abraham Lincoln* (New Brunswick, N. J.: Rutgers University Press, 1953–55), 4-419. President Abraham Lincoln met with two Chicago ministers at the White House on September 13, 1862. Remarks by the president were reported at a meeting at Bryan Hall in Chicago on September 20, 1862: Abraham Lincoln papers: Series 1. General Correspondence, 1833–1916, Library of Congress.
7. Ezra A. Carman, and Thomas G. Clemens, ed. *The Maryland Campaign of September 1862. Volume 1, South Mountain* (El Dorado Hills, Calif.: Savas Beatie, 2010); John M. Priest, *Before Antietam, The Battle for South Mountain* (Shippensburg, PA: White Maine Publishing, Inc., 1992); D. Scott Hartwig, *To Antietam Creek* (Baltimore: The Johns Hopkins University Press, 2012); Sears, *Landscape Turned Red*; Brian M. Jordan, *Unholy Sabbath: the Battle of South Mountain in history and memory, September 14, 1862* (El Dorado Hills, CA: Savas Beatie, 2012).
8. Alexander B. Rossino, *Their Maryland: The Army of Northern Virginia From the Potomac Crossing to Sharpsburg in September 1862* (El Dorado Hills, CA: Savas Beatie, 2021). Rossino indicated that Indiana troops found the lost copy of Special Order No. 191 at a place erroneously thought to be where Major General D. H. Hill's men camped.
9. Curtis L. Older, *The Land Tracts of the Battlefield of South Mountain* (Westminster, MD: Heritage Books, Inc., 2008), 42.
10. Maryland Hall of Records, BC & GS 40, 114, Grim's Fancy, Alexander Grim, surveyed February 27, 1764, 50 acres. The Grim's Fancy deed was the only proof John Fox lived near Fox's Gap; Daniel G. Fox, *The Fox Genealogy including the Metherd, Benner, and Leiter Descendants* (n. p. 1914), Appendix One, 169.
11. Curtis L. Older, *The Braddock Expedition and Fox's Gap in Maryland* (Westminster, MD: Heritage Books, Inc., 2019), 5–6.
12. Older, *The Land Tracts*, 45–6.
13. Ibid., 46–9.
14. Ibid., 51–4.

15. Jacob D. Cox, *Military Reminiscences of the Civil War* (New York: Charles Scribner's Sons, 1900), 1:279.

16. Fox, *The Fox Genealogy*, (n. p. 1914). Fox's Gap received its name from John Frederick Fox and his nearby family. John Frederick Fox was a fifth great-grandfather of mine. Frederick Fox, a son of John Fox and my fourth great-grandfather, first obtained a survey for a tract of land named Fredericksburg near the South Mountain crest on Fox's Gap's east side. Fox obtained a patent for the Fredericksburg tract on March 13, 1794. On May 11, 1795, he received a special warrant to resurvey 34 acres of his Fredericksburg tract and add contiguous vacancy. Fox decided to keep his patent for Fredericksburg and to create a new parcel of land that he named Addition to Friendship for 202 acres, surveyed on May 9, 1797. Fox obtained a patent for this tract on May 7, 1805.

17. Steven Stanley, 6:00 am to 9:00 am, Fox's and Turner's Gaps.

18. Older, *The Land Tracts*, 206–10.

19. Ibid., 217–25.

20. Maryland State Archives, Special Collections (Maps) No. 504 Road from Williamsport to Turner's Gap, 1791 [MdHR 1427-504, B5-1-3]. The 1791 map of the road Lleading from Williamsport to Turner's Gap in the South Mountain identified almost one mile of road on the mountain's west side as "up through the gap."

21. Cox, *Military Reminiscences of the Civil War*, 1:290.

22. The reader cannot directly convert the contour measurement or designation used on the 1872 *Atlas Map* to the actual "feet above sea level" used on modern maps. The contour measurement or tag used was accurate in showing the *general* contours. Otherwise, readers comparing the maps from different eras will notice discrepancies and question the validity of either or both. Modern topographical maps are measured as feet above sea level for those unfamiliar, using bold lines every 100 feet and faint lines between every 20 feet in elevation.

23. *OR* 19, 1:1020, Report No. 293, Daniel H. Hill, 1862.

24. Carman and Clemens, *The Maryland Campaign of September 1862*, 1:315.

25. Priest, *Before Antietam*, 109–13.

26. Allen S. Cutts, "The Number of Guns in Cutts Battalion at Sharpsburg," *Southern Historical Society Papers*, (1882), Vol. 10, 430.

27. Hartwig, *To Antietam Creek*, 680.

28. Priest, *Before Antietam*, 325; Hartwig, *To Antietam Creek*, Appendix B, September 2 strength.

29. Walter Clark, ed. *Histories of the Several Regiments and Battalions from North Carolina in the great war 1861–1865* (Goldsboro: Nash Brothers, not dated), 2:220.

30. Priest cites George D. Grattan, "The Battle of Boonsboro Gap or South Mountain," *Southern Historical Society Papers*, XXXIX, 1914, 33–5.

31. *Southern Historical Society Papers*, Vol. III, No. 1 (Richmond: Virginia Historical Society, 1876–1959), 281; *OR* 19, 1:814, Report No. 206, MG J. E. B. Stuart, February 13, 1864.

32. Joseph L. Harsh, *Sounding the Shallows: A Confederate Companion for the Maryland Campaign of 1862* (Kent, Ohio: The Kent State University Press, 2000), 89.

33. *OR* 19, 1:814, Report No. 206, James E. B. Stuart, February 13, 1864, report covering August 30 to September 18, 1862; *OR* 19, 1:1052, Report No. 304, A. H. Colquitt, October 13, 1862; Judge George D. Grattan, "Boonsboro Gap, or South Mountain," *Southern Historical Society Papers* vols. 39–40, (Richmond: Virginia Historical Society, 1876–1959). People living near Fox's Gap referred to the gap as Fox's Gap, while people living outside the immediate vicinity of Fox's Gap referred to the gap as Braddock's Gap. Another mountain pass called Braddock's Gap was on the road over the Catoctin Mountains near Braddock Heights.

34. Hartwig, *To Antietam Creek*, 673.

35. Ezra A. Carman and Joseph Pierro, ed. *The Maryland Campaign of September 1862: Ezra A. Carman's Definitive Study of the Union and Confederate Armies at Antietam* (Routledge, 2012), 145. "Hill sent him the two brigades of Garland and Colquitt and the four-gun batteries of Captains James W. Bondurant (Alabama) and John Lane (Georgia)"; also see Carman and Clemens, *The Maryland Campaign of September 1862*, Chapter 8, South Mountain (Fox's Gap).

36. Hartwig, *To Antietam Creek*, 306.
37. Sarah M. Vinton became Admiral John A. Dahlgren's wife in 1865. Admiral Dahlgren invented the Dahlgren gun and died in 1870. Mrs. Dahlgren acquired 60 acres of land at Turner's Gap, including the Mountain House; Washington County Land Records, 74-264, April 19, 1876, from George F. Smith; Madeleine V. Dahlgren oversaw the building of the Dahlgren Chapel in 1881 across the Turnpike from the Mountain House. Today, Dahlgren Road runs from just east of the Dahlgren Chapel at Turner's Gap to intersect Frostown Road at Frostown, MD.
38. Older, *The Land Tracts*, 217.
39. Ibid. McClellan's Headquarters were about half a mile north of the Fox Inn. George Fox, a three-times great grandfather of mine and a son of Frederick Fox, briefly owned the Fox Inn from 1805 to 1807. McClellan's headquarters stood on a land tract first owned by Bartholomew Booker, the father-in-law of Frederick Fox.
40. George B. McClellan, and William Cowper Prime, *McClellan's Own Story: The War for the Union* (New York: C. L. Webster & Company, 1887), 612. September 15, Monday, 9:30 am, Bolivar, MD.
41. *OR* 19, 1:416, Report No. 137, Ambrose E. Burnside, September 30, 1862.

Chapter 2: Fox's Gap—Union Perspective

1. Cox, *Military Reminiscences of the Civil War*, 1:278.
2. Ibid., 1:290.
3. Ibid., 1:277–281.
4. *OR* 19, 1:208, Report No. 8, Alfred Pleasonton, September 19, 1862.
5. Ibid, also S. Rep. No. 1189, 50th Cong., 1st Sess. (1888).
6. Ibid.
7. Cox, *Military Reminiscences of the Civil War*, 1:288–9.
8. *OR* 19, 1:208 and 210, Report No. 8, Alfred Pleasonton, September 19, 1862; Cox, *Military Reminiscences of the Civil War*, 1:279.
9. Cox, *Military Reminiscences of the Civil War*, 1:281.
10. Edward O. Lord, *History of the Ninth Regiment, New Hampshire Volunteers in the War of the Rebellion* (Concord, NH: Republican Press Association, 1895), 79.
11. William J. Bolton, and Dr. Richard A. Sauers, ed., *The Civil War Journal of Colonel William J. Bolton* (Conshohocken, PA: Combined Publishing, 2000), 83.
12. Priest, *Before Antietam*, 134.
13. Ibid., 137–8.
14. Cox, *Military Reminiscences of the Civil War*, 1:281–4.
15. Wikipedia, Military Crest.
16. Bradley M. Gottfried, *The Maps of Antietam: An Atlas of the Antietam (Sharpsburg) Campaign, including the Battle of South Mountain, September 2–20, 1862* (El Dorado Hills, CA: Savas Beatie LLC, 2012), e-book page 50 of 241.
17. Ibid., e-book page 49 of 241.
18. Curtis L. Older, *News from Fox's Gap* (Heritage Books, Inc., 2018); various articles related to the Battle of South Mountain: Issue 8, Vol. 1, December 1, 1999, "Lost Legion, The Phillips Legion Infantry Battalion at Fox's Gap Maryland, September 14, 1862," by Kurt Graham; Issue 9, Vol. 1, June 1, 2000, "Death of a Brigade" by Kurt Graham; Issue 10, Vol. 1, December 1, 2000, "Casualties in the 50th Georgia Regiment at the Battle of South Mountain, September 14, 1862," by Kurt Graham; Issue 1, Vol. 2, June 1, 2001, "Casualties in the 51st Georgia Regiment during the Maryland Campaign, September 14, 1862," by Kurt Graham; Issue 2, Vol. 2, December 1, 2001, "The Third (James) South Carolina Infantry Battalion Takes a Licking at Fox's Gap September 14, 1862," by Sam B. Davis.
19. Cox, *Military Reminiscences of the Civil War*, 1:290.
20. Homer C. Hockett, "Jacob Dolson Cox," *Dictionary of American Biography* (New York: Charles Scribner's Sons, 1930), 4:476–8.

21. *OR* 19, 1:458, Report No. 154, Jacob D. Cox, September 20, 1862.
22. Cox, *Military Reminiscences of the Civil War*, 1:290.
23. Ibid.
24. Ibid., 1:289–90.
25. Bolton and Sauers, *The Civil War Journal of Colonel William J. Bolton*, 81.
26. Ibid., 82.
27. Cox, *Military Reminiscences of the Civil War*, 1:290.
28. Ibid., 1:283.
29. *OR* 19, 1:1,031, Report No. 295, Roswell S. Ripley, September 21, 1862.
30. Lord, *History of the Ninth Regiment*, 79.
31. Daniel E. Hurd, "My Experiences in the Civil War," 8, William Marvel Collection, USAMHI, 4. "The next morning we were on the march again and went down the so-called 'sunken road' where we saw the Rebel dead piled on each side of the road. Perhaps piled is extravagant but they lay in vast numbers."
32. Cox, *Military Reminiscences of the Civil War*, 1:283.
33. Ibid., 1:291.
34. Jordan, *Unholy Sabbath*, Chapter Seven, first page, John McQuaide, 8th Pennsylvania Reserves.
35. Cox, *Military Reminiscences of the Civil War*, Preface, Vol. 1.
36. "John F. Holahan Diary, 1861–1865," Accession No. 1981/10.0345, Special Collections Department, Marshall University, Huntington, WV.
37. Ibid.
38. George W. Whitman to Louisa Van Velsor Whitman, September 21, 1862, Trent Collection of Whitmaniana, Duke University Rare Book, Manuscript, and Special Collections Library.
39. Hartwig, *To Antietam Creek*, 677. Sept. 2—2nd Brigade— Ferrero. See Footnote 1, page 678.
40. Ibid., 677. Sept. 2—2nd Division—Sturgis. See Footnote 1, page 678.
41. *OR* 19, 1:429, Report No. 139, Orlando B. Willcox, September 21, 1862.
42. George W. Whitman to Louisa Van Velsor Whitman, September 21, 1862.
43. James Wren and John M. Priest, ed., *From New Bern to Fredericksburg: Captain James Wren's Diary: B Company, 48th Pennsylvania Volunteers, February 20, 1862 – December 17, 1862* (Shippensburg, PA: White Mane Pub. Co., 1990).
44. Ibid., 82–5.
45. *James Wren diary, September 14, 1862.* Manuscript, Antietam National Battlefield, 104; Oliver C. Bosbyshell, *The 48th in the War* (Philadelphia: Avil Printing Co., 1895), 76–7.
46. Older, *The Land Tracts*, 14.
47. Wren and Priest, *From New Bern to Fredericksburg: Captain James Wren's Diary*, 85–6.
48. Washington County Land Records, Y 723-725, made May 8, 1813; LBN 2 177, made May 9, 1867; KK 663, made March 30, 1869; and VJB 649, p. 525, made November 21, 1977.
49. Wren and Priest, *From New Bern to Fredericksburg: Captain James Wren's Diary*, 86.
50. Wren and Priest, *From New Bern to Fredericksburg: Captain James Wren's Diary*, 86.
51. Carman and Clemens, *The Maryland Campaign of September 1862*, 1:335.
52. William F. McConnell, *Remember Reno: A Biography of Major General Jesse Lee Reno* (Shippensburg, PA: White Mane Publishing, 1996); Tim Ware, mountainaflame.blogspot.com; The Pennsylvania Historical & Museum Commission website, www.phmc.pa.gov, contains the Hartranft-Stockman Shireman Collection Photographs. Photograph number 58 was taken at the Dedication of the Reno Monument at South Mountain, MD, September 14, 1889. General Hartranft was in the row just behind the second man from the right sitting on the fence. The photograph was taken less than a month before the death of General Hartranft and possibly was the last known photo taken of him. Photo on Matte. 12½" × 5".
53. Oliver C. Bosbyshell, *Miner's Journal*, Schuylkill County, Pennsylvania, September 21, 1862.
54. Joseph Gould, *The Story of the Forty-Eighth: A Record of the Campaigns of the Forty-Eighth Regiment Pennsylvania Veteran Volunteer Infantry During the Four Eventful years of its service in the War for the Preservation of the Union* (Sagwan Press, 2018), 87.

55. Curtis Clay Pollock, *Dear Ma: The Civil War Letters of Curtis Clay Pollock: First Defender and First Lieutenant, 48th Pennsylvania Infantry*, ed. John D. Hoptak (Boiling Springs, PA: Sunbury Press, 2017).

56. George A. Hitchcock, *The Civil War Diary of an Andersonville Survivor* (Jefferson, NC: McFarland & Co., Inc., 2014), 27.

57. Lord, *History of the Ninth Regiment*, 91.

58. Bolton and Sauers, *The Civil War Journal of Colonel William J. Bolton*, 84.

59. Thomas H. Parker, *History of the 51st Regiment P.V. and V.V* (Philadelphia: King & Baird, Printers, 1869), 224.

60. *OR* 19, 1:458, Report No. 154, Jacob D. Cox, September 20, 1862.

61. Brainyquote.com. William T. Sherman. "A battery of field artillery is worth a thousand muskets."

62. *OR* 19, 1:447–48, Report No. 148, Edward Ferrero, September 19, 1862.

63. William Alfred Robinson and Robert J. Taylor, *The Civil War Letters of William A. Robinson and the Story of the 89th NYVI* (Bowie, MD: Heritage Books, Inc., 2000), 40–1.

64. David L. Thompson, "All about us grew pennyroyal," *In the Ranks to the Antietam*. In *Battles and Leaders of the Civil War*, ed. Ned Bradford (New York: Appleton-Century, 1956), 238.

65. Ibid., 237–8.

66. *OR* 19, 1:416, Report No. 137, Ambrose E. Burnside, September 30, 1862.

67. Lord, *History of the Ninth Regiment*, 71.

68. *OR* 19, 1:49, Report No. 2, George B. McClellan, October 15, 1862.

69. McClellan and Prime, *McClellan's Own Story*, 612. September 15, Monday, 9:30 am, Bolivar, MD.

70. Cox, *Military Reminiscences of the Civil War*, 1:290.

Chapter 3: Fox's Gap—Confederate Perspective

1. William Shakespeare, *The Tempest*. Probably about 1611.

2. Hartwig, *To Antietam Creek*, 312–15.

3. *OR* 19, 1:1020, Report No. 293, Daniel H. Hill, 1862.

4. *OR* 19, 1:49, Report No. 2, George B. McClellan, October 15, 1862.

5. Robinson and Taylor, *The Civil War Letters of William A. Robinson*, 40–1.

6. Benjamin B. Ross, BrakeColl (Corporal's memoirs, Apr 15, 1861–Apr 9, 1865), Civil War Unit: 4th North Carolina Infantry Regiment, U.S. Army Heritage & Education Center, Carlisle Barracks, PA

7. *OR* 19, 1:1,049, Report No. 301, Bryan Grimes, October 13, 1862.

8. *OR* 19, 1:1,049–50, Report No. 302, A. J. Griffith, 1862.

9. *OR* 19, 1:1,050–1, Report No. 303, W. W. Sillers, October 13, 1862.

10. Clark, *Histories of the Several Regiments and Battalions*, 1:245.

11. Carman and Clemens, *The Maryland Campaign of September 1862*, 1:341.

12. Ibid.

13. Priest, *Before Antietam*, 325.

14. *OR* 19, 1:1,050–1, Report No. 303, W. W. Sillers, October 13, 1862.

15. *OR* 19, 1:1,031–2, Report No. 295, Roswell S. Ripley, September 21, 1862.

16. Ibid.

17. Stephen D. Thruston, report of September 27, 1862, "Letter addressed to Governor Zebulon Vance, North Carolina," William L. DeRossett Collection, North Carolina State Archives, Raleigh. Possibly found in N. C. Archives, Governors' Papers, Box No. G. P. 160, Correspondence, September 21, 1862–September 30, 1862; Chet Bennett, *Resolute Rebel: General Roswell S. Ripley, Charleston's Gallant Defender* (Columbia, SC: The University of South Carolina Press, 2017), Chapter Fifteen, Maryland Campaign.

18. George C. Smith, "A Fighting Chaplain—Experience at the Battle of South Mountain—Fierce Mortar Duels." From an 1886 anthology of Civil War reminiscences titled "Camp Fire Sketches & Battlefield Echoes."

19. *OR* 19, Part 1, 1,031–2, Report No. 295, Roswell S. Ripley, September 21, 1862.

20. Older, *News from Fox's Gap*, Issue 9, Volume 1, June 1, 2000, "Death of a Brigade" by Kurt Graham; Kurt D. Graham and Richard M. Coffman, *To Honor These Men*, (Mercer University Press, Macon, Georgia 2007), 87–102; Ezra A. Carman, *The Maryland Campaign of September 1862: Volume One: South Mountain* ed. Thomas G. Clemens, (Savas Beatie, New York and California, 2010), 1:336. Chapter Eight, footnote 44.

21. Frederick County Land Records, WBT-1, 100, April 1, 1845, Susan Miller, et al. to John Miller, Bowser's Addition and part of Addition to Friendship, 13¼ acres.

22. Priest, *Before Antietam*, 190.

23. *OR* 19, 1:427–9, Report No. 139, Orlando B. Willcox, September 21, 1862.

24. Graham and Coffman, *To Honor These Men*, 98–100.

25. Older, *News from Fox's Gap*, Issue 9, Volume 1, June 1, 2000, "Death of a Brigade" by Kurt Graham.

26. Orlando B. Willcox and Robert G. Scott, ed., *Forgotten Valor, The Memoirs, Journals, & Civil War Letters of Orlando B. Willcox*, (Kent, Ohio & London, The Kent State University Press, 1999), 355.

27. Willcox and Scott, *Forgotten Valor*, 355.

28. Cox, *Military Reminiscences of the Civil War*, 1:279. Cox's Map, Battle of South Mountain.

29. Ibid., 1:289–90.

30. *OR* 19, 1:839, Report No. 212, James Longstreet, October 10, 1862.

31. Cox, *Military Reminiscences of the Civil War*, 1:290.

32. Carman and Clemens, *The Maryland Campaign of September 1862*, 1:377. See table and footnote 76.

33. Older, *News from Fox's Gap*, various articles related to the Battle of South Mountain: Issue 8, Volume 1, December 1, 1999, "Lost Legion, The Phillips Legion Infantry Battalion at Fox's Gap Maryland, September 14, 1862," by Kurt Graham; Issue 9, Volume 1, June 1, 2000, "Death of a Brigade" by Kurt Graham; Issue 10, Volume 1, December 1, 2000, "Casualties in the 50th Georgia Regiment at the Battle of South Mountain, September 14, 1862," by Kurt Graham; Issue 1, Volume 2, June 1, 2001, "Casualties in the 51st Georgia Regiment during the Maryland Campaign, September 14, 1862," by Kurt Graham; Issue 2, Volume 2, December 1, 2001, "The Third (James) South Carolina Infantry Battalion Takes a Licking at Fox's Gap September 14, 1862," by Sam B. Davis; Graham and Coffman, *To Honor These Men*, 87–102.

34. Bolton and Sauers, ed., *The Civil War Journal of Colonel William J. Bolton*, 81–2.

35. J. Evans Edings, *History of Drayton's Brigade from 1862 to _____ from the Diary of Capt. J. E. Edings, A.A.G., General Thomas F. Drayton's staff*. Library of Congress.

36. *OR* 19, 1:908–11, Report No. 243, George T. Anderson, September 30, 1862.

37. Ibid., 1:908–9.

38. Carman and Clemens, *The Maryland Campaign of September 1862*, 1:377. See Table and Footnote 74.

39. *OR* 19, 1:1,039, Report No. 297, Duncan K. McRae, October 18, 1862.

40. Priest, *Before Antietam*, 326. Priest estimated 27 casualties in the 5th VA Cavalry and Pelham's artillery.

Chapter 4: Brigadier General John Bell Hood's Advance

1. James Longstreet, *From Manassas to Appomattox; Memoirs of the Civil War in America* (Philadelphia: Lippincott, 1896), 226.

2. John Bell Hood, *Advance and Retreat. Personal Experiences in the United States and Confederate States Armies* (New Orleans: Published for the Hood Orphan Memorial Fund by G. T. Beauregard, 1880), 39.

3. Carman and Clemens, *The Maryland Campaign of September 1862*, 1:342.

4. Priest, *Before Antietam*, 325. Priest lists 864 men in Wofford's Brigade and 1,493 in Law's Brigade.

5. *OR* 19, 1:922, Report No. 248, John B. Hood, September 27, 1862.

6. Longstreet, *From Manassas to Appomattox*, 226.

7. James Longstreet, "A field of blue as far as the eye could see," *The Invasion of Maryland*. In *Battles and Leaders of the Civil War*, ed. Ned Bradford (New York: Appleton-Century, 1956), 263.

8.   *OR* 19, 1:922, Report No. 248, John B. Hood, September 27, 1862.
9.   Ibid.
10. Hood, *Advance and Retreat*, 40–1.
11. *OR* 19, 1:922, Report No. 248, John B. Hood, September 27, 1862.
12. Hood, *Advance and Retreat* 40–1.
13. Ibid.
14. *OR* 19, 1:1,021, Report No. 293, Daniel H. Hill, 1862.
15. Hood, *Advance and Retreat*, 40–1.
16. Priest, *Before Antietam*, 165 and 169.
17. Hood, *Advance and Retreat*, 40–41.
18. Ibid.
19. Ibid.
20. Ibid.
21. Bolton and Sauers, *The Civil War Journal of Colonel William J. Bolton*, 84.
22. Ibid., 81.
23. Richard William Lobst, Louis H. Manarin, and Wade Lucas, *The Bloody Sixth: The Sixth North Carolina Regiment,* Confederate States of America (Raleigh: North Carolina Confederate Centennial Commission, 1965), 94.
24. *OR* 19, 1:925, Report No. 249, Major B. W. Frobel, October 1, 1862.
25. Hood, *Advance and Retreat*, Chapter 2.
26. Ibid., 40–1.
27. *OR* 19, 1:1,021, Report No. 293, Daniel H. Hill, 1862.
28. Hood, *Advance and Retreat*, 40–1.
29. Ibid.
30. Ibid.
31. Ibid.
32. Older, *News from Fox's Gap*, Issue 9, Volume 1, June 1, 2000, "Death of a Brigade" by Kurt Graham.
33. Carman and Clemens, *The Maryland Campaign of September 1862*, 1:314.
34. Hood, *Advance and Retreat*, 40–1.
35. Gould, *The Story of the Forty-Eighth*, 89–90. The 48th suffered 11 wounded and one missing at South Mountain; Bosbyshell, *The 48th in the War.*
36. Older, *The Braddock Expedition*, 78.
37. Nicholas A. Davis and Donald E. Everett, *Chaplain Davis and Hood's Texas Brigade* (San Antonio: Principia Press of Trinity University, 1962), 51. Engagement at Boonsboro Gap.
38. *OR* 19, 1:443, Report No. 146, Samuel D. Sturgis, September 22, 1862. "When morning broke the enemy had withdrawn, leaving his dead in ghastly numbers scattered on the field."
39. Ibid.
40. Longstreet, *From Manassas to Appomattox*, 226.
41. Ibid.
42. Edmund DeWitt Patterson, *Yankee Rebel, The Civil War Journal of Edmund DeWitt Patterson*, ed. John G. Barrett (Chapel Hill: The Univ. of NC Press, 1966), 64–5. Under his entry of September 22, 1862, at Gordonsville, northeast of Charlottesville. Patterson was not at Antietam.
43. Thompson, "All about us grew pennyroyal," *In the Ranks to the Antietam.*
44. Randolph A. Shotwell, Joseph Gregoire de Roulhac Hamilton, and Rebecca Cameron, *The Papers of Randolph Abbott Shotwell,* Publications of the North Carolina Historical Commission (Raleigh: North Carolina Historical Commission, 1929), 1:340–1. Shotwell was in Garnett's brigade of D. R. Jones's division.
45. Library of Congress, Digital Collections, *Civil War Manuscripts, A Guide to Collections in the Manuscript Division of the Library of Congress*, compiled by John R. Sellers, page 215, item 772—David A. Rice—Private 108th NY—Antietam.
46. Thomas F. Toon, *North Carolina 20th Regiment Infantry roster and history* (Signal Mountain, TN: Mountain Press, 2019), 111.

47. Lord, *History of the Ninth Regiment*, 125.
48. Older, *News from Fox's Gap*, Issue 9, Volume 1, June 1, 2000, "Death of a Brigade" by Kurt Graham.
49. John W. Stevens, *Reminiscences of the Civil War* (Hillsboro, TX: Hillsboro Mirror Print, 1902), Chapter XVI.
50. MERLIN (Maryland Environmental Resource & Land Information Network). Analysis by Ted Ellis.
51. Smith, "A Fighting Chaplain."
52. Priest, *Before Antietam*, 325.
53. Hartwig, *To Antietam Creek*, Appendix B.
54. George W. Whitman to Louisa Van Velsor Whitman, September 21, 1862.
55. *OR* 19, 1:1,021, Report No. 293, Daniel H. Hill, 1862. "Encouraged by their successes in that direction, the Yankees thought that it would be an easy matter to move directly up the turnpike, but they were soon undeceived. They were heroically met and bloodily repulsed by the Twenty-third and Twenty-eighth Georgia Regiments of Colquitt's brigade."
56. Bolton and Sauers, *The Civil War Journal of Colonel William J. Bolton*, 81.
57. *OR* 19, 1:1,021, Report No. 293, Daniel H. Hill, 1862. "The Yankees on their side lost General Reno, a renegade Virginian, who was killed by a happy shot from the Twenty-third North Carolina."
58. Clark, *Histories of the Several Regiments and Battalions*, 2:221.
59. Hoptak, John D. *The Battle of South Mountain*. The History Press Civil War Sesquicentennial Series. Charleston, SC: History Press, 2011.
60. Cox, *Military Reminiscences of the Civil War*, 1:291.
61. R. T. Coles and Jeffrey D. Stocker, *From Huntsville to Appomattox: R. T. Coles's History of 4th Regiment, Alabama Volunteer Infantry, CSA, Army of Northern Virginia* (Voices of the Civil War Series). 1st ed. (Knoxville: University of Tennessee Press, 1996), 62.
62. Ibid., 62.
63. Ibid., 62.
64. Hood followed a relatively level course along the east side of the East Ridge below the peak until the boulders prevented him from continuing that course. South from Old National Pike, the East Ridge bowed slightly to the west, then back to the east and beyond a straight line drawn directly south from the Mountain House as it continued curving southeast toward Fox's Gap one mile away. The ridge ascended steeply just behind the Mountain House from 1,050 feet at Old National Pike to over 1,220 ft at the peak several hundred yards south. This steep peak was, however, very narrow and rocky. This rocky peak extended about 400 yards south of the Mountain House, then began to descend just as rapidly on the south as it ascended north. The crest then began sloping gradually until culminating at the Saddle, half a mile south. Just beyond the south end of the peak at about 500 yards from the Mountain House was the large boulder field extending from the crest down the east side of the mountain about 200 yards. The speculated course of Hood's advance in a straight line from Keedy's orchard would have been 20–40 feet lower in elevation than the crest when Hood approached the boulder field. The east slope of the East Ridge generally continued steep and rocky as before, but the spine and west slope from this point south became very gently sloping and relatively rock-free by comparison.
65. Coles, *From Huntsville to Appomattox*, 64.
66. Ibid.
67. Ibid.
68. All data on MoonPosition.com was based on the high-precision NASA/JPL DE-405 Ephemeris model. This model is used to compute the annual astronomical almanacs published by the U.S. Naval Observatory and Her Majesty's Nautical Almanac Office (HMNAO). The Ephemeris provides accurate data in the years ranging from 1600 to 2200.
69. nineplanets.org
70. Maryland State Archives, MSA c2201_000001. S. M. Hockman, Blank Book Manufacturer and Bank Stationer, Hagerstown, MD. The 1851 Road Survey appeared in Volume 4, Number 33; Washington County Court (Road Record), 1819–1871, Book OHW-1, MSA Citation: C2201-1.
71. Coles and Stocker, *From Huntsville to Appomattox*, 62.
72. *OR* 19, 1:927, Report No. 250, W. T. Wofford, September 20, 1862.

73. *Confederate Veteran*, "Hood's Texas Brigade at Sharpsburg," by W. R. Hamby, Vol. XVI, page 19. "After the battle of South Mountain, September 14, 1862, we were the rear guard of the army on the march to Sharpsburg."

74. Hood, *Advance and Retreat*, 40–1.

75. Ibid.

76. Carman and Clemens, *The Maryland Campaign of September 1862*, 1:344. Carman's footnote 61: "A detailed account of casualties is appended to the chapter, but the Union totals here are taken from *OR* 19, 1:187. The Confederates did not report separate casualties for each battle in the Maryland Campaign and are thus necessarily imprecise."

77. Ibid., 1:387.

78. *OR* 19, 1:908–11, Report No. 243, George T. Anderson, September 30, 1862.

79. Ezra A. Carman and Joseph Pierro, ed. *The Maryland Campaign of September 1862: Ezra A Carman's Definitive Study of the Union and Confederate Armies at Antietam* (Routledge, 2012), 166.

80. Thruston, "Letter addressed to Governor Zebulon Vance."

81. Carman and Clemens. *The Maryland Campaign of September 1862*, 1:389. Footnote 15 referenced G. T. Anderson's report at *OR* 19, 1:908.

82. *OR* 19, 1:908–11, Report No. 243, George T. Anderson, September 30, 1862.

83. Carman and Clemens, *The Maryland Campaign of September 1862*, 1:389.

84. Ibid.

85. Ibid., 1:390.

86. Longstreet, *From Manassas to Appomattox*, 226.

87. *OR* 19, 1:1,031-32, Report No. 295, Roswell S. Ripley, September 21, 1862.

88. Thruston, "Letter addressed to Governor Zebulon Vance."

89. Clark, *Histories of the Several Regiments and Battalions*, 1:224.

90. *OR* 19, 1:1,031–2, Report No. 295, Roswell S. Ripley, September 21, 1862.

91. Cox, *Military Reminiscences of the Civil War*, 1:290.

92. Michael R. Brasher, *The Second Mississippi Infantry Regiment* (Coonewah Creek Publishing, 1994).

93. North Carolina Digital Collections, "Bloody Sixth: the 6th NC Regiment, CSA, p. 284–450," digital. ncdcr.gov; Tim Ware, https://mountainaflame.blogspot.com.

94. Willis Brewer, *Brief historical sketches of military organizations raised in Alabama during the Civil War* (Montgomery: Alabama State Dept. of Archives and History, 1966), 594.

95. Robinson and Taylor, *The Civil War Letters of William A. Robinson*, 40–1.

96. George W. Whitman to Louisa Van Velsor Whitman, September 21, 1862.

97. For an account of the Confederate Army in Frederick, Maryland, see Dr. Charles E. Goldsborough of Hunterstown, PA, "Fighting Them Over," *National Tribune*, October 1886, digitized by the Library of Congress.

98. Shotwell, de Roulhac Hamilton and Cameron, *The Papers of Randolph Abbott Shotwell*, 1:313.

99. Hartwig, *To Antietam Creek*, 116–17.

100. Carman and Clemens, *The Maryland Campaign of September 1862*, 1:107; *New York Times*, September 14, 1862, page 1.

101. Lord, *History of the Ninth Regiment*, 89.

102. Carman and Clemens, *The Maryland Campaign of September 1862*, 1:376.

103. Priest, *Before Antietam*, 326. Priest listed 27 casualties for the 5th VA Cavalry and Pelham's Artillery.

104. Clark, *Histories of the Several Regiments and Battalions*, 1:141.

105. Lyman Jackson, *History of the Sixth New Hampshire Regiment in the War for the Union* (Concord, NH: Republican Press Association, 1891).

106. Charles F. Walcott, *History of the Twenty-First Regiment, Massachusetts Volunteers, in the War for the Preservation of the Union, 1861–1865. With Statistics of the War and of Rebel Prisons* (Boston: Houghton, Mifflin and Co., 1882), 190.

107. Ibid.

108. Ibid., 191.

109. Ibid., 190–2.

110. Hood, *Advance and Retreat*, 39.

111. *OR* 19, 1:428, Report No. 139, Orlando B. Willcox, September 21, 1862: Cox, *Military Reminiscences of the Civil War*, 1:187–8.
112. Cox, *Military Reminiscences of the Civil War*, 1:192.
113. Gould, *The Story of the Forty-Eighth*.
114. Ibid.
115. Brit Kimberly Erslev, "'Nearly There:' Daniel Harvey Hill, Proponent and Target of the Lost Cause." PhD Dissertation. (Chapel Hill, 2011), 166.
116. Washington D.C. *Evening Star*, September 18, 1862, front page, upper right column: "The late battle field of Sunday presents a most sickening aspect, the work of burying the dead having not yet been half finished." "At one point in a mud road to the left of the turnpike, nearly four hundred bodies are strewn thickly over less than an acre of ground, all of them in the unmistakeable Rebel garb."
117. Cox, *Military Reminiscences*, 1:290.
118. Ted Ellis, March 20, 2022.

Chapter 5: The Confederate Dilemma at Turner's Gap

1. Shotwell, de Roulhac Hamilton, and Cameron, *The Papers of Randolph Abbott Shotwell*, 1:339.
2. Thruston, "Letter addressed to Governor Zebulon Vance"; Bennett, *Resolute Rebel*, Chapter Fifteen, Maryland Campaign.
3. Priest, *Before Antietam*, Maps 50 through 54.
4. Hartwig, *To Antietam Creek*, 395 and map page 400.
5. Ibid., 395; *OR* 19, 1:1018–30, Report No. 293, Daniel H. Hill, 1862.
6. *OR* 19, 1:51, Report No. 2, George B. McClellan, October 15, 1862.

Chapter 6: After South Mountain

1. *OR* 19, 1:417, Report No. 137, Ambrose E. Burnside, September 30, 1862.
2. Sears, *Landscape Turned Red*, 150.
3. Carman and Clemens, *The Maryland Campaign of September 1862*, 1:381–2.
4. Sears, *Landscape Turned Red*, 150.
5. Ibid., 151.
6. *OR* 19, 1:213–16, Joseph Hooker, Washington City, D. C., November 7, 1862.
7. *OR* 19, 1:422–23, A. E. Burnside, Falmouth, VA, January 20, 1863.
8. Jacob D. Cox, *Military Reminiscences of the Civil War*, 1:291–93.

Afterword

1. Howard K. Beale, ed., *Diary of Gideon Welles* (New York: Norton, 1960), 1:143.
2. North Carolina State Archives, Raleigh, NC. Reverend Daniel Worth to Abraham Lincoln, September 12, 1862; Tolbert, Noble J. "Daniel Worth: Tar Heel Abolitionist." *The North Carolina Historical Review* 39, no. 3 (1962): 284–304. Reverend Daniel Worth was my second cousin, four generations removed. Reverend Worth and I were descendants of those who arrived on the famous ship *Mayflower* in 1620.
3. Basler, *The Collected Works of Abraham Lincoln*, 4–419. Remarks by the president were reported at a meeting at Bryan Hall in Chicago on September 20, 1862.
4. La Moille, Bureau County, Illinois, Citizens to Abraham Lincoln, Sunday, September 14, 1862, Memorial and Resolution recommending emancipation. Library of Congress.
5. United States War Department, George B. Davis, Calvin D. Cowles, and J. A Caldwell, *Atlas of the war of the Rebellion giving Union and Confederate armies by actual surveys by the Union and Confederate*

engineers, and approved by the officers in command, of all the maps herein published (New York: Atlas Pub. Co, 1892), Battlefield of South Mountain.

6. Middletown, MD, newspaper, Sept. 19, 1862. These reports also are in the Official Records.

7. McClellan and Prime, *McClellan's Own Story*, September 15, Monday, 9:30 am.

8. Brown University Library, Brown Digital Repository. Abraham Lincoln to Jesse K. Dubois: September 15, 1862.

9. Library of Congress, Public Domain Archive. Richard Yates to Abraham Lincoln, Monday, September 15, 1862.

10. *OR* 19, 2:312, McClellan to Halleck, 1:20 pm; Stephen W. Sears, ed., *The Civil War Papers of George B. McClellan: Selected Correspondence, 1860–1865* (New York: Ticknor & Fields, 1989), 467.

11. Beale, *Diary of Gideon Welles*, 1:143.

12. Basler, *Collected Works of Abraham Lincoln*, 4:424. While riding the court circuit in Danville, Illinois, Abraham Lincoln attended the Presbyterian Church on the northwest corner of North and Franklin Streets. I was baptized at the First Presbyterian Church at the same location on Easter Sunday in 1948 and later became a member of that church.

13. Ibid., 4:438. Lincoln spent most of his time writing the Emancipation Proclamation at the "Lincoln Cottage" near the Soldier's Home in Washington, D.C. Two brothers of Chesterfield Worth, my great-grandfather, were in the Union Army and both died of typhoid fever in November 1861 in Washington, D.C. They were James W. Worth and Seth Worth. Both were buried at the Soldier's Home near the "Lincoln Cottage"; Matthew Pinsker, *Lincoln's Sanctuary* (Oxford University Press, 2003), 63–6; Elizabeth Smith Brownstein, *Lincoln's other White House* (Hoboken, NJ: John Wiley & Sons, Inc.), 113–18.

14. George B. McClellan, *McClellan's Own Story*, 27.

15. Refer to the original text, Plate 23, Vol. One, *Gardner's Photographic Sketch Book of the War* (Washington: Philp & Solomons, 1865–66).

Appendix A

1. Maryland State Archives, IC #P 672–3, May 9, 1797; Friendship—Unpatented Certificate #238, June 8, 1795; Frederick Fox obtained a survey dated July 6, 1792, for a tract of land named Fredericksburgh containing 75 acres near the South Mountain crest on Fox's Gap's east side. Fox obtained a patent for the Fredericksburgh tract on March 13, 1794. On May 11, 1795, he received a special warrant to resurvey 34 acres of his Fredericksburgh tract and add contiguous vacancy. Fox decided to keep intact his patent for Fredericksburgh, consisting of 75 acres, and to create a new parcel of land that he named Addition to Friendship for 202 acres, surveyed on May 9, 1797. Fox obtained a patent for this tract on May 7, 1805.

2. Older, *The Land Tracts*, 206.

3. Maryland State Archives, BC & GS 44, 439–440, Flonham, Philip J. Shafer, patented April 20, 1774, 36 acres.

4. Older, *The Land Tracts*, 36–7. David's Will land tract.

5. Cox, *Military Reminiscences of the Civil War*, Vol. 1, Chapter XIII, Map of South Mountain.

6. *Atlas of the War of the Rebellion to Accompany the Official Records*, map of the Battlefield of South Mountain, Library of Congress, www.loc.gov/item/2009581111/.

7. *OR* 19, 1:1,031–2, Report 295, Roswell S. Ripley, September 21, 1862.

8. Maryland State Archives, BC & GS 27, 396, David Bowser, David's Will, December 24, 1763, 49 acres.

9. Maryland State Archives, BC & GS 44,439–40, Philip J. Shafer, Flonham, April 20, 1774, 36 acres.

10. Older, *The Braddock Expedition*, 191.

11. MdHR, BC & GS #1, 177, Daniel Dulaney Esqr., The Exchange, surveyed October 5, 1742, 100 acres.

12. Maryland State Archives, Special Collections (MSA Map Collection) No. 507, "Road from Swearingen's Ferry on the Potomac River through Sharpsburg to the top of the South Mountain at Fox's Gap." [MSA G1427-507, B5-1-3], August 13, 1792.

13. Older, *The Land Tracts*, 40. Fox's Gap.

14. MERLIN (Maryland Environmental Resource & Land Information Network). Analysis by Ted Ellis.

15. Frederick County Land Records, THO-1-103, Joseph Swearingen Esqr., Mount Pelier, surveyed November 8, 1790, 90 acres.

16. Frederick County Land Records, WBT-1, 100, Susan Miller, et al. to John Miller, Bowser's Addition and part of Addition to Friendship, April 1, 1845, 13¼ acres.

17. Cox, *Military Reminiscences of the Civil War*, 1:290.

18. Older, *The Land Tracts*, 217. The Mountain House at Turner's Gap.

19. Washington County Land Records, LBN-2-133, Edward L. Boteler to George F. Smith, recorded May 14, 1867, 60 acres. Line 10 was "33 perches to the north side of the public road leading from said turnpike to Daniel Rent's farm." Also see WCLR 74-264, George F. Smith to Madeleine Dahlgren, April 19, 1876, 60 acres.

20. Older, *The Land Tracts*, 51.

21. Ibid., 46.

22. Ibid., 42.

23. Cox, *Military Reminiscences of the Civil War*, 1:290.

24. Older, *The Braddock Expedition*, 189.

25. Washington County Land Records, 74-264, George F. Smith to Madeleine Dahlgren, April 19, 1876, 60 acres. See Battlefield of South Mountain Map included in the *Atlas to Accompany the Official Records*. "D. Rent" appears near the bend in Dahlgren Road east of the Mountain House.

26. Cox, *Military Reminiscences of the Civil War*, 1:290.

27. Older, *The Land Tracts*, 45. Maryland State Archives, Special Collections (Maps) No. 504, Road from Williamsport to Turner's Gap, 1791 [MdHR 1427–504, B5-1-3]. The 1791 map of the road leading from Williamsport to Turner's Gap in the South Mountain identified almost one mile of road on the west side of the mountain as "up through the gap."

28. Older, *The Land Tracts*, 189 and 208.

29. Ibid, 179.

30. Library of Congress, map, South Mountain, 1872, copy1.

Bibliography

Primary Sources

Basler, Roy P., ed. *The Collected Works of Abraham Lincoln*. New Brunswick, N.J.: Rutgers University Press, 1953.

Beale, Howard K., ed. *Diary of Gideon Welles*. New York: Norton, 1960.

Bolton, William J., and Sauers, Dr. Richard A., ed. *The Civil War Journal of Colonel William J. Bolton*. Conshohocken, PA: Combined Publishing, 2000.

Bosbyshell, Oliver C. *The 48th in the War*. Philadelphia: Avil Printing Co., 1895.

Coles, R. T., and Jeffrey D. Stocker, ed. *From Huntsville to Appomattox: R. T. Coles's History of 4th Regiment, Alabama Volunteer Infantry, CSA, Army of Northern Virginia*. Knoxville: University of Tennessee Press, 1996.

Cox, Jacob D. *Military Reminiscences of the Civil War*. Two Vols. New York: Charles Scribner's Sons, 1900.

Cutts, Allen S. "The Number of Guns in Cutts Battalion at Sharpsburg." *Southern Historical Society Papers*, 40 vols. Richmond: Virginia Historical Society, 1882.

Davis, Nicholas A., and Donald E. Everett, ed. *Chaplain Davis and Hood's Texas Brigade*. San Antonio: Principia Press of Trinity University, 1962.

Edings, Captain J. Evans. "A Manuscript History of General Thomas F. Drayton's Brigade". Edward Willis Papers, 1860–65. *Civil War Manuscripts* compiled by John R. Sellers, Library of Congress.

Gardner, Alexander. *Gardner's Photographic Sketch Book of the Civil War*. Mineola, New York: Dover Publications, Inc., 1959.

Grattan, George D. "The Battle of Boonsboro Gap or South Mountain". *Southern Historical Society Papers*, XXXIX, 1914, 33–5.

Hayes, Rutherford B., and Charles Richard, ed. *Diary and Letters of Rutherford Birchard Hayes: nineteenth President of the United States*. Columbus, OH: Ohio State Archaeological and Historical Society, 1922.

Hitchcock, George A. *From Ashby to Andersonville: The Civil War Diary and Reminiscences of Private George A. Hitchcock, Company A, 21st Massachusetts Regiment, August 1862–January 1865*. Campbell, CA: Savas Publishing Company, 1997.

Holahan, John F. "Diary, 1861–1865." Accession No. 1981/10.0345, Special Collections Department, Marshall University, Huntington, WV.

Hood, John Bell. *Advance and Retreat. Personal Experiences in the United States and Confederate States Armies*. New Orleans: Published for the Hood Orphan Memorial Fund by G. T. Beauregard, 1880.

Hurd, Daniel E. "My Experiences in the Civil War." *Daniel Emerson Hurd Diary*, William Marvel Collection, 1861–1865, USAMHI.

Kerr, Jr., Richard E. "Wall of Fire—The Rifle and Civil War Infantry Tactics." Fort Leavenworth, Kansas, 1990.

Longstreet, James. *From Manassas to Appomattox; Memoirs of the Civil War in America*. Philadelphia: Lippincott, 1896.

McKee, L., and C. G. Robertson. "A map of Washington Co., Maryland. Exhibiting the farms, election districts, towns, villages, roads, etc., etc." Library of Congress, 1859.

MERLIN—Maryland Environmental Resource & Land Information Network.

McClellan, George B. *McClellan's Own Story*. New York: Webster, 1887.

Older, Curtis L. *The Land Tracts of the Battlefield of South Mountain*. Westminster, MD: Heritage Books, Inc., 2008.

Patterson, Edmund DeWitt, and John G. Barrett, ed. *Yankee Rebel, The Civil War Journal of Edmund DeWitt Patterson*. Chapel Hill: The Univ. of NC Press, 1966.

Pollock, Curtis Clay and John D. Hoptak, ed. *Dear Ma: The Civil War Letters of Curtis Clay Pollock: First Defender and First Lieutenant, 48th Pennsylvania Infantry*. Boiling Springs, PA: Sunbury Press, 2017.

"Road from Swearingen's Ferry on the Potomac River through Sharpsburg to the top of the South Mountain at Fox's Gap, August 13, 1792." Special Collections (MSA Map Collection) #507 [MSA G1427-507, B5-1-3]. Annapolis: Maryland State Archives.

Robinson, William Alfred, and Robert J. Taylor. *The Civil War Letters of William A. Robinson and the Story of the 89th NYVI*. Bowie, MD: Heritage Books, Inc., 2000.

Shotwell, Randolph A., and Joseph Gregoire de Roulhac Hamilton and Rebecca Cameron, ed. *The Papers of Randolph Abbott Shotwell*. Raleigh: North Carolina Historical Commission, 1929.

Stevens, John W. *Reminiscences of the Civil War*. Hillsboro, TX: Hillsboro Mirror Print, 1902.

"The 1851 Road Survey, Rohrersville Road." Maryland State Archives or Washington County Land Records. Possibly MSA c2201_000001. Volume 4, Number 33, published by S. M. Hockman, Hagerstown, Md.

Thruston, Stephen D. "Report of Stephen Decatur Thruston, September 27, 1862." Letter addressed to Governor Zebulon Vance, North Carolina. Raleigh: William L. DeRossett Collection, North Carolina State Archives.

United States. War Department. *The War of the Rebellion. Official Records of the Union and Confederate Armies*. Washington: Government printing office, 1899.

Whitman, George Washington. "Letter to Louisa Van Velsor Whitman, September 21, 1862." Trent Collection of Whitmaniana, Duke University Rare Book, Manuscript, and Special Collections Library.

Whitman, George Washington and Jerome M. Loving, ed. *Civil War Letters of George Washington Whitman*. Durham, NC: Duke University Press, 1975.

Willcox, Orlando B. and Robert G. Scott, ed. *Forgotten Valor, The Memoirs, Journals, & Civil War Letters of Orlando B. Willcox*. Kent, Ohio & London, The Kent State University Press, 1999.

Worth, Reverend Daniel. "Reverend Daniel Worth to President Abraham Lincoln, September 12, 1862." Raleigh: North Carolina State Archives.

Wren, James, and John M. Priest, ed. *From New Bern to Fredericksburg: Captain James Wren's Diary: B Company, 48th Pennsylvania Volunteers, February 20, 1862–December 17, 1862*. Shippensburg, PA: White Mane Pub. Co., 1990.

Secondary Sources

Bennett, Chet. *Resolute Rebel: General Roswell S. Ripley, Charleston's Gallant Defender*. Columbia, SC: The University of South Carolina Press, 2017.

Brasher, Michael R. *The Second Mississippi Infantry Regiment: An Introduction to the Full Annotated Roster (History of the Second Mississippi Infantry)*. United States: Coonewah Creek Publishing, 1994.

Brewer, Willis. *Brief historical sketches of military organizations raised in Alabama during the Civil War*. Montgomery: Alabama State Dept. of Archives and History, 1966.

Brownstein, Elizabeth Smith. *Lincoln's Other White House*. Hoboken, NJ: John Wiley & Sons, Inc., 2005.

Carman, Ezra A., and Thomas G. Clemens, ed. *The Maryland Campaign of September 1862. Volume 1, South Mountain.* El Dorado Hills, Calif.: Savas Beatie, 2010.

Carman, Ezra A., and Joseph Pierro, ed. *The Maryland Campaign of September 1862.* New York: Taylor & Francis Group, 2008.

Clark, Walter. *Histories of the Several Regiments and Battalions from North Carolina in the Great War, 1861–65.* Wilmington, NC: Broadfoot Publishing Co., 1996.

Cumulative Index: The Confederate Veteran Magazine 1893–1932. Wilmington: Broadfoot Pub. Co., 1986.

Freeman, Douglas Southall. *R. E. Lee: A Biography.* New York: Scribner's, 1937.

Fox, Daniel G. *The Fox Genealogy including Metherd, Benner, and Leiter Descendants.* N.p., 1924.

Goldsborough, Dr. Charles E. "Fighting Them Over". *National Tribune,* October 1886, Library of Congress.

Gottfried, Bradley M. *The Maps of Antietam: An Atlas of the Antietam (Sharpsburg) Campaign, including the Battle of South Mountain, September 2–20, 1862.* New York: Savas Beatie, 2013.

Gould, Joseph. *The Story of the Forty-Eighth: A Record of the Campaigns of the Forty-Eighth Regiment Pennsylvania Veteran Volunteer Infantry During the Four Eventful years of its service in the War for the Preservation of the Union.* Sagwan Press, 2018.

Graham, Kurt. "Death of a Brigade at Fox's Gap, September 14, 1862." *News from Fox's Gap,* Issue 9, Volume 1, June 1, 2000. Berwyn Heights, MD: Heritage Books, Inc., 2018.

Graham, Kurt, and Richard M. Coffman. *To Honor These Men: a History of the Phillips Georgia Legion Infantry Battalion.* Macon, GA: Mercer University Press, 2007.

Harsh, Joseph L. *Sounding the Shallows: A Confederate Companion for the Maryland Campaign of 1862.* Kent, Ohio: The Kent State University Press, 2000.

Hartwig, D. Scott. *To Antietam Creek: The Maryland Campaign of September 1862.* Baltimore: The Johns Hopkins University Press, 2012.

Hill, Jr., Daniel H. *Bethel to Sharpsburg.* Raleigh: Edwards & Broughton Co., 1926.

Hockett, Homer C. "Jacob Dolson Cox." *Dictionary of American Biography.* New York: Charles Scribner's Sons, 1930.

Hoptak, John D. *The Battle of South Mountain.* The History Press Civil War Sesquicentennial Series. Charleston, SC: History Press, 2011.

Jackson, Lyman. *History of the Sixth New Hampshire Regiment in the War for the Union.* Concord, NH: Republican Press Association, 1891.

Johnson, Robert Underwood, Clarence Clough Buel, and Roy F. Nichols. *Battles and leaders of the Civil War: being for the most part contributions by Union and Confederate officers.* New York: Thomas Yoseloff, 1956.

Jordan, Brian M. *Unholy Sabbath: The Battle of South Mountain in History and Memory, September 14, 1862.* New York: Savas Beatie LLC, 2012.

Lord, Edward O. *History of the Ninth Regiment, New Hampshire Volunteers in the War of the Rebellion.* Concord: Republican Press Association, 1895.

Marvel, William. *Burnside.* Chapel Hill: University of North Carolina Press, 1991.

Morgan, H. Wayne. *William McKinley and his America.* Kent, OH: The Kent State University Press, 1998.

Older, Curtis L. *News from Fox's Gap.* Berwyn Heights, MD: Heritage Books, Inc., 2018.

Older, Curtis L. *The Braddock Expedition and Fox's Gap in Maryland.* Westminster, MD: Heritage Books, Inc., 2019.

Parker, Thomas H. *History of the 51st Regiment of P.V. and V.V.: From its organization, at Camp Curtin, Harrisburg, PA., in 1861, to Its Being Mustered Out of the United States Service at Alexandria, VA, July 27th, 1865.* Philadelphia: King & Baird Printers, 1869.

Pinsker, Matthew. *Lincoln's Sanctuary, Abraham Lincoln and the Soldiers' Home*. Oxford: Oxford University Press, 2003.

Priest, John M. *Before Antietam, The Battle for South Mountain*. Shippensburg: White Mane Publishing Company, Inc., 1992.

Rice, David A. Library of Congress, Digital Collections, Civil War Manuscripts, A Guide to Collections in the Manuscript Division of the Library of Congress, compiled by John R. Sellers, page 215, item 772—Private 108th NY—Antietam.

Rossino, Alexander B. *Their Maryland, The Army of Northern Virginia from the Potomac Crossing to Sharpsburg in September 1862*. El Dorado Hills, CA: Savas Beatie, 2021.

Sears, Stephen W. *Landscape Turned Red, The Battle of Antietam*. New York: Ticknor & Fields, 1983.

Stotelmyer, Steven R. *Too Useful to Sacrifice*. El Dorado Hills, CA: Savas Beatie, 2019.

Stotelmyer, Steven R. *The Bivouacs of the Dead*. Baltimore: Toomey Press, 1992.

Toon, Thomas F. *North Carolina 20th Regiment Infantry roster and history*. Signal Mountain, TN: Mountain Press, 2019.

Walcott, Charles F. *History of the Twenty-First Regiment, Massachusetts Volunteers, in the War for the Preservation of the Union, 1861–1865*. Boston: Houghton, Mifflin and Co., 1882.

Index

2 1982 32412 7079